REVOLUTIONS IN THE ATLANTIC WORLD

Revolutions in the Atlantic World

A Comparative History

NEW EDITION

Wim Klooster

NEW YORK UNIVERSITY PRESS
New York

NEW YORK UNIVERSITY PRESS
New York
www.nyupress.org

References to Internet websites (URLs) were accurate at the time of writing. Neither the author nor New York University Press is responsible for URLs that may have expired or changed since the manuscript was prepared.

Library of Congress Cataloging-in-Publication Data
Names: Klooster, Wim, author.
Title: Revolutions in the Atlantic world : a comparative history / Wim Klooster.
Description: New edition. | New York : New York University Press, 2017. |
Includes bibliographical references and index.
Identifiers: LCCN 2017008033| ISBN 9781479875955 (cloth : acid-free paper) |
ISBN 9781479857173 (paperback : acid-free paper)
Subjects: LCSH: Revolutions—America—History—18th century. | Revolutions—America—History—19th century. | Revolutions—Cross-cultural studies. | Sovereignty—Cross-cultural studies. | United States—History—Revolution, 1775–1783. | France—History—Revolution, 1789–1799. | Haiti—History—Revolution, 1791–1804. | Latin America—History—Wars of Independence, 1806–1830.
Classification: LCC E18.82 .K55 2017 | DDC 973.3—dc23
LC record available at https://lccn.loc.gov/2017008033

New York University Press books are printed on acid-free paper, and their binding materials are chosen for strength and durability. We strive to use environmentally responsible suppliers and materials to the greatest extent possible in publishing our books.

Manufactured in the United States of America

10 9 8 7 6 5 4 3 2 1

Also available as an ebook

CONTENTS

Acknowledgments   vii

1. Introduction: Empires at War   1

2. Civil War in the British Empire: The American Revolution   12

3. The War on Privilege and Dissension: The French Revolution   49

4. From Prize Colony to Black Independence: The Revolution
   in Haiti   91

5. Multiple Routes to Sovereignty: The Spanish American
   Revolutions   126

6. The Revolutions Compared: Causes, Patterns, Legacies   169

   Notes   189

   Index   243

   About the Author   253

ACKNOWLEDGMENTS

When I first arrived in the United States on a Fulbright fellowship in 1995, the John Carter Brown Library in Providence, Rhode Island, was my new academic home. An unrivaled repository of books published on the Americas from Columbus's days to those of Bolívar, the JCB also offered a superb environment for intellectual exchange with fellow Americanists and Atlanticists. It was therefore no punishment to return to Providence during the academic year 2006–2007 on a Mellon InterAmericas fellowship. I would like to thank Director and Librarian Ted Widmer and his staff for providing all the conditions in which scholarship can thrive. Most of this book was written at the library, upstairs and downstairs, inspired by conversations with other scholars using the collection. Particularly stimulating were the discussions I had with Guillaume Aubert and Lyman Johnson, experts respectively on French and Spanish America. Outside of Providence, Mark Peterson and one of the manuscript's anonymous reviewers helped me tremendously with their comments and insights. Last but not least, I have benefited from the support of Aviva Ben-Ur, Alison Games, and Philip Morgan.

This book also bears the imprint of Clark University, where I teach a seminar every other year on the Age of Atlantic Revolutions. Different cohorts of students have thus contributed to my ideas about the individual revolutions and their connections. I am grateful as well to my colleague Thomas Kühne for inviting me to speak about the revolutions in our department's colloquium, which offered plenty of food for thought. Finally, my thanks to Debbie Gershenowitz, the history editor at NYU Press and herself a Clark alumna, for approaching me about this book project and then shepherding it through the publication process.

1

Introduction

Empires at War

On July 11, 1791, an elaborate spectacle unfolded in revolutionary Paris. On a triumphal car twenty-five feet high, the remains of the great philosophe Voltaire (1694–1778) were carried around the city. One hundred thousand residents defied the pouring rain to witness the procession, many of them dressed in classical outfits in front of, beside, or behind the carriage. There were multiple stops en route to the Panthéon, under whose dome Voltaire's coffin would be left for eight hours, so it could be viewed by all who wanted. One of the intermediate stations was at a new theater, whose columns were decorated with crowns and garlands. A song was sung there from the opera *Samson*, for which Voltaire had written the libretto, but which had never been performed due to censorship. It included the words: "People, wake up, break your irons / Rise again to your former greatness / Liberty calls on you / You who were born for it."[1]

The cortege also halted at the ruins of the Bastille. As a major symbol of arbitrary rule, this old royal prison had been the target of an angry crowd just two years before. The storming of the Bastille had marked the start of a particularly tumultuous decade in European history: the French Revolution (1789–1799). This revolution was no isolated series of events. Revolutionary turmoil also left its mark on British North America (1775–1783), Saint-Domingue (1791–1804), and Spanish America (1810–1824). This book offers an overview of these four revolutions, followed by a comparative perspective.[2] Although each uprising (or set of uprisings) had its own causes, traits, and impact, they all created sovereign states that professed hostility to privilege and began to question black slavery. Between the first shots fired in Lexington and Concord in 1775 and the departure of the last Spanish troops from mainland America in 1826, these revolutions changed the Atlantic world beyond recognition.

It had been a deliberate choice that the procession would stop at the Bastille. Not only had Voltaire once been imprisoned in the prison for almost a year, his name was now inextricably bound up with the revolution. As the Constituent Assembly put it: "The glorious revolution has been the fruit of his works."[3] We may wonder whether that was true. More broadly, we can ask what the role of ideas was in the various revolutions. What is clear is that they shared an ideological background: the Enlightenment.

The author of an entry in the *Encyclopédie*, the famous eighteenth-century work that was aimed at incorporating all existing knowledge, painted a contrasting picture of two kinds of thinkers. Some men "are carried away by their passions, without their actions being preceded by reflection: these are men who walk in the shadows." The representative of the Enlightenment, however, "acts only after reflection; he walks in the night, but he is preceded by a torch."[4] The Enlightenment sought to achieve progress and utility through the use of reason. Its most conspicuous protagonists were the philosophes—the public intellectuals who were active in a broad range of disciplines, including science, economics, philosophy, theater, and politics.

By rationally penetrating, ordering, and controlling the world, educated people who embraced Enlightenment thought worked to increase the happiness of mankind through material advancement.[5] Although it has often been portrayed as a movement largely confined to France and the British Isles, the Enlightenment led to debates all over Europe and the European colonies in Asia and the Americas. There was no single center, but multiple centers around the world.[6] If not all participants were interested in the same topics or stressed the same points, it would be wrong to conclude that there were multiple Enlightenments, each one embedded in a separate national tradition. The Enlightenment was too cosmopolitan in nature for that. The production of its written works and the correspondence between its protagonists took place in what contemporaries called the Republic of Letters, a polity transcending borders whose ideas applied to the wider world.

No consensus was ever reached about many topics. The philosophes disagreed so often that we should actually conceive of the Enlightenment as a series of problems and debates, not as a stream of conclusions. One such debate was inspired by men's equality in the state of nature as described by Thomas Hobbes (1588–1679). Jean-Jacques Rousseau (1712–1778), Denis Diderot (1713–1784), Claude-Adrien Helvétius (1715–1771), and Jean d'Alembert (1717–1783) regarded equality as an inalienable natural right. It was necessary, they thought, to provide freedom and equality with a solid foundation by allowing everyone access to education. Voltaire, on the other hand, argued that equality was perhaps natural, but that in practice there would always be a class who command and a class who obey.[7]

The Enlightenment derived its dynamic in part from the massive reaction it brought about in conservative circles. A true Counter-Enlightenment came about, shaped by thinkers who emphasized belief, piety, and obedience to worldly authorities. They criticized abstract rights and accused the philosophes of destroying religion and thereby removing all obstacles for anarchy and lawlessness. National governments sought to keep new ideas at bay, but compared to the past struggle against heretical opinions, it was much harder to judge whether Enlightenment notions, which were more philosophical than theological in nature, undermined the established order.[8] At the same time, monarchs took their cues from enlightened ideas in their quest of national reform, often achieving libertarian ends by autocratic means. Unintentionally, state-sponsored reform in some parts of Europe was more successful than the works of the philosophes in instilling enlightened values in the educated part of the population. In Austria, Sweden, Denmark, Spain, Portugal, and Germany's Roman Catholic states, the enlightened minds were almost exclusively tied to the state.

Was the French Assembly right in claiming that their revolution had been the fruit of Voltaire's work? The question whether Enlightenment thought was actually instrumental in bringing about the revolutionary turmoil was already debated during the age of revolutions itself. The Catholic German theologian and philosopher Jakob Salat (1766–1851) wrote in 1802: "The Enlightenment is the source of revolutions, its opponents shout; yes, sooner or later it necessarily leads to revolution, assert even some of its friends. Other supporters, however, argue that the Enlightenment does not spawn revolution, but is instead the best way to thwart it."[9] Most contemporary intellectuals, however, saw the events occurring in revolutionary France as the outcome and fulfillment of the philosophes' agenda. Especially Rousseau's footprints were everywhere.[10]

Prior to the outbreak of a revolution, very few people actually dreamed of a violent overthrow of the existing order. The focus on ideals such as equality that can be associated with the French Revolution should not blind us to the fact that most celebrated Enlightenment thinkers did not challenge the status quo. Two years into the revolution, one of Rousseau's admirers even wrote that one could reproach the author of *Social Contract* and other best sellers for not having spoken of insurrection, "the legal instrument of an oppressed people."[11] Nor did the philosophes place their hope of social reform in the illiterate majority, but instead on the traditional elite. Nonetheless, enlightened ideas shaped the revolutions around the Atlantic Basin in the five decades after 1775. Often combined in new ways or watered down and linked to elements from other ideologies, they made it possible to call into question a world based on tradition, hierarchy, and corporatism. They did not inevitably cause the various revolutions, but they did give the insurgents an ideological reservoir that they could tap as they improvised to set up new forms of government.

The objective of this book is to present the four above-mentioned revolutions on their own terms, while emphasizing four aspects:

1. They cannot be understood outside the realm of international politics. Inter-imperial warfare called for reforms, which exposed the foundations of empires and jeopardized their existence by revealing and exacerbating enduring social, political, and ethnic inequities. In addition, individual events that were taking place an ocean away created a favorable climate for the revolutions.[12]

2. None of the revolutions was foreordained. Even if active fault zones were visible, the political earthquakes could have been avoided until the very moment that they hit. Nor were the revolutions guaranteed success once they broke out. Loyalty to the empire was considerable in the American colonies, and it was only in the course of wars that the revolutions triumphed.

3. Divided loyalties meant that these wars often had the overtones of civil wars, whose main protagonists were previously voiceless popular classes fighting for their own reasons, which often did not square with those of the elites.

4. In his classic and still influential *Age of the Democratic Revolution* (2 vols., 1959–1964), historian R. R. Palmer presented the age of revolutions as the triumphal march of democracy.[13] But democracy is no appropriate prism through which to see these uprisings. It was hardly more than a temporary by-product of some insurrections.

Which social factors made the Atlantic world ripe for revolution? Although eighteenth-century Europe was undergoing rapid change, agriculture remained the livelihood of the majority. From time immemorial, clergy and nobility owned most land, which had given them access to economic resources. Villages had originally had a lord, who let peasants work on his land and derived his income from the demesne, the section of his lands that tenants could not cultivate for their own sake and that the lord kept for his use, and from head taxes levied among all households within the lord's jurisdiction. But by the eighteenth century, over half of the land was owned by peasants themselves, most of whom had become smallholders. In much of Western Europe, the lord's traditional sources of income had been reduced, due in part to peasant resistance. Many French peasants had, for instance, managed to gain control of their holdings at fixed rents, but at a price. By raising or reintroducing fees, the landlords made up for lost income after the middle of the eighteenth century.[14]

A lasting medieval legacy was that landownership entailed not only economic power for the landlord, but judicial authority over the peasants living on his lands. The nobility's principal privileges were different, however, consisting of the right to be judged by one's peers and exemption from some, though by no means all, taxes. Privilege was the organizing principle of the European kingdoms and their overseas colonies. Privilege was typical of all the corporate bodies that composed society in a manner seen as divinely inspired. These corporations included guilds, confraternities, the military, ecclesiastical bodies (including universities, monasteries, and the Inquisition), cities, rural communities, and family clans. Such bodies all had their own rights and duties, some of which had been formally recognized while others were based on tradition or tacit agreement. Keeping a firm grip on their privileges, the corporations ultimately obeyed the king, who regulated privilege and guaranteed the proper social hierarchy among the corporations. The social order and hierarchy were therefore closely connected.[15]

Clergymen and noblemen were therefore not the only beneficiaries of privilege. What is more, they did not necessarily lead privileged lives. In the eighteenth century, only a small section of the nobility was well-to-do. Numerous noble families had been impoverished and moved into trade and industry to make a living.[16] Among the clergy, it was also a small elite that was affluent: the bishops, abbots, and priors who owed their benefices to family wealth. The vast majority of clergymen were village priests who shared the living standards of their flock. Their chief legal privilege, exemption from taxation, was not even universally observed. So-called voluntary contributions to the national treasury, especially in wartime, were often substantial.

The old idea that two social classes bled the third has therefore been dismissed. Historians have shown that urban middling groups—merchants, goldsmiths, drapers, among others—acquired much land in early modern Europe, usually as an investment, but also to gain status. Some lent money to peasants and other landowners, receiving a fixed annual payment in return. Town and country did not always see eye to eye. Peasants associated the city with unscrupulous tax collectors and absentee landowners, urban dwellers saw the countryside as the root of the exorbitantly high grain prices. These prices, townspeople believed, had to be regulated and grain sold at a just price, not the prices peasants allegedly demanded. In reality, the rural population was also weighed down by rising prices.[17]

Privilege was also the main organizing principle of the Euro-American societies that sprang up across the Atlantic Ocean. Unlike in Europe, it had an ethnic component throughout the Americas. Whites assigned servile or otherwise subordinate roles to blacks, mulattoes, Indians, and mestizos. Until the late eighteenth century, the term *español* ("Spanish") was used officially to refer to a white person in the Spanish colonies.[18] Nor did official ethnic discrimination abate as colonial societies matured. Authorities did not question the connection between blackness and slavery, allowing African slavery to continue to thrive from Boston to Bahia and Buenos Aires; free mulattoes in the Caribbean even experienced an increase in legal discrimination in the 1760s and 1770s.

Apart from the Swiss cantons and the Dutch provinces, kings held sway in the European countries and their empires. They controlled foreign policy and the armed forces, appointed ministers and officials, and regulated trade and industry. Monarchical power began to expand in the sixteenth century, but could be achieved only in close collaboration with local institutions.[19] The ascendance of monarchies, therefore, went hand in hand with the strengthening of local representative bodies, as kings bestowed rights, privileges, and representative institutions where they had not existed before. Indirect rule also marked the way in which European states governed their American colonies. Consent rather than coercion was the preferred instrument of empire. The term "colonialism" obscures the working of the administrative machinery in the overseas provinces. Colonies generally formed their own power base before metropolitan authority was established. Even then, the combination of distance, local interests, and the small size of the bureaucracy made it impossible for the mother countries to impose their will on their colonies. Only by negotiating with colonial elites could metropolitan authorities hope to achieve policy goals. The inevitable price they paid was to recognize the right of settlers to enjoy some form of self-government.[20] As long as the mother countries did not tamper with the principle of negotiation, colonial elites would not call into question their loyalty to the imperial center.

Prior to the French Revolution, reform, rather than revolution, was in the air all over Europe. Sweeping domestic and international changes made the reorganization of the European states inevitable. Rapid population growth, a serious food shortage that affected much of Southern Europe, competition over colonies, and, perhaps most important, demands of military expenditure to keep up with powerful neighbors compelled governments to introduce the reforms. French king Louis XIV (1638–1715) had set an example to others, privileging four areas of domestic reform: the police, poor relief, education, and public works. Reforms required not only raising existing taxes but tapping new sources of money. Church and nobility, however, stood in the way, each tenaciously defending its vested interests. In their battles with these estates, monarchs often availed themselves of enlightened ideas to achieve their objectives. The Enlightenment lent an air of legitimacy to the destruction of old privileges.[21]

What opened the door to reform in the middle decades of the eighteenth century was international warfare, lasting from 1739 through 1763 and interrupted by only six years of peace (1748–1754), with theaters in Europe, the Americas, and India. European rivalry assumed a global character, inaugurating a contest over colonies that would last into the twentieth century. Riches from other continents had occasionally tempted Europe's main powers to engage in colonial hostilities in earlier eras, but never on this scale. Louis XIV spent an extraordinary amount of time and energy on warfare, but exclusively on the European mainland—the two wars that he fought with Britain saw fighting in the Low Countries, southern Germany, Spain, Italy, and the Mediterranean.

In the course of the eighteenth century, relations between France and Britain deteriorated largely because of the similarity of the two countries' economic and geopolitical interests. Both French and British ships depended for their masts and timber on the Baltic, both nations had strategic interests in the Mediterranean, and both were large producers and sellers of textiles and, as the eighteenth century advanced, also of sugar. Increased French competition in the West Indies seemed irreversible and could not be offset by British commerce with the Spanish Empire.[22] During the War of the Austrian Succession (1740–1748), France became anti-British and Britain anti-French. The French seized numerous British oceangoing ships, conquered the Austrian Netherlands (today's Belgium), placing themselves just across from England, fomented the Jacobite rebellion in Britain, and tried unsuccessfully to invade Britain. The French government also had British Madras in India occupied in 1746, primarily in response to the French loss of the North American fort of Louisbourg on Isle Royale (now Cape Breton Island), close to the cod fisheries off Newfoundland and those in the Gulf of Saint Lawrence.[23]

The Peace of Aix-la-Chapelle (Aachen) of 1748 that concluded the War of the Austrian Succession solved nothing. Britain and France swapped their conquests of Louisbourg and Madras, France had to give up the Austrian Netherlands, and generally everything was restored to prewar conditions. The enormous war effort therefore seemed entirely in vain to the Britons—many of whom thought King George II's chief concern had been to protect his native Hanover, of which he was the elector—but even more to the French, who coined the popular expression "stupid as the peace." Although Austria was left a weaker power at war's end, the price France paid was high, her treasury facing a bill of ten million livres, or the equivalent of almost four years of royal income. In addition, the war saw the emergence of Prussia and Russia as dangerous French rivals to the east. Finally, irregular warfare had taken place between British and French forces (both helped by Indian allies) in North America, whetting Britain's appetite for expansion, leaving New France in jeopardy, and creating a climate of hate and fear.[24]

The root cause of the rivalry in North America was that the peace of 1748 failed to solve one long-standing issue: the boundaries between French and British territories. Where was the border between eastern Canada and New England? Who had a legitimate claim on the Ohio Valley? France had previously had the upper hand in the area between Lake Erie and the Allegheny Mountains, cultivating close relations with a great many indigenous nations, but during the latest war, the French had found it difficult and expensive to maintain the practice of gift-giving in exchange for furs. To make matters worse, British encroachments began to occur on "French" lands. In order to preempt this and maintain communications between Canada and Louisiana, the French in 1753 started the construction of a string of forts, further alienating local groups such as the Shawnees and the Delawares, which now allied themselves with the British.

The French were dealing not only with British policymakers here. They also faced American colonists, who were eager to move into unexplored lands from Pennsylvania and Virginia. Wealthy planters and speculators formed the Ohio Company, a land speculation company that began building a fort in the upper Ohio Valley. To protect the fort against the French, Virginia's Lieutenant Governor Robert Dinwiddie, one of the Company speculators, sent an expedition of Virginia volunteers to the upper Ohio Valley in 1754. Commanded by a young George Washington, the Virginians tasted defeat and retreated. The British cabinet made heavy weather of these hostilities, viewing them as evidence of French aggression. The dispatch of six hundred fresh French soldiers to reinforce the garrison in Louisbourg seemed to offer only further proof. In reality, however, the French also acted out of self-preservation.[25]

Skirmishes in America did not cause the war that was soon to start in Europe. The seeds for the Seven Years' War had been planted earlier, in Aix-la-Chapelle.[26] The new war was preceded by a spectacular reversal of alliances. In January 1756, Britain abandoned her old Austrian ally and signed an alliance with mighty Prussia, followed by an alliance in May between France and her old Austrian foe. Compared to the last war, this one had more pronounced global dimensions. The war theaters in India, the Caribbean, and North America forced France to fight a war on multiple fronts, benefiting Prussia, which had little to fear from its west. But before that became clear, Frederick the Great had struck with a lightning campaign against Saxony. He exploited his new conquest to the fullest, incorporating Saxon soldiers into his army and using its economic resources to continue the war. And those resources came on top of Prussia's gigantic military budget and large subsidies from Britain.[27] Still, Prussia did not win the war in 1756. In the years ahead, her fortune waxed and waned as both Russia and Austria invaded the country, both occupying the capital city of Berlin.[28]

Britain was again mostly concerned about Hanover, the target of the French war machine. The French rationale was to restore lost territories in the Americas by means of military pressure in Europe. That was a wise strategy that ultimately persuaded the British to abandon their course to monopolize the Newfoundland fisheries. The French navy, smaller than the British but still respectable, was thereby saved from ruin, since those fisheries were the nursery of French seamen, whom French statesmen were, of course, eager to use in times of war. Strengthened after 1763, the French navy would intervene in the War of American Independence to Britain's detriment.[29] Naval activity was widespread in the Caribbean, where Britain and France were out to destroy each other's sugar colonies or, if that proved impossible, to starve the enemy of slaves and provisions, thereby hurting sugar production. Exploiting its naval superiority and competence in amphibious warfare, Britain managed to capture both Guadeloupe (1759) and Martinique (1762) as well as two other, tiny, islands. In the latter year, the Royal Navy also conquered the Spanish colonial towns of Havana (Cuba) and Manila (Philippines). Spain had entered the war only in early 1762, when Britain declared war on the Bourbon monarchy after King Charles III signed a new Family Compact with his French neighbors, joining them in a military alliance. Although Spain's main reason for entering the war was the fear that a British victory in Canada would increase British power in the New World, it seriously underestimated Britain's military capability.[30]

Prior to her Caribbean victories, Britain had made great strides against France in North America, beginning with the implementation of a Western Squadron off the British Isles, which enabled the capture of Fort Beauséjour (in present-day New Brunswick), leaving Britain in control of most of Acadia. Eventually, Britain completely removed the French from Canada due to superior troop strength and the erosion of Indian support for New France. Traders from the Thirteen Colonies moved in to supply goods to native groups, who were also impressed by British successes on the North American battlefields after 1758. At the same time, British forces settled scores with those Indians opposing them in the most ruthless ways, as they did with the Cherokees in 1760–1761.[31]

Britain and Prussia emerged as victors of the Seven Years' War in February 1763, when two treaties put an end to the hostilities. Prussia retained possession of Silesia, but not of Saxony, Austria lost power, France surrendered all of Canada, the political control she had wielded in India, as well as possession of some minor Caribbean islands (Tobago, Dominica, Saint Vincent, and the Grenadines), but regained those captured by Britain during the war. France's status as a world power remained intact, however, since she retained her main Caribbean colonies as well as the island of Gorée in West Africa, the important center of the Atlantic slave trade that British forces had seized during the war.[32]

As the recipient of French-held areas, the former Spanish colony of Florida, and all other Spanish territories east of the Mississippi River, Great Britain, once a typical seaborne empire, overnight became a territorial empire in America. But the price was high. Britain spent much more than in the previous three major wars: eighty-two million pounds compared to thirty-two million in the Nine Years' War (1688–1697), fifty million in the War of the Spanish Succession (1701–1714), and forty-three million in the War of the Austrian Succession. Like in the earlier three wars, about two-thirds of the war was financed by income and only one-third by debt.[33] In other countries, the war exacerbated existing economic woes. Much of Europe's credit system was built on a shaky base that was exposed as the war progressed. The resulting economic recession left its mark around the continent, forcing numerous banks and industrial firms to close down.[34] Europe's main powers were thus compelled to embark on ambitious programs of fiscal and military reform to pay for the previous war and prepare for the next. These reforms would help undermine the stability of the old regimes.

2

Civil War in the British Empire

The American Revolution

In the eighteenth century, continental British America was in a state of constant demographic flux. Free and indentured immigrants arrived from Germany and the British Isles, enslaved blacks from the Caribbean and Africa. Africans were brought against their will to spend their days in servitude. Whites were lured by the freedom to worship, to settle and work the land for themselves, and to elect and reject those in political office. Their continual immigration pushed the frontier (zones of intensive interaction) with Indians ever farther to the west, setting off numerous migrations among native groups.

Indians and whites had been neighbors since the beginning of European settlement. By the middle of the eighteenth century, their lives were intertwined in myriad ways. Indians adopted European commodities, using linen, woolens, and cotton in their clothing, while white frontiersmen led a life that was heavily influenced by Indians. Their lifestyles may have had much in common, but the interests of both groups were incompatible. Natives wanted to remain on their ancestral lands, but colonists wanted to turn those lands into pastures for cattle or fields for grain. The intensification of their commercial relationship spelled doom for the Indians, who first traded away all their products and were then forced to give up part of their lands, as settlers benefited from a steady increase in land grants to wealthy speculators.[1] Oneida chief Conoghquieson complained in 1768 that his young men hunting in their own country could no longer procure "Venison to Eat, or Bark to make huts, for the Beasts are run away and the Trees cut down."[2]

Land grants, protected by judges and lawyers, boosted the British presence in the Ohio Country, where the conflict between France and Britain came to a head. Both believed that whoever controlled the Ohio Valley would control the continent. It was here, in the frontier area west of the Appalachians encompassing modern-day Ohio, western Pennsylvania, eastern Indiana, and northwestern West Virginia, that the Seven Years' War began.[3] The Europeans were not the only aliens to claim possession of the Ohio Country. The Iroquois Confederacy, also known as the Six Nations, based its claim on conquest, but never proceeded to occupy the territory. It did, however, lend legitimacy to the expansion of Pennsylvania into the lands along the Susquehanna and Delaware rivers after 1732.

Vacated by natives in the mid-seventeenth century, the Ohio Country remained no-man's-land until the immigration of Delaware and Shawnee Indians in the 1720s. Two decades later, some Iroquois known as Senecas also moved from the north into Ohio Country, perhaps to move close to French traders or to resettle ancestral lands. In these decades, regional indigenous identities developed that were not really tied to Delaware, Shawnee, and Seneca kinfolk in the east. Midcentury native communities were often multitribal and based on kinship networks.[4] Suspicious of French and British ambitions and wary of Six Nations pretensions, the Indians were also threatened by traders and speculators from various colonies on the eastern seaboard. The number of peddlers grew dramatically as natives appreciated their superior affordable goods. The price was high: the Europeans' hunger for fur forced Indians to hunt beavers—their livelihood—almost to extinction, and the native addiction to liquor caused social disruption.

The presence of British subjects stirred up bad blood among the French in Canada, who perceived the Ohio Country as vital to their connection with Louisiana. French military leaders were willing to risk their peaceful relations with Pennsylvania by inciting their native allies to remove British interlopers, only to find natives not very willing to engage in acts of violence against the British. Instead of British traders, it was French peddlers whom the Indians resented, not merely due to their expensive, low-grade wares, but especially because of their lack of fairness. Anti-French sentiment ran so high that Senecas, Shawnees, Delawares, Mingos, and other Ohio Indians formed an alliance in 1747.[5] Encroachments by British subjects eventually turned the tide. With French help, the Indians successfully waged war against the "British" colonists, killing seven hundred of them in the mid-1750s. This slowed down but did not halt the flow of colonists moving into the backcountry, where they settled into a life of raising crops and livestock. Divided by ethnic backgrounds—the largest group was made up of the Scotch-Irish (or Ulster Scots), followed by Irish, Germans, Scots, Welsh, and English—they were also separated by denomination: Presbyterians, Anglicans, Baptists, Quakers, Mennonites, and Roman Catholics all found their way to the frontier.[6]

Whether they remained on the eastern seaboard or moved west, European settlers found a combination of conditions in Britain's North American provinces that set them apart from other New World colonies: "Weakness of royal authority relative to local assemblies, an extensive territory, widespread property ownership, relatively high degrees of social mobility, explosive population growth, growth of settlements and high levels of internal migration, and a less stratified society."[7] Similar to Australia and New Zealand in a later era, the emptiness of mainland British America produced a relatively egalitarian society. A remarkable number of white North Americans were yeoman farmers, smaller farmers, artisans, and others who were socially independent. Social values were consequently largely those of the middling groups.[8] Yet this was not a classless society. The lives of planters, landlords, merchants, and lawyers contrasted markedly with those led by free laborers, servants, and slaves. In the South, the differences between haves and have-nots were the most conspicuous. Chesapeake planters differed from other colonial elites not only in their ownership of large numbers of slaves but also in their lifestyle and aspirations, trying to emulate (but never equaling) the English landed gentry. Noting that planters on both banks of the James River in Virginia treated their slaves cruelly, one foreign observer added in 1782 that the "whites believe that they debase themselves if they engage in the work they say is fit only for these wretched beings."[9]

England's Glorious Revolution of 1688–1689, which had established freedom from arbitrary power, religious toleration, and the maxim of representation, promoted belief in an ideology that the colonies clung to, each in its own way. Representation originated in the early days of the colonies, when assemblies were set up in Virginia and Bermuda that assumed tasks such as taxation, local administration, and the maintenance of public order. These experiences set the tone for colonies founded afterward, so that by 1640, eight assemblies were functioning in the colonies, seven of which were in North America.[10] In the nascent colonial societies, where virtually all white males who were not indentured owned freehold property, qualifications for voting were much more generous than in England itself. By the middle decades of the eighteenth century, up to 75 percent of all adult males in Pennsylvania, over 75 percent in Massachusetts, and between 50 and 80 percent in New York enjoyed the right to vote in town elections. In the main cities, the percentages were even higher. Popular participation in colonial politics was made possible by the rise in the eighteenth century of the lower houses of the assembly at the cost of royal authority.[11]

This rise of the assemblies was part of a trend that diminished royal authority, thus reversing a process of enhancement of royal authority that had developed since the restoration of the power of the Crown in Britain after 1660. Bent on reducing the autonomy of the New England colonies, the Crown established the Dominion of New England in 1686, which dissolved existing assemblies and set up a royal government. This was not to last. After two and a half years, an organized rebellion overthrew the Dominion (which also included New York and New Jersey), and the autonomy of the individual colonies was restored in most cases after 1692. Elsewhere, no action was taken against colonial assemblies, yet all but five charter and proprietary colonies in North America were royalized, and governors were installed wielding vast powers, such as the right to veto laws and fire judges. In the course of the eighteenth century, however, they had to hand over more and more authority to the legislative assemblies. Since the Crown needed support from these representative bodies to finance local government and imperial warfare, the metropolis could not thrust its policies on the mainland colonies. The era of what historians have dubbed "salutary neglect" of the colonies was born. The Navigation Acts were, for example, evaded on a large scale without any retaliatory measures from royal appointees.[12] Those who attempted to properly perform their tasks usually encountered obstruction, not cooperation, from the local colonial authorities, who used the entire legal apparatus to have their way.[13]

In other respects as well, authority was weak in early America, shown "in the widespread lack of respect or deference of inferiors to their social betters and political officials."[14] This mentality extended to the imperial relationship, as a traveling Englishman noted: "The public or political character of the Virginians, corresponds with their private one:

they are haughty and jealous of their liberties, impatient of restraint, and can scarcely bear the thought of being controuled [*sic*] by any superior power. Many of them consider the colonies as independent states, unconnected with Great Britain, otherwise than by having the same common king, and being bound to her with natural affection."[15] North Americans thus revealed the importance of their independence, defined in practice as the freedom from others. The achievement of independence was the life story of the bulk of the white settlers, many of whom had risen from modest beginnings by means of hard work.[16] They were not going to give that up.

The average free male in colonial British North America was not just fiercely independent; he and his family were also well-off. Their standard of living may have been higher than anywhere else in the world up until that time.[17] If Spain valued her colonies as producers of silver, Britain cherished her North American provinces as consumers of English exports and reexports, although the production of cash crops was not insignificant. The Chesapeake stood out for the value of its tobacco exports to the metropolis, accounting for £756,128 per year from 1768 to 1772, ten times the amount of all exports from New England. At the same time, West Indian sugar exports to Great Britain, worth £3 million, easily eclipsed exports from the Chesapeake.[18]

Colonial imports initially did not count for much, but their value grew considerably in the eighteenth century, from 11 percent of English exports in 1700–1701 and 16 percent in 1750–1751 to 38 percent in 1772–1773. Of British goods consumed in the North American colonies, 90 percent were (semi)manufactured commodities, such as woolens, linens, silk, cottons, and hardware.[19] These exports helped compensate for the decline in continental European demand for English manufactures. Finished manufactures were far less important in the trade of the West Indian islands from Britain, accounting on average for only 19 percent of imports. Foodstuffs were much more prominent, with grain, hops, and fish making up more than half of all imports from Britain.[20] The importance of the export trade to the Thirteen Colonies was such that English caricatures commonly represented America as barrels or piles of goods.[21]

Dramatic population growth was an important factor in the rising economic significance of British North America. Virginia grew from

130,000 (1750) to over 400,000 (1775) and New York from 73,000 (1749) to 168,000 (1771).[22] By 1775, all of British America had 3 million inhabitants, distributed as follows: 1.3 million in the South (Maryland, Virginia, North and South Carolina, and Georgia), 700,000 in the Middle Colonies (Delaware, New Jersey, New York, and Pennsylvania), 600,000 in New England (New Hampshire, Massachusetts, Connecticut, and Rhode Island), 400,000 in the Caribbean, including Bermuda and the Bahamas, and 30,000 in Newfoundland and Nova Scotia.[23]

The Seven Years' War

The Seven Years' War was a watershed on the frontier. Thousands of settlers fled east when Indian fighters used massive violence against squatters. The actions of natives were mostly reactive. Their numbers dwindling everywhere, they were forced to ally themselves with the two warring European powers, both colonial militias and regular forces. As warfare destroyed entire villages, Indian dependence on European supplies grew at the same time that Indians' resentment over the continuous theft of their lands found an outlet in raids of white settlements. In Pennsylvania and Virginia, they burned cabins, barns, and fields, took whites captive, and killed others in campaigns of psychological warfare.

Meanwhile, the fortunes of the British army changed in a spectacular fashion in 1759, as the Six Nations, including warriors who had aided the French earlier in the war, allied themselves with their traditional foes. Their decision was prompted by the fear that a powerful new Indian confederacy was forming in the west. With the help of the Iroquois, Britain's troops—now including numerous colonists—beat the French decisively. Their victories laid the foundation for the Treaty of Paris (1763), in which France surrendered New France and all of her North American territories east of the Mississippi River, amounting to a loss of half a billion acres. French defeat also left the Indians much more vulnerable than they had ever been, since the danger that British measures would drive Indians into the arms of the French was no longer a factor.[24]

A revolt that broke out after hostilities ended between the French and the British showed continued Indian strength. In May 1763, at least seven nations joined in surprise attacks on British posts, capturing several and laying siege to others. Within two years, the charismatic Ottawa war chief Pontiac, for whom the revolt was named, and his men reclaimed hunting grounds on the frontiers of Pennsylvania, Maryland, and Virginia, taking British forts and killing or capturing two thousand traders and settlers along the way.[25] For their part, settlers wreaked havoc in native communities, such as a group of Scotch-Irish farmers known as the Paxton Boys who killed some twenty native Conestoga men, women, and children without any provocation. Pontiac's War exacerbated tensions between settlers and the metropolis, as the "redcoats" proved unable to sufficiently guard colonists against native violence and even protected Indians and their hunting grounds. Still, it would be wrong to suggest that the British army sided with the Indians. Commander-in-chief Jeffrey Amherst even considered germ warfare to put them in their place, but the natives were stricken with smallpox before he could act.[26] The King's Proclamation of October 7, 1763, explicitly sought to limit the land grants and prevent more warfare between colonists and Indians by prohibiting settlement west of the Appalachians and recognizing Indians' rights to unceded lands. But although the Proclamation deterred land companies, whose members included George Washington, Thomas Jefferson, and other speculators, settlers continued to ignore metropolitan dictates. In fact, the British victory in the Seven Years' War opened the floodgates of settlement from Quebec and Maine to the Floridas. Meanwhile, traders from all walks of life poured into Indian country in the South, availing themselves of the Proclamation's stipulation that the Indian trade was open to all British subjects.[27]

In two provinces, the Seven Years' War led to major changes. If Pennsylvanians and Virginians had little prior exposure to their provincial assemblies, warfare changed that (especially in Pennsylvania, whose legislature had never engaged in warfare before), as assemblies assumed the task to raise and provision armies. The war also bred mutual suspicion between British subjects on either side of the ocean. British officials blamed colonists for their small financial contributions to the war effort and criticized them for their reluctance to defend themselves. Settlers, for their part, lost their confidence in the redcoats, whose performance was at times unconvincing and awkward, as impressive as the capture of Havana and other campaigns may have been. Tensions with the mother country mounted as the Crown annulled several land grants, British soldiers removed some squatters, and settlers wondered why they

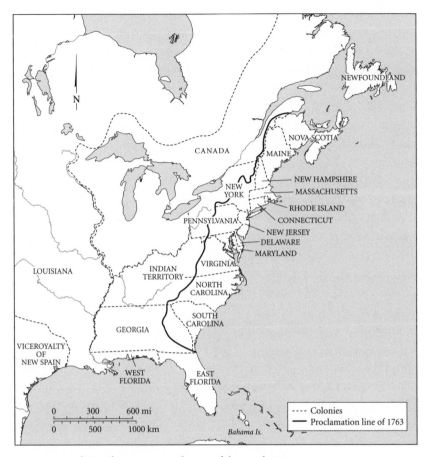

Map 2.1. British North America on the eve of the revolution.

had fought in the Seven Years' War in the first place. The war also left a legacy of violence between colonists and natives, which was bolstered by incidents during Pontiac's War. Consequently, frontier settlers now saw Indians, and not the colonial elite or distant Britain, as their main enemy.[28]

The impact of the Seven Years' War on all Thirteen Colonies was to end the long reign of salutary neglect. With theaters in Europe, North America, the Caribbean, and the Indian subcontinent, warfare had far-reaching financial consequences for the countries involved.[29] Although Britain emerged victorious and obtained, it seemed, unrivaled global military superiority, her war expenditures would haunt her. Her commitment to preserving the conquests made during the war and safe-guarding the frontier areas, which colonists allegedly had been unable to do, required a large naval and military presence. Given the economic malaise, politicians wanted to spare British taxpayers and make the wealthy Americans pay for their own defense. This happened without much reflection, since policymakers assigned a subordinate role in the empire to the American provinces. This position was summarized in the Declaratory Act of 1766 as follows: "that the king's majesty, by and with the advice and consent of the lords spiritual and temporal, and com-mons of Great Britain, in parliament assembled, had, hath, and of right ought to have, full power and authority to make laws and statutes of sufficient force and validity to bind the colonies and people of America, subjects of the crown of Great Britain, in all cases whatsoever."[30]

The Declaratory Act was part of a string of laws enacted for North America in the decade after the Seven Years' War. With every act, the metropolis and the colonies came to loggerheads before repeal brought about reconciliation. At first, nobody in North America was interested in revolution. Independence was inconceivable, as Andrew Eliot of Bos-ton remonstrated in a sermon in 1765: "We highly value our connection with Great-Britain, there is perhaps not a man to be found among us, who would wish to be independent of our mother-country, we should regret the most distant thought of such an event."[31] Nevertheless, the adoption in London of the Sugar Act in the previous year had damaged the imperial relationship. The Sugar Act was intended to replace the Mo-lasses Act of 1733, which had imposed a heavy tax of six pence per gallon on all foreign rum, molasses, and sugar imported into British America, but had hardly been enforced. The extent of official neglect was shown in Salem, Massachusetts, in 1758, when merchants rose in rebellion after customs officers began to collect 10 percent of the tax.[32] The solution ad-opted was to lower the duty on foreign molasses to three pence per gal-lon, to be enforced rigorously. Continued smuggling would induce the ministry to lower the tax even further, to one pence, in 1766. But other provisions of the original law hurt American merchants much more, such as the stipulation that logwood, boards, and staves, all commodi-ties in which the Americans enjoyed a lively trade with foreign colonies, could be transported only from the British Caribbean to the mother country. Besides, new rules were approved to enforce the law. Merchants who were unable to produce the correct shipping manifests were to be prosecuted and their sentence pronounced not by a jury but by a royally appointed judge of a vice-admiralty court.[33]

In the following years, customs officials, who had never been well-liked, were the target of popular anger, directed at them because they put ships under embargo on suspicion of iniquities. In one incident in May 1769, none of the neighbors, except for one servant, came to the rescue when the house of Boston's customs collector Henry Hulton caught fire. And when he moved his family to Brookline, five miles away, a Boston mob assaulted Hulton in his own home. Other customs officials were tarred and feathered, though none as brutally as John Malcom. In New Hampshire, Malcom first underwent this treatment in 1773 after seizing a brig that was not registered, then again when a crowd seized him in Boston in January 1774 for violently attacking a shoemaker. The Bostonians stripped and flogged Malcom, then carted him around for several hours. As a result, he lost strips of skin and suffered frostbite.[34]

Such uprisings, in which urbanites took part in the conviction that their actions were for the common good, were a time-honored way to protest British policies. They constituted an important form of American resistance against British policies up to the outbreak of the revolution. Largely an urban phenomenon, the riots were usually directed against customs officials or impressment of Americans for the Royal Navy.[35] The mobs, in which sailors and free and enslaved blacks featured prominently, did not act autonomously, but cooperated with the leaders of the colonial opposition movement, who in Boston did their utmost to unleash the mob against the British. They achieved this goal only after the North End and South End mobs made peace in 1765, allowing for a united front against the introduction of the so-called Stamp Act later that year.[36] First, the Sons of Liberty, a group made up of workers, artisans, and shopkeepers, hanged in effigy stamp collector Andrew Oliver and battered his home, and later attacked the homes of three other officials, including that of Deputy Governor Thomas Hutchinson. The crowds had been energized by a sermon by Jonathan Mayhew. From Boston, riots spread elsewhere. Mobs opposed to the Stamp Act also held sway in New York for many months.[37]

Growing directly out of the Seven Years' War, the Stamp Act was devised to tap the economy of the American colonies on an unprecedented

Figure 2.1. Customs officer John Malcom was first tarred and feathered by sailors in New Hampshire in November 1773 for seizing a brig for lack of registration. He underwent the same ritual in Boston on January 25, 1774, after violently attacking a shoemaker. On the second occasion, depicted here, Malcom was stripped, flogged, and carted around for several hours. As a result, he not only lost strips of skin but also suffered frostbite. Unsurprisingly, Malcom never joined the cause of the revolution and retired to England. Courtesy of the John Carter Brown Library at Brown University.

scale by requiring payment of a stamp for a wide variety of documents to obtain legal force, including land transactions, probate orders, articles of apprenticeship, liquor licenses, documents bearing on court cases, passports, newspapers, and notarizations. To add insult to injury, the stamp had to be paid in sterling, and not in the form of a bill of exchange, foreign currency, or local tender. And few residents of the colonies disposed of hard British cash. Whereas the Sugar Act made an impact in port cities, especially in Massachusetts, Rhode Island, and New York, the Stamp Act brought about a direct confrontation between Britain and all American towns.[38]

The two reforms deepened the economic crisis of the 1760s. As manufacturers and merchants in England saw business decline, the ministry in London set about to reverse the Stamp Act. That was no simple task, since British Parliament roared with anger about the "ingrate" Americans who resented "taxation without representation." What the Americans meant was that they had not had any say in the new taxes, nor could they have been heard. Delegates from several American colonies meeting in New York therefore agreed that the Stamp Act was unconstitutional. Only their own assemblies, in which they were represented, had the right to tax the colonists. British Treasury Secretary Thomas Whately argued, however, that the Americans were virtually represented in Parliament just like the many men and all women in Britain who played no direct part in electing its members. On the other hand, William Pitt the Elder, Secretary of State during the Seven Years' War and now a member of the opposition, agreed wholeheartedly with the overseas rioters, rejoicing, as he said, that the Americans had resisted. And he added: "I desire to know when they were made slaves?" In combination with the testimony of Benjamin Franklin and the numerous petitions by merchants and manufacturers that sketched the Stamp Act's negative impact, Pitt's speech convinced a majority in the Houses of Commons and Lords to vote for repeal. In March 1766, the act was canceled.[39]

Ironically, the most serious financial impact of the Stamp Act was felt in the Caribbean colonies, but apart from protests in two of the Leeward Islands (Saint Kitts and Nevis), no serious objections were raised there, nor did anybody bring up the colonists' rights. It was in North America that the new law set off a deep crisis, in which British sovereignty was disputed for the first time. The act's ultimate repeal made no difference, especially since Britain's policymakers did not give up on their attempts to raise revenue from the American colonies. This task was now entrusted to Charles Townshend, Chancellor of the Exchequer, who suggested levying duties on items of which England monopolized the trade and whose overall economic significance was small, thus leaving trading patterns unharmed. The articles included china, glass, paper, lead, painters' colors, and tea. To enforce the tax, an American Board of Customs Collectors was established, based in Boston. In June 1767, the bill sailed through Parliament and on July 2, King George III signed it, not in the least expecting that this revenues act would provoke another storm of protest on the other side of the ocean.[40]

Individuals all over America decided to curtail luxury and stimulate local industries by boycotting silk and satin clothes, "English" tea, foreign wines, clocks, mirrors, jewelry, funerary goods, and other imported luxuries. This boycott went hand in hand with encomiums on locally made goods. Women were encouraged to lead the way, newspapers imploring them to save rags for papermaking. In dozens of spinning meetings they were urged to take the lead in manufacturing clothing.[41] The most important form of resistance was nonimportation of British goods, which had been successfully pioneered three years earlier during the Stamp Act crisis. Back then, New York's merchant community had taken the initiative and Philadelphia and Boston had followed the example. In early 1768, Boston was the first to boycott British goods, with the merchants of New York following suit, but those of Philadelphia put off a decision, joining the boycott only in March 1769 after large stocks of British commodities had been received. The campaign was not effective everywhere. Many inland towns did not observe it, and in Virginia, the boycott was a total failure. Nor were any nonimportation associations set up in the West Indies, where the successive acts—except for the Stamp Act—had caused little distress, in part because the newly formed American Board of Customs Collectors had no authority over the islands.[42]

In North America, nonimportation was more than a protest against British legislation. By means of nonimportation, patriot leaders and ordinary urban dwellers became allies. As the little activities of everyday life such as drinking tea and spinning were linked to the larger constitutional issue, they became politically charged. In addition, nonimportation allowed merchants to dispose of goods that had not sold well and, because bills of exchange were cheaper now, it enabled them to pay the debts they had in Britain.[43] Designed as a temporary relief measure, the boycott had outlived its usefulness in 1770, when it began to fade and trade with Britain resumed everywhere.

Before nonimportation had stopped, the ministry in London once again came to the rescue of metropolitan merchants who had suffered under nonimportation. In March 1770, it canceled the duties on glass, lead, painters' colors, and paper, laying the foundation for a peaceful interval, although the Townshend Acts had not been repealed in full. The years 1770 to 1773 were marked by imperial harmony, predicated on the remarkable growth in trade, manufacture, mining, and banking in Britain and the European continent, which rubbed off on America.

This was accompanied by a seemingly unlimited availability of credit, leading to immense speculation. The bubble burst in 1772, setting off a credit crisis that spread unchecked and thereby accelerated the conflict with the mother country. If the issues at stake in this conflict were of a constitutional nature, it is clear that the most serious opposition came from colonies hit hardest by the crisis, including Massachusetts, Virginia, and Maryland, while a port city like Philadelphia, which did not suffer economically, failed to produce a movement lambasting British policies.[44] The planters in Virginia, where the value of tobacco was almost halved in the span of one year, conflated the economic and political woes, branding British merchants as agents of an oppressive regime. Planters had always consigned their tobacco to the merchants, who were willing to extend credit to the planters, enabling these to weather hard times. But now that the crisis had touched the merchants, they dared to call in long-standing debts, which caused a breakdown in the traditional relationship.[45]

If Virginia's planters vented their displeasure on British merchants, the port cities of the eastern seaboard declared war on a new law introduced in London: the Tea Act of May 10, 1773. The rationale for this law was to provide relief for the struggling East India Company, which was losing its fight against smugglers. The Company derived her earnings from the sale of Chinese tea in England, tea accounting for 90 percent of her commercial profits. But inland and customs duties in England were so high that much tea was smuggled into the British Isles from the continent. The Company's condition was so bleak that the Bank of England refused to grant another extension on a loan after the onset of the 1772 credit crisis. At this juncture, the ministry intervened, first by attempting to sell Company tea duty-free on the European mainland—a plan that failed—and then by sending it to North America and granting the Company the monopoly of selling tea there. That is how the Tea Act came about.[46]

The adoption of the act put an end to three years of peaceful transatlantic relations. A first violent confrontation between "redcoats" and American settlers in Boston had occurred in 1770. British soldiers had stayed in North America after the war for a variety of reasons. They were to occupy and defend the newly acquired territories of the North (Canada, Nova Scotia) and South (Florida) and those in the interior.

And since they found themselves on American soil, they were also responsible for policing the trading posts west of the settled areas where Indians and whites exchanged goods. That policy aimed at discouraging settlers from stealing Indian lands and at preventing white traders from abusing their Indian counterparts by enabling only traders licensed by the local governor or the British commander-in-chief to engage in business deals. The plan was, in other words, for the army to function as a police force, but that proved unfeasible. By 1768, the fur trade was still unregulated and the army did not thwart illegal squatters in any way.[47]

In the East, soldiers were to combat lawlessness in Boston. They were called upon after customs officials in that city fled in March 1768, having failed to arrest a sloop of John Hancock. The arrival of more than four battalions from Halifax and Ireland did not spark protests, but the measures army commanders took to fight their desertion, sentineling guards all over the city, ultimately alienated the population.[48] The tense situation boiled over in March 1770 when soldiers fired into a hostile crowd, killing five civilians: the "Boston Massacre." Although the regiment's captain and the soldiers won acquittals, three years without hostilities ensued. The Tea Act proved that old sensibilities had not vanished. In the eyes of many Americans, there was no disguising the fact that Parliament did not care about the rights of colonial subjects. Fond of "English" tea, Bostonians made heavy weather of the new act. During a mass rally on December 16, 1773, they decided to dump East India Company tea in the harbor. A few dozen males dressed as Mohawks spent hours on board three ships casting ninety thousand pounds of tea into the water. Parliament's reaction to the Tea Party (as the dumping would be labeled decades later) was to close Boston Harbor, alter the Massachusetts charter, and occupy the town with British troops. According to the new charter, the Crown would henceforth nominate the Council—the upper house of the legislature, which had always been elected; the governor, instead of a popularly elected committee, would appoint civil officials; towns could not meet unless with royal approval; and sheriffs would select juries. Self-governance in the Bay State thus effectively ceased to be.[49]

Like their predecessors, the new soldiers had to deal with an ill-disposed population. Even the unemployed sailors, dockworkers, and other mechanics exhorted by British colonial officials to build barracks for the four regiments arriving in August 1774 declined the jobs they were offered. Carpenters and bricklayers had to be imported all the way from Nova Scotia. Solidarity against perceived British injustice was also on display farther south, in Virginia. The legislature, the House of Burgesses, decided that June 1, 1774, was to be a colony-wide day of fasting and prayer. Most important, the British overreaction made all Thirteen Colonies, except for Georgia, send delegates to a Continental Congress in Philadelphia.[50]

The delegates quickly agreed on a Declaration of Rights. London, they contended, had no right to tax and legislate the colonies, whose rights originated from the laws of nature, the British Constitution, and the colonial charters.[51] This declaration was followed six days later, on October 20, 1774, by a momentous decision, when Congress recommended the colonies to form so-called associations. These new bodies' task was to make sure that a boycott of British goods was effective, while pursuing an economic program that had to reduce dependence on those same items while encouraging the production and consumption of goods made in America. Everywhere, associations sprang up like mushrooms, producing texts that were distributed in all the townships, counties, and villages, as "associators" persuaded the male residents to sign the documents. Outside of Georgia, whose governor's loyalty to the metropolis did not waver, the Carolina backcountry and pockets of New York State, the willingness to sign was large. In Virginia, for example, the support for nonimportation was widespread, due especially to the economic recession that had set in two years before. The lack of imported British goods actually made it easy to proclaim a "boycott," just as the old strategy to withhold the crop could now be presented as patriotic "nonexportation."[52]

Emboldened by their unprecedented success, the associations or committees began to concern themselves with politics in 1775, producing new texts that stressed the natural and constitutional liberties and rights of the Americans. All men who refused to sign risked exile or other punishments. When war broke out, they were disarmed and branded as Tories, the enemies of the movement that was gaining momentum against British rule. The committees constantly swung into action, raiding Tory communities, and chiding or punishing individual Tories who defended British policies, bypassed the trade boycott, or rejected the authority of the Continental Congress. A German officer wrote in 1777: "Heaven help him who is suspected of being a Tory! Many families are now living under this suspicion. At their command the minister leaves the altar, and the male members of his congregation grasp the musket and the powder-horn."[53]

In Philadelphia, the committees shaped anti-British opposition. Neither rich nor poor, their members tended to be radicals, who in speeches, broadsides, and newspaper articles persuaded the general population to support a "continental congress." They helped create a united front among people who had always been divided along ethnic, religious, and class lines.[54] In other towns, the committees were also the engines of the revolution, their members preaching the vices of British politics and the virtues that America and her inhabitants represented.[55] Ministers were no less outspoken in their sermons, and their audiences were larger than those of other rebel activists. The Massachusetts House of Representatives recognized this when it urged the clergy to sermonize about the rights of the colonies and the oppressive conduct of the mother country. Ministers eagerly obliged, stressing that the colonies had originated as bulwarks of freedom and that freedom had to be defended at all costs. Along with other ideologues, they forged a philosophy that praised the British Constitution, while criticizing British policies. Shared allegiance had always bound Britons and Americans together, but Britain was only one part of this community and thus unable to claim jurisdiction over the whole community of allegiance. Americans could not be subjects of subjects. The only connecting principle of the empire was the king, whose role was that of mediator in conflicts.[56]

But the king's reputation was irreparably damaged. In the course of 1775, George III became the target of frontal assaults. By giving up the protection of his people and ignoring humble petitions, he was said to have revealed himself as a tyrant. He had become the complete opposite of the "Good Prince." Nor did his standing improve after the war broke out. On July 9, 1776, twenty-six indictments of the king were read aloud in New York City, after which a crowd tore down an equestrian statue of the king that had been erected only six years before. His image hit rock bottom by the end of the war, when George was quoted in an anonymously published dialogue with the devil, confessing that he had destroyed at least fifty thousand people in his attempt to enslave America. Nor did he plan to stop. "And should I succeed," he added, "I'll surpass in barbarity any tyrant that ever lived."[57]

One of the rabble-rousers who directed his venom at the king was corset-maker Thomas Paine (1737–1809), an Englishman who had moved to Pennsylvania in October 1774. He absorbed the growing anti-British feelings, putting them into words in his pamphlet *Common Sense* (January 1776), which sold 150,000 copies. Paine's unambiguous judgment helped steer the revolutionary movement on the path to independence, revealing the evils of monarchy and subordination, and underscoring that no advantage could be derived from reconciliation with the mother country. Instead of "the Royal Brute of Britain," law would rule in America. A rift with Britain, Paine went on, would clear the way for the foundation of a republic, whose rulers were bound by written charters and chosen by popular election. Most pressing, given the reality of the war, was a declaration of independence, since it would enable the support of France and Spain. As long as Americans professed themselves subjects of the British king, foreign countries would remain aloof and see them as rebels.

British tyranny was a pervasive theme of contemporary American pamphlet literature, just like British corruption. The Americans defined liberty as the exercise of natural rights within limits set by laws. Defeated elsewhere sooner or later, the rule of law had triumphed in Britain thanks to a constitution that balanced the Crown, the nobility, and the democracy. But it was a precarious victory that did not last. Britain had "sunk in corruption," resembling decadent Rome before the fall, led by self-interest and indulging in luxury. Freedom was at risk, since wealth and inequality had spawned greed and dependency. Britain's degeneracy contained the warning that corruption could easily spread among Americans as well. They had to guard against moral decline by behaving in a frugal, industrious, temperate, and simple way, and sacrificing private interests to the revolutionary ideal. That was one aspect of republicanism. It also stood for a society in which every man enjoyed the right to property, whereby he rid himself of dependence on others and qualified to participate in politics. Individual freedom was not much stressed in the revolutionary heat of 1775 and 1776. The focus was on the struggle against British privileges, the trampling of the public rights of an entire people.[58]

Much of this was of course propaganda. The men who were mapping out the road to revolution did not identify with the entire people, fearing the sailors and slaves who had kept alive revolutionary fervor during the crisis with Britain. Even Paine turned against mobs after a riot in Philadelphia in 1779. Once the revolution was consolidated, the shock troops were no longer needed and had to be disbanded.[59]

The Revolutionary War in the West

Indigenous Americans did not belong to "the people" either. Patriots did not respect native land rights and did all they could to seize frontier territories. One reason they were upset about the Quebec Act adopted by Parliament in 1774 was that it extended the frontier of Quebec south to the Ohio River and west to the Mississippi, rendering activities by traders and speculators there illegal. The Act came six years after the Fort Stanwix Treaty, signed by the Six Nations and Great Britain, which settled a boundary much farther west than the Proclamation Line, allowing settler migration across the Susquehanna River and the Allegheny Mountains into Kentucky. Considered by Britain's negotiators as the paramount power in the Ohio Country, the Iroquois signed away the hunting grounds of Delawares, Shawnees, and Ohio Iroquois, whom in reality they did not control at all but whose obstinacy they had always resented.

As many settlers poured into the Ohio Country beyond the new border, some moving even farther, Shawnees and Mingos refused to sign the treaty.[60] Their resistance to any form of white immigration led the Virginia House of Burgesses to declare war at the request of Governor John Murray, Earl of Dunmore. After a year of fighting, the Virginia militia emerged victorious in October 1774, sparking increasingly desperate acts of native violence against settlers.

The colonists' pressure on their lands made support of many Indian groups for Britain inevitable once the war was under way. But with both rebel and British forces courting them, Indians ended up fighting on both sides of the war.[61] Rifts occurred within and between Indian communities, entailing civil wars among both the Iroquois and the Cherokee. Few Indian nations were as fortunate as the Abenaki, who managed to maintain their neutrality throughout the war.[62]

The Revolutionary War was devastating for the natives of North America. Time and again, they were victimized either for allying with

Britain or the rebels, in retaliation for destruction wrought by Indian war parties or—as so often in the past—when native communities were destroyed in order to make new lands available. The Americans' strategy was essentially the same as the one the French and British had tried before, not merely obliterating Indian villages, but burning Indian crops (corns, beans, and squash) late in the season, so no crop could be grown before winter. Starvation and disease were the obvious results.[63]

Some nations suffered more than others. The Cherokees were still reeling from the territory they had lost during the Seven Years' War, after defeat by a combined British-colonial army in 1761. By the mid-1770s, they witnessed the arrival of ever larger numbers of illegal settlers from Virginia, Georgia, North and South Carolina, who began a tragic "cycle of retaliation."[64] The squatters provoked punitive expeditions by small Cherokee bands in the summer of 1776, assisted by British forces. In response, the governments of Virginia and the two Carolinas, afraid that Britain would use the Cherokees as soldiers but mostly reacting to rumors about an impending Indian invasion, sent a joint army and ordered the soldiers to take harsh, even unprecedented, action. In South Carolina, William Henry Drayton advised his troops sent against the Cherokees: "Cut up every Indian cornfield, and burn every Indian town."[65] Historian Wayne E. Lee writes: "Three separate columns marched over the mountains and into the Cherokee towns. . . . The violence that these forces visited upon the Cherokees exceeded anything meted out to Loyalists and Tories in the same period, despite the fact that none of the columns met with serious resistance. . . . In general, the great majority of the Cherokees dispersed and refused to come to close quarters with the Rebel militia. What the Whig forces did do over the course of September and October 1776, however, was to destroy more than thirty-six Cherokee towns and lay waste their stores and crops."[66]

Less than three years passed before the Cherokees were attacked again. In April 1779, an American force led by Evan Shelby burned eleven towns in Chickamauga Cherokee country, killing half a dozen men and looting goods worth £25,000. Farther north, Colonel Goose Van Schaick raided the Onandaga settlements, killing cattle and horses and taking thirty-three prisoners. The fall of 1779 saw another two simultaneous invasions of Indian territory. General John Sullivan, having received instructions from Washington for "the total destruction and devastation" of indigenous settlements, took five thousand soldiers into Iroquois country and burned forty towns and an estimated 160,000 bushels of corn as well as a large amount of vegetables, while Colonel Daniel Brodhead destroyed at least sixteen Lenape and Seneca towns in eastern Ohio, looting goods worth £30,000. In addition, American commanders and Kentucky militia overran villages of Shawnee Indians to carry out the orders of Thomas Jefferson, governor of Virginia, that they be exterminated or removed from their lands.[67]

Indians sometimes responded with violence of their own, raiding settler communities and forcing them to fortify their villages. They had engaged in such attacks before the revolution and would continue to do so afterward, striking fear into white towns with raids that colonists called "massacres." In the face of Indian attacks, Loyalism quickly melted away in the Ohio River valley, as those faithful to the Crown began to cooperate with patriots. Even the most peaceful Indians suffered at the hands of these revolutionaries. In the spring of 1781, Brodhead raised hell in the area around Coshocton, Ohio, which had become a refuge for Delawares and Shawnees. He killed fifteen young men and later massacred twenty old men, women, and children he had taken prisoner. In all, thirty-eight residents were killed, only one of whom was a combatant. On March 8, 1782, a few days after four Indians had killed the wife and baby of an illegal squatter in Ohio, the Pennsylvania Third Militia regiment, under the command of Colonel David Williamson, murdered ninety-six children, women, and men in the towns of Gnadenhütten and Salem. All but ten of them were Moravians, predominantly Munsee and Unami Delawares.[68]

Between the loss of life, large-scale migration, and the string of crop failures, the impact of the Revolutionary War on Indian country was immense. If that were not enough, the end of the war saw an acceleration of the theft of Indian lands, now legitimized by the Indian wartime alliances with Britain and condoned by laws adopted by the Continental Congress and the Virginia assembly. As many as eighty thousand people therefore settled in Shawnee hunting territories from 1775 through 1790. And yet, Indian groups who had allied themselves with the Americans did not fare better. By 1788, the territory of the Oneida Indians had been reduced from 6 million acres to 250,000.[69] Former allies or not, Indians were seen as savages who stood in the way of the destiny of the new nation. The old British practice of cultivating relations with them as equals was therefore to be discontinued, James Duane, chairman of the Committee on Indian Affairs in the Continental Congress, insisted. Natives, as the Declaration of Independence put it, were after all "merciless Indian savages, whose known rule of warfare is an undistinguished destruction of all ages, sexes, and conditions."[70] Southerners like Jefferson were primarily concerned about westward expansion, which was integral to their plans for the new republic. Conquest of the West, they reasoned, would ensure settler loyalty to Congress and prevent foreign powers from posing a threat to the new nation.[71] The achievements of the revolution would thus be saved.

The Eastern Theater

"And you will find," a "British Bostonian" argued in late 1772, "that the *Americans* will not submit to be SLAVES: They know the use of the gun, and the military art as well as any of his Majesty's troops at St. *James's*: And where his Majesty has one soldier, *America* can produce fifty free men, and all volunteers; and raise a more potent army of men in three weeks, than *England* can in three years."[72] The Americans were soon to prove that they were ready for war.

The indignation of most New Englanders about British measures taken in response to the Boston Tea Party was such that by the end of 1774, General Thomas Gage asked the ministry to send twenty thousand new troops and revoke the "Intolerable Acts." Neither request was granted. While the king, fed up with the general, went looking for a successor, the Earl of Dartmouth, Secretary of State for the Colonies, wrote to Gage that it was time to take action. On April 18, 1775, interpreting that message his own way, Gage sent nearly a thousand troops in the dead of night to seize Massachusetts Provincial Congress's ammunition depots in the inland town of Concord. But as the local population quickly alarmed the rebel leaders, militias from various towns rushed to Concord. There and in the neighboring town of Lexington, the first armed confrontations occurred between Britons and Americans. Most of the 368 casualties were on the British side.[73]

As the bloodshed reduced the possibility of reconciliation, Thomas Paine and other pamphleteers did all they could in the following months to head for a breakup. But when the Second Continental Congress met in Philadelphia on May 10, 1775, few of its members favored independence. The number of radicals grew, however, as the war spread. Among them were men such as John and Samuel Adams. Samuel (1722–1803) was a prolific contributor to newspapers, known for his plain clothes and sober living conditions. Very popular among craftsmen and laborers, he had publicly hinted at independence as early as 1769, coined the term "Boston Massacre," and helped organize the Boston Tea Party. John (1735–1826), his second cousin, was a learned lawyer who had been elected to the Massachusetts Assembly in 1770 and to the First and Second Continental Congresses. He advocated the creation of new state governments that should join hands in a confederacy that was to declare a sovereign state. Opponents of a complete rift with the British enemy argued that the middle colonies were not ripe yet, but these critics were increasingly marginalized, and by June 1776, Congress appointed a committee that would prepare a declaration of independence. Illustrious members of that committee were Benjamin Franklin and John Adams, but the document's main author was Thomas Jefferson (1743–1826), the thirty-three-year-old planter and former governor of Virginia who had formally studied law but informally read everything under the sun. The document was one that could appeal to many different Americans, arguing in Enlightenment fashion: "We hold these truths to be self-evident, that all men are created equal, that they are endowed, by their Creator, with certain unalienable Rights, that among these are Life, Liberty, and the pursuit of Happiness." At the time, however, the declaration was less important as a domestic rallying cry than as a message to the wider world that a new nation had joined the international community. Jefferson's document was approved by Congress, with some revisions, on July 2, and promulgated two days later, after the colonies that had opposed independence had given way in the previous weeks. Only New York, of the thirteen mainland colonies that joined, did not commit to the final step until July 15.[74]

Independence was thus declared in the midst of warfare. Americans had the advantage of rapid mobilization of their own men, while the British army was made up in part of young Germans. More than thirty thousand German soldiers from Hesse and Brunswick entered British ranks, constituting 33 percent of the North American army in 1778 and

37 percent in 1781.[75] Many of them were prone to desertion when the opportunity presented itself. A German army surgeon in Canada noted in his diary in the summer of 1776 that the Brunswick auxiliary troops confused New Spain with Spain and thought it possible to walk from Canada to New Spain and from there, via France, back to Germany: "This erroneous belief tempted some to desert but they could not even get out of Canada. Because no bridges had been built across the rivers they found in the wilderness, they either had to starve to death in the wilderness or be brought back by the Savages or Canadians that had been sent after them."[76]

Often serving against their will in a strange land, these mercenaries formed a sharp contrast with the first Continental Army that they faced. Here were soldiers resembling the citizens of Classical Antiquity who served the public cause by taking up arms. But heavy losses forced the American commanders to form a new army in 1776, which looked more like that of the enemy. More than half of the troops were of German or Irish origin and a large proportion "represented ne'er-do-wells, drifters, unemployed laborers, captured British soldiers and Hessians, indentured servants, and slaves," lured by the promise of free land or freedom. In all, some 200,000 men served for at least six months in the militia or nine consecutive months in the Continental Army during the war.[77] That seems an appreciable number for a population of some 350,000 adult males between the ages of sixteen and fifty, but this figure obscures the difficulties that army recruiters experienced as early as the fall of 1775. By December of that year, fewer than 4,000 men had signed up for campaigns in 1776, precisely because these were fiercely independent landowners. The army of 75,000 men that Congress desired was therefore not realistic. And even when a number of states introduced conscription, men of better means could avoid service by paying fines or sending substitutes. In Virginia, smallholders and planters fought tooth and nail against the draft. The strength of the American war effort, then, lay not as much in the Continental Army as in the militias. Their men numbered in the tens of thousands and they saw most action during the war.[78]

The rebels obtained much of their gunpowder from the warehouses of Sint Eustatius, a Caribbean island of twenty-one square kilometers, or one-quarter the size of Manhattan. Nicknamed the "Golden Rock," Sint Eustatius benefited from official Dutch neutrality in the American

War of Independence, absorbing cash crops from Britain's mainland and island possessions, and sending large amounts of military stores to the North American rebels. At least four thousand barrels of gunpowder left Sint Eustatius in the first half of 1775 alone, and by the end of the year, daily shipments of Dutch and French gunpowder were sent to North America. Many more were to follow in the years ahead.[79]

The Americans held their ground in Atlantic waters. According to an estimate that may well be too low, 792 privateering vessels captured or destroyed 600 British ships worth eighteen million dollars and took sixteen thousand prisoners. American ships even harassed enemy ships in British waters, forcing Britain to escort shipping between Ireland and England.[80] The prospect of making a living and, perhaps, a fortune must have lured many sailors. Among the thousands of privateers were men like schoolteacher William Russell and shoemaker George Robert Twelves Hewes, who had both taken part in the Boston Tea Party and were now in search of money and possibly a better station in life.[81]

In 1776, when George Washington (1732–1799), a Virginia veteran of the Seven Years' War, set about organizing the Continental Army, the British left hostile Boston and established their headquarters in New York City, known to have good lines of communication with the interior. Seventy-three warships with thirteen thousand sailors and several hundred vessels carrying thirty-two thousand troops disembarked. The Americans did not immediately yield to superior numbers, but at the Battle of Brooklyn Heights (August 27, 1776), Washington had to acknowledge the superiority of the forces led by the British commander-in-chief William Howe, barely escaping Brooklyn at all. After a battle on Manhattan Island (November 16), Washington abandoned New York City and retreated through New Jersey. His campaign had been a great fiasco. Although the British war machine now seemed to be heading for victory, Washington managed to cross the Delaware River with his army and find shelter in neighboring Pennsylvania. But the dismal situation in which Washington found himself, commanding few soldiers, whose morale was low and many of whose terms were about to expire, induced him to attempt a risky enterprise. With timely reinforcements, he crossed the Delaware River again, now to launch a surprise attack on the British. His courage was rewarded. The American army, fighting in the bitter cold, achieved resounding victories over their Hessian and British foes at Trenton (December 26) and Princeton (January 3, 1777), thus significantly reducing Howe's hold on New Jersey.[82] The British troops faced more than these battles alone. Although Howe did receive, as he had expected, Loyalist support for his men, they were also constantly harassed by ambushes and raids from local militia.[83]

After Howe evacuated New Jersey in the spring of 1777, the tide turned again for Britain, with successes at Brandywine Creek (September 11, 1777) and Germantown (October 3), enabling their forces to occupy Philadelphia, from where Congress had been evacuated. By failing to clear the lower Hudson Valley and attacking Philadelphia from the sea, however, Howe made it easy for his enemies to regroup in the interior. The American Northern Army won two battles against the British forces of General John Burgoyne, who had moved his men from Canada and across the Hudson River. Faced with regular enemy troops, ubiquitous rural militias, and the prospect of warfare in the wilderness, Burgoyne surrendered his entire army to General Horatio Gates (1728–1806) at the village of Saratoga in New York (October 17). The loss thwarted the British attempt to isolate New England and gained the rebels so much international credibility that France was willing to sign an alliance with the North Americans. This Treaty of Amity and Commerce, approved by Congress in May 1778, changed the course of the war. Prior to 1778, naval supremacy in the Atlantic might still have won Britain the war, but after the signing of the treaty, Britain could not deploy her home fleet in America because of the perceived danger of a French invasion of the mother country. Other concerns were raised about Britain's Mediterranean garrisons of Gibraltar and Minorca and her Caribbean colonies, where metropolitan authorities had started diverting men and ships. To make matters worse for Britain, Spain entered the war on the French side in 1779 and in that summer, a Franco-Spanish fleet threatened an invasion of old England.[84]

Meanwhile, the American army began a process of professionalization in 1778 with the arrival of Friedrich von Steuben (1730–1794), a Prussian staff-officer appointed as the army's inspector-general. Steuben taught the American soldiers the drill procedures for which the Prussians were known, albeit adapted to local conditions, and instructed them how to use the bayonet in battle. The American armed forces did not become Prussia's peers overnight. What *was* shaped was an army that made the most of the available men and means. European-style battles were never its strong suit; in fact, the Continental Army, as it was called, would not win a single battle during the war fought according to European rules. Apart from Prussian expertise, the Americans, obviously, also benefited tremendously from French help, even if the eventual victory was no automatic outcome. In 1780, a succession of defeats coupled with financial chaos and a lack of soldiers and supplies almost brought about the collapse of the Revolutionary War effort.

In view of the French participation in the conflict, the British retooled by shifting the emphasis of the war to the southern mainland colonies. The troops were first to capture the lower South, then the Chesapeake. Fighting, at least so it was assumed, would thus take place in an area with a large presence of Loyalists, who could police the country. Their tasks included maintaining surveillance against slave revolts and preventing blacks from running away. After the conquest of Georgia passed off smoothly in the winter of 1778–1779, a Franco-American assault on Savannah miscarried, and Charles Town in South Carolina fell in the lap of the British when an American commander surrendered before a shot was fired. But the Americans' resistance, kept alive by militias and guerrilla fighters, was not broken. When General Charles Cornwallis (1738–1805), in charge of the British troops in the South, embarked on the subjection of Virginia in order to complete the conquest of the Carolinas, General Washington abandoned his plan to attack New York City. Instead, he devised the masterful plan to surprise the British in their new headquarters in Yorktown, Virginia, by combining American forces with French troops, stationed in Newport, Rhode Island, and commanded by the Count de Rochambeau (1725–1807) and a French fleet of twenty-nine ships and three thousand soldiers led by Admiral Count de Grasse (1722–1788). De Grasse's fleet was to sail from the Caribbean and transport French and American regiments from the Chesapeake Bay to the James River. That operation was successful, after which the Franco-American artillery, sixteen thousand men in all, prevailed over the British. On October 17, 1782, Cornwallis and his eight thousand men surrendered.[85]

Admiral Sir George Rodney should have intercepted de Grasse's fleet, but he was too busy with the spoils of his successful raid of Sint Eustatius in February 1781. The island's barely disguised aid to the rebel Americans had provoked the ire of British commanders. Adding insult to injury, the Dutch saluted the Grand Union flag in November 1776, when the brigantine *Andrew Doria* arrived in the island's Orange Bay, which in British eyes was tantamount to recognizing the rebel states' independence. In the early stages of the Fourth Anglo-Dutch War, Rodney's fleet forced the residents of Sint Eustatius to surrender, settling old scores by confiscating cash, ships, and other property. Rodney then made two mistakes that could have changed the course of the war by failing to intercept the French naval force before it reached Martinique and neglecting to chase it en route from Saint-Domingue to Virginia. In both cases, motivated by concerns arising from the merchandise he had seized in Sint Eustatius, he delegated the task to Sir Samuel Hood, saddling the admiral with faulty instructions.[86]

The rebel siege of Yorktown was also enabled by the loss of West Florida, a colony Britain had wrested from Spain at the end of the Seven Years' War. In May 1781, the roles were reversed as a Spanish army that included blacks from Cuba and Louisiana won the Battle of Pensacola. In the wake of this victory, Spanish forces sailed into the Gulf of Mexico and the Caribbean to protect French shipping.[87]

The loss at Yorktown ushered in overall British defeat. On February 27, 1782, Parliament decided to stop the offensive war in North America, and soon peace negotiations began, leading to an agreement on November 29 by which Great Britain acknowledged U.S. independence. As the last British troops left New York City the next year, a Hessian recalled: "On all corners one saw the flag of thirteen stripes flying, cannon salutes were fired, and all the bells rang. The shores were crowded with people who threw their hats in the air, screaming and boisterous with joy, and wished us a pleasant voyage with white handkerchiefs. While on the ships, which lay at anchor with the troops, a deep stillness prevailed as if everyone were mourning the loss of thirteen beautiful provinces."[88]

A bloody war had come to an end. Historian Howard Peckham counted a total of 25,674 military deaths: 6,090 in military engagements, 1,084 in naval engagements, 10,000 in camp, and 8,500 in prison.[89] But these numbers do not tell the whole story, because twice as many "war victims" died of smallpox and other diseases. Besides, the war regularly spilled over into looting and atrocities committed by either side. Patriot and pro-British militiamen and deserters on both sides were guilty of plunder from Virginia to upstate New York. From 1780 through 1782, one scholar maintains, militiamen in the South "who voluntarily went on active duty seemed to have scarcely any motivation other than to plunder with impunity."[90]

Apart from plundering and burning private houses and public buildings, rebels and Loyalists executed some prisoners and tortured others, justifying this conduct by reference to previous misdeeds committed by the other side. The two armies did not behave differently. The plunder of his soldiers reached such dimensions that Washington was not able to control them with occasional hangings. For their part, British soldiers sometimes took out their frustration on a hostile population.[91] It was perhaps not remarkable, therefore, that even in communities that had enthusiastically supported the revolution, war weariness set in after 1777.[92]

Independence created a split among the former British colonies, since East Florida, Nova Scotia, Newfoundland, Quebec, and the Caribbean islands stuck with the metropolis. The West Indies had seen widespread initial island opposition to Britain's policy in North America, motivated by the close local commercial ties to the North Americans. The islands' dependence on provisions from North America made the West Indian elites question the wisdom of metropolitan policies. Without regular shipments of salt fish and guinea corn, the staples of the slave diet, there was a threat of starvation. And inadequate food supplies, the elites feared, might give rise to slave revolts, their ultimate nightmare. But it was the same anxiety that prevented the islands from breaking up with Britain. The elites were, after all, tiny white groups facing a large black majority—in the 1770s, blacks made up 95.7 percent of the population in the Neutral Islands (Dominica, Grenada, Saint Vincent, and Tobago), 93.9 percent in Jamaica, 89 percent in the Leeward Islands, and 78.2 percent in Barbados.[93]

The fear of the Caribbean elites was not misplaced. In a number of islands, slaves and maroons took advantage of the imperial crisis. Slaves even staged a general revolt in Jamaica that lasted for seven weeks, angry, as one of them put it, "with the white people, because they had taken from them their bread." Seventeen blacks paid with their lives. The revolt, which had been carefully planned to coincide with the embarkation of soldiers destined for the North American war in 1776, forced the whites in the British Caribbean to abandon their campaign to assuage the British ministry in its confrontation with the Thirteen Colonies. There were other reasons for this change in course. Soon after the war broke out, North American privateers stopped distinguishing between ships from Britain and those from the British West Indies, and even invaded Tobago and Nassau in the Bahamas. Not only was the trade of the West Indians interrupted, they saw their cash crops reach their lowest value in the century, underscoring the islands' dependence on British markets and their natural position within the British Empire.[94] Loyalism was therefore an obvious choice.

Loyalists and Neutrals

Loyalists had occupied an important place in the British strategy in the South. The British army was to break the power of the rebels and then support the Loyalists, whose task it would be to control the countryside. It is clear that the British overestimated the Loyalists' numerical strength, although by no means did they constitute a small force. A lot of them were tied to Britain by way of commerce, while others were foreigners with no roots in North America. In New York City, many of the men "who chose Britain were powerful and honored as well as rich, and they owed power, honor, and wealth alike to the tie with the mother country."[95] Still, Loyalism was not based on class. We have data for 544 Loyalists in Norfolk, Virginia, and two adjacent counties. Of these, 361 were white men, 111 black male slaves, 2 free black men, and 70 women—20 white women and 50 black slaves! Of the Loyalists, 64 are known to have been born in Scotland and England, and at least 25 of them had wives who were native Virginians. In Deerfield, Massachusetts, the Loyalist ("Tory") group comprised rich and poor, all making a living in commerce and retail trade, and distinguishing themselves from the Patriot ("Whig") farmers who preferred to till the land. Sometimes economic reasons made entire towns and regions put their weight behind Britain. For example, on Daufuskie Island, South Carolina, indigo growers cherished the protection by Parliament against foreign competition, while local shipbuilders hoped Britain would construct a naval base and a shipyard.[96]

The number of Loyalists waxed and waned according to the circumstances. Loyalist strength increased when the British army appeared, often only to dwindle again due to British misbehavior. Here and there, like in Pennsylvania in 1776, men alienated by the course of the revolution swelled Loyalist ranks. The British apparently believed that Loyalists would forever maintain their unswerving allegiance to the Crown, not realizing the conditional character of their support. To categorize men or communities as either Patriot or Loyalist or split between them would be incorrect, however. Historian John Shy has written that the great middle group of Americans almost certainly formed a majority of the population. These "were the people who were dubious, afraid, uncertain, indecisive, many of whom felt that there was nothing at stake that could justify involving themselves and their families in extreme hazard and suffering."[97] This would describe various parts of New York State, such as Queens County. In Flushing, more than three-quarters of the population remained neutral, with only 13 percent supporting Britain and less than 10 percent backing the rebels. Still, such indifference was not tolerated in large parts of revolutionary America. Residents with a dissident opinion were frequently ostracized, and five states denied them the vote.[98]

Some British sympathizers, notably in Georgia, the Carolinas, and New York, formed their own militias, but Loyalist organization was generally inferior to that of their enemies, who exiled not a few Loyalists to other states. Others moved voluntarily to New York and Philadelphia, where they sought protection from British troops after suffering indignities at home. Their peregrinations continued just before the Paris peace treaty of 1783, when British ships moved some five thousand Loyalists to East Florida, along with runaway slaves who outnumbered them (six thousand). After the British surrender, another exodus involving twenty-five thousand men, women, and children took place from New York to Nova Scotia, which had remained on the British side. The arrival of these refugees and of another ten thousand who settled in Loyalist Quebec, all provided by the British with large tracts of land and free provisions for two years, led to a huge population increase in the area of present-day Canada.[99]

The Political Transformation

Thirteen colonies may have been united in their declaration of independence in 1776, but there was little coherence to their federation. Federate institutions were lacking altogether, apart from the Continental Congress and the army, until Congress adopted the Articles of Confederation, drafted in 1777 and approved by the states four years later. These endowed the new United States of America, a name coined by Thomas Paine, with the most basic constitution, but nothing else. Under the articles, the Union looked more like an association of sovereign states than a republic. Congress was not allowed to tax the people directly, nor were executive or judicial powers created.[100]

In *L'Esprit des Lois*, the Baron de Montesquieu had distinguished between the legislative, executive, and judicial powers of a state, which had to be separated to guarantee liberty. Their admiration for the Frenchman notwithstanding, the Americans did not follow his recipe. If colonial assemblies had tried to combine their proper legislative function with control over law courts and judges, assemblies after the revolution continued as before. Their position was even enhanced by the curtailment of most gubernatorial powers. Governors were now little more than administrators.[101]

Virtually all state constitutions provided for annual assembly elections that changed the expectations for candidates. Historian Richard Ryerson has written: "The fundamental purpose of pre-Revolutionary elections was to allow freemen to choose, from among two or more contenders who were in effect nominated by their social position, the morally superior candidate." But during the revolution, voters came to prefer candidates who shared their vision and they demanded to know the candidates' position on various issues. The franchise was further widened, as in Pennsylvania and North Carolina, where all male taxpayers could now go to the polls. Most males in New Hampshire and Georgia were also entitled to vote, but other states did not see an expansion of the electorate. New York's constitution excluded sailors, farmworkers, and the urban poor, while voters in South Carolina had to possess a plantation of a hundred acres, although that disqualified no more than 20 percent of free white men. Broadening the franchise did not yield high turnouts on election day. From 1776 through 1779, only 10 to 15 percent of voters showed up, although those years were marked by the absence of soldiers. But even in the late 1780s, the figure had climbed to only 20 to 30 percent.[102]

After independence was declared, the committees of correspondence ceased to be, and an electoral process began that gave a legal force to the new state legislatures. In Philadelphia, a remarkable phase of the revolution thus came to an end, in which radical associators had gained the upper hand, even ousting the old elite. For a long time, they were too extreme for the general public, which was not convinced of the need for independence. Elsewhere, the colonial elites remained in power, even if new men came to join them. They feared the radical democracy practiced in Philadelphia and were bent on maintaining social gradations.[103]

What especially alarmed the revolutionary leaders was the violence to which mobs were prone. During the economically difficult war years, many crowds, often dominated by women, had gone after local merchants and speculators who hoarded flour and other products in order to sell these at the opportune moment. The crowds confronted the merchants with popular justice, forcing them to lower the prices or make the goods available. To steal popular thunder, state and town governments introduced embargoes and anti-monopoly laws. The state of New York instituted price controls and confiscated estates of landowners who had not sided with the revolution.[104]

These landowners were not the only ones left in the cold. Many nameless men who had helped the war effort were disappointed by the advent of peace. Promises of land were not redeemed and discharged soldiers were kept waiting so long that necessity made them exchange their land warrants for cash. Poverty-stricken veterans did not get a pension until 1818, and only in 1832 did Congress grant all veterans, including militiamen, an old-age pension.[105] Women were also left empty-handed despite their manifold contributions to the revolutionary cause, by nursing, cooking, and washing near the front lines, and by staying home and sustaining family-based agricultural economies in the absence of enlisted men.[106] If women in New Jersey were allowed to vote—a privilege withdrawn in 1807—everywhere else they lacked a formal political identity. The role reserved for them was that of republican mothers, instilling republican values in their children and husbands.[107]

Blacks and the Revolution

When the English army returned to Britain, eight to ten thousand blacks came along, constituting about half of the slaves who had run away from their American masters during the war. England had held great attraction for slaves ever since the Somerset case in 1772. James Somerset, a slave who had sailed with his owner from Boston to England, fled on the other side of the ocean in 1771. Captured, he faced transportation as a slave to Jamaica, but before he could embark, Somerset brought his case before a court. The presiding judge, Lord Mansfield, decided that slavery was illegal in England and restored Somerset's freedom. One year later, Virginian blacks tried to board English vessels in order to secure their freedom an ocean away. From Massachusetts to Georgia, the revolution and the war only increased rebelliousness among slaves. While the patriots questioned their subordination to the metropolis, African Americans began to challenge their owners' authority. In South Carolina, tensions ran so high during the Stamp Act crisis that the legislature imposed a three-year ban on importation of African slaves.[108] Many more slaves than before managed to run away from their masters, turning maroon or, if possible, joining the British army, although British officers did not receive with open arms every slave seeking shelter. Among those defecting to Britain were some of George Washington's slaves, who left America on a British ship, and twenty-three of Thomas Jefferson's, who fled to Cornwallis's headquarters in Virginia.[109]

When rebel troops invaded Virginia in 1775, Virginia's Governor Dunmore fled aboard a British warship in Norfolk. From there, he put the spark to the tinder by issuing a proclamation on November 7, in which he called on those loyal to the king to come to his side. More important, Dunmore (himself a slaveholder) added the promise that slaves who served the king by taking up arms would be manumitted. The effect was to frighten slave owners throughout the South and encourage blacks—and white indentured servants—to flee to Dunmore's temporary headquarters in the port of Norfolk. Fifteen hundred slaves, often fleeing with entire families and many of them convinced that the British had come to liberate them, managed to reach Norfolk. Sadly, two-thirds of them fell victim to an epidemic of typhoid fever. The surviving males either were enrolled in the so-called Ethiopian Corps, or were assigned civilian chores, as were the women.[110]

In the years that New York was in British hands, countless slaves again tried to escape and join their supposed liberators. Dunmore's proclamation was known here as well, and those unfamiliar with it would have heard about General Howe's declaration of 1778, which offered freedom to slaves who deserted in exchange for military service. As many as two thousand blacks reached New York, where they would enjoy unprecedented liberties for the duration of the British occupation. After war's end, they moved with British help to Nova Scotia, but saw their dream of a better life vanish into thin air.[111] In all, twenty-four thousand blacks served the British cause during the war, half of whom fought in the Caribbean theater. The blacks' share was thus relatively small, representing 4 percent of the British war effort. On the American side, six thousand blacks, also 4 percent, served as soldiers, privateers, and auxiliaries. The patriots were hesitant to deploy more blacks, especially the officers who benefited from slavery themselves. In the northern states, where slaves were a small minority, the Americans' willingness to put them into action was greater.[112]

If many black males attempted to obtain their freedom on the battlefield, they received support from free New Englanders of African descent, who argued that blacks should also enjoy the rights to life, liberty, and the pursuit of happiness. In four separate petitions from 1773 through 1777, these men confronted their white brothers with their own revolutionary rhetoric by stressing that real slavery was irreconcilable with the inalienable rights of man.[113] Some whites did act consistently by freeing their own slaves. The Quakers of Philadelphia prohibited their own members from owning slaves in 1774, and Methodist leaders called on their members in 1780 to release all their slaves, in 1784 excommunicating those who had not complied.[114] Some Founding Fathers, like Benjamin Franklin, advocated an end to slavery, but most were slaveholders themselves and not eager to abolish the institution. The delegates to the Constitutional Convention in 1787 never considered addressing the issue of slavery.[115]

Only in New England, home to relatively few slaves, did egalitarian ideas lead to abolition, with Vermont as the lone state to incorporate it in its constitution (July 8, 1777), and then only implicitly. Too much has been made of this step, one historian even writing that "for the first time in the whole history of the western hemisphere, there was a place where being black automatically meant that a person was free rather than a slave."[116] The many generations of blacks who lived and died in maroon communities all over the Americas would have been surprised to hear that. Since the start of black slavery in the New World, slaves had liberated themselves not just by running away but by forming more or less stable maroon societies. Those in Jamaica and Suriname were eventually recognized by the white colonial governments. And since these governments never reversed their decisions, being born in those territories meant being free.

In Massachusetts and New Hampshire, the process of abolition followed a more gradual and circuitous trajectory. Even in these states where slavery was not a crucial economic institution, it did form a system of social control that seemed hard to replace in the eyes of the white elite.[117] Where slavery was more integral to the economy, abolition was a protracted process, inducing numerous slaves (as in New York State) to run away from their masters. The otherwise radical lawmakers of Pennsylvania agreed in 1780 on a law that did not give a single slave immediate freedom and forced all slave children to spend their lives in bondage. Each child born to a slave after the adoption of the law was to remain enslaved for twenty-eight years. Not until 1847 did all black Pennsylvanians enjoy freedom. Connecticut, Rhode Island, New York, and New Jersey passed similar laws.[118] In the South, no emancipation decrees, however moderate, were passed. What is more, in spite of the dislocation brought by the war—only five thousand of Georgia's fifteen thousand slaves were, for example, still around by 1783—the overall number of slaves in the South actually grew from half a million in 1776 to nearly seven hundred thousand in 1790. Southern slavery became so firmly entrenched that it would take a bloody civil war some four score years later to abolish the institution.[119]

The contours of that conflict were visible by 1787, when the question arose who could be counted and who not in determining the apportionment of state delegates to the U.S. House of Representatives and the Electoral College. Supporters of slavery wished to include all slaves; opponents refused. Emotions ran high as the very survival of the new republic seemed in doubt over this issue. The compromise reached was to count three out of every five slaves, which was both to the advantage of the southern states, whose delegates in Congress thereby increased in number, and to their detriment, since any tax levied by state population was to also count slaves as three-fifths persons. The next day, the Continental Congress, still in session in New York, adopted the Northwest Ordinance, which included the stipulation that slavery was banned north of the Ohio River. This implied, of course, that slavery was allowed in all territories south of the Ohio as well as those yet to be formed in the West. Even in the North, no slaves were freed as a consequence of the ordinance.[120]

For all the support settlers showed for the war against the British that began in 1775, a remarkably large number of men and women, white or black, remained faithful to the British Empire. Thousands of them chose exile over a life in the new republic. Indians lacked that option. For them, the revolution was another episode in their extended decline, and an especially devastating one. The Patriot camp was shaped by the events that transpired after 1763, when the actions of the British army and policies enacted by Parliament combined to alienate many settlers. The new laws required Americans to help pay for their own defense, albeit without their consent, and the new tasks of the redcoats—protecting Indian lands against squatters and occupying the town of Boston—caused increasing resentment. But resentment in itself did not breed revolution, and few would have conceived of a total rupture with Britain until General Gage's troops provoked a bloody military encounter in Massachusetts in 1775.

3

The War on Privilege and Dissension

The French Revolution

Colonial uprisings such as the American Revolution can, as I have stressed, be understood only in an international context. But the same is true of the various revolts that rocked Europe during that period. A war with Great Britain set the stage for the rise of the Patriot revolt in the Dutch Republic in the 1780s. Likewise, international warfare precipitated the revolution in France, Europe's most populous country, with twenty-six million men, women, and children. Her almost uninterrupted warfare in the eighteenth century came at a high price, not only economically but financially. The main problem of public finance in France, as in Britain (see chapter 2), was how to pay for the wars. In practice, they were financed by a mixture of borrowing and taxation. The nobility was exempted from most taxes, but what manifestly inhibited the French monarchs from raising taxes was the need to consult the *parlements*, the chief law courts that registered royal edicts and ordinances, thus lending them the force of law. The alternative—suppressing the *parlements*—was tried unsuccessfully between 1770 and 1774. In practice, the kings ordinarily chose neither option, only introducing emergency taxes in wartime. The tax system that was in place proved inadequate, in part because indirect taxes counted for little. Less than 50 percent of the total increase in royal revenues in the period 1700 to 1789 came from indirect taxes, compared to 90 percent in England in the same years. The tax system also depended far too much on revenues from agriculture, the weakest economic sector. Trade and industry could have been taxed much more heavily.[1]

The French state repeated the same sequence of moves in every eighteenth-century war: borrowing heavily to finance the war effort, seeking in vain to raise taxes during the war to pay the debt, borrowing even more to service the debt, and finally defaulting on payments after war's end. The scale of the financial predicament had grown with every war, reaching the dimensions of an outright crisis in 1776, when a Protestant foreigner was appointed as finance minister. Jacques Necker, the resident minister of the Republic of Geneva in Paris, owed his mandate to his excellent reputation as a banker. Necker broke with precedent by not raising taxes during the war with England over the Thirteen Colonies. He paid for the war almost exclusively by borrowing, offering high yields to investors on life annuities and thus avoiding a clash with the Paris *parlement*. Necker was, however, dismissed in 1781. His successors tried in vain to find prescriptions for the persistent financial headache. In May 1787, Loménie de Brienne, archbishop of Toulouse and friend of Necker, attempted to accomplish this task, but he could not perform magic either. His efforts to raise taxes and issue new long-term loans met with resistance from the *parlement* of Paris. After the *parlement* also opposed numerous other reform measures of the government, the government drastically curtailed its jurisdiction and that of the other *parlements*, provoking protests in various provinces.[2]

In their protests over one of the laws Brienne proposed—a stamp act—the *parlement* of Paris drew inspiration from the arguments American pamphlets had used. Its outcry resonated not only with those who would obviously be affected, such as business owners, but also with a variety of employees. Since contracts, bills of exchange, and even ordinary invoices and receipts would be taxed, it was feared the act might bring about widespread economic suffering, and possibly a financial disaster for the country, with an avalanche of bankruptcies in its wake. Artisans with various trades, some already out of work, others dreading the same fate, took the helm in September 1787, and violent clashes ensued with the Paris Guard, whose task it was to maintain law and order. The timing of these confrontations was curious, occurring as they did after the stamp act had been declared null and void. The demonstrations actually took place as people celebrated this decision. Along with similar disturbances in August and September 1788, these crowd actions provided a training ground for those that took place during the revolution. A tradition of revolt had not existed prior to these riots.[3]

Two historians have argued that Louis XVI still could have opted for bankruptcy at this stage, thereby repeating the old pattern. One may even speculate that the entire revolutionary crisis, which was soon to break out, could have been avoided.[4] But the king refused, calling instead in August 1788 for a meeting of the nation's three estates: clergy, nobility, and the Third Estate. That move did little to solve the kingdom's financial crisis. Following Brienne's resignation later that month, Necker was called back to pick up the pieces. Like his colleagues, Necker tried desperately to find new fiscal resources, but like them he did not revamp the tax system. All finance ministers relied in part on the old tradition to sell offices as a way to borrow money. In the process, by strengthening and spreading privilege, they unwittingly promoted the idea of fundamental social change.[5] Receptivity to this idea was growing rapidly. It was ominous that the Paris *parlement*, long a buttress of the monarchy, adopted the rhetoric of representative government, extolling individual liberty and denouncing arbitrary rule.[6] "The authorities from July 1788 on cleared the way for a truly national discussion of public issues by granting broad freedom to the press, liberating most booksellers and pamphleteers who had recently been incarcerated for disseminating antiministerial writings, and tolerating 'clubs,' 'societies,' and other associations in the capital and elsewhere."[7] Shedding its old guise as a vague abstraction, public opinion was suddenly everywhere.

No single factor contributed more to the subsequent course of events that eventually led to the French Revolution than the calling of the Estates General on August 8, 1788. The king resuscitated a tradition that had been dormant since 1614, the last time the estates had convened to advise the king on the issues at hand.[8] As on previous occasions, the meeting was a last resort for a king in dire straits. But unlike what had happened in the remote past, the announcement changed the country greatly in the period between August 8 and May 1, 1789, when the representatives were to convene in Versailles. As economic problems deepened, public opinion became more vociferous. All the king's subjects were empowered to express their opinions in January 1789, when the estates were advised to prepare *cahiers de doléances*, lists of grievances that would assist their representatives with the advice that they gave.

Divided into the traditional three estates, the male inhabitants of every French parish drew up *cahiers* of their own, and chose deputies who compiled a general *cahier* in each of the 150 French bailiwicks and elected the deputies to the Estates General. All adult tax-paying males had the right to vote. Two out of every three men elected to represent the First Estate (the clergy) were parish priests. Only one in seven was a bishop. The noble deputies were dominated by men who had served in the army and could trace back their ancestry to at least 1500. The latter feature made them hardly representative for their estate, 70 percent of which had been ennobled since 1600. Among the deputies of the Third Estate, men with legal training predominated.[9]

The tens of thousands of *cahiers* present us with a unique snapshot of French opinions on the eve of the revolution. Local issues exercised minds everywhere: in the town of Fraize (Lorraine), the Third Estate requested to be indemnified for rebuilding its parish church after the old one was lost in a fire.[10] What is remarkable, though, is how many issues of national concern were taken up in the *cahiers*. The three estates stressed distinct matters. The clergy's first demand was often the continued and exclusive protection of the Roman Catholic religion. Half of the noble *cahiers* mention the importance of symbolic deference. The noblemen insisted on rights enabling them to distinguish themselves from others in dress or behavior, such as the right to bear arms. The Third Estate, on the other hand, refused to accept any degrading social distinctions.[11] Social differences as such were not disputed. Grievance lists of the peasantry did not challenge the existing social structure; on the contrary, they considered the traditional distinction among the estates essential to the kingdom. Symbolic expressions of noble status were less of a concern to the kingdom's rural dwellers than privileges of the landlords that actually had an impact, such as the lord's right to hunt, his monopolies, the tolls he levied, and the labor services he demanded. The collection of dues traditionally had been justified by the protection the lord offered to the peasantry, but since midcentury the state had progressively assumed many of the seigneur's political, judicial, and administrative tasks. Stripped of these functions, the landlords came to be viewed by the villagers as mere proprietors. The seigneurial dues owed them were seen as remnants of a now defunct relationship with the lord.[12]

What peasants resented even more than the rights claimed by the lords was taxation by the central government, a leitmotiv of their grievances. Rural communities did not advocate the abolition of tithes, appreciating that pastoral activities had to be financed in some way. Urban notables were more likely to view priests as pariahs and tithes as yet another needless burden on the peasantry. Because their objective was to rid society of all impediments to the free flow of goods, the urbanites argued that landlords should be deprived of their privileges, albeit not without compensation.[13]

The convocation of the Estates General had been announced with some ambiguity. It was left unresolved whether the estates were to be organized along traditional lines. A royal decree allowed the Third Estate in December to double the number of its delegates compared to the other estates, but it remained unclear whether their estate would have two votes in the deliberations with the monarch instead of one. If not, they could and would be outvoted by the privileged orders. Others had misgivings about the time-honored principle that motions in the Estates General could not pass unless all orders agreed. The members of the Third Estate did not yet expect the meeting of the orders to turn into the formation of a permanent legislative body. Nobody could have foreseen that. Few *cahiers* even proposed giving the Estates General legislative authority, and those that did were not based on a clear rationale.[14]

The upcoming meeting of the Estates General produced debate and discussion in workshops, on the streets, in salons and coffeehouses, and on paper. The first months of 1789 saw an unprecedented output of pamphlets. Earlier in the decade, perhaps 12 pamphlets had appeared annually in all of France, but as the 1780s advanced, that number rose steadily, reaching 819 in 1788. Between January and April 1789, the time of the elections for the estates, no fewer than 2,000 pamphlets were published. The most skilled pamphleteer was Emmanuel-Joseph Sieyès (1748–1836), a priest who published a stream of incendiary pamphlets in late 1788 and early 1789. He focused on what seemed to be the central fissure in French society: the split between the privileged and the unprivileged. In his indictment of the Old Regime, Sieyès took into account the three dominant contemporary political discourses. The main discourse was that of justice, as espoused especially by the *parlements* who indicted ministerial despotism. This discourse emphasized the need to limit royal power, but did not question the separation of the orders. An alternative discourse was that of will, stressing—as Rousseau had—that liberty was the expression of a general political will. Despotism, it maintained, occurs when an individual or particular will is paramount. The discourse of reason, finally, championed the idea of founding public life on reason and nature, as for instance in the form of the adoption of civil rights and equal taxes. Sieyès drew on the latter two languages, maintaining in his *Qu'est-ce que le Tiers Etat?* ("What Is the Third Estate?") that since citizenship presupposes equality, the two privileged orders cannot be part of the nation. The Third Estate could fill all roles in society. In fact, he wrote, because it represented 95 percent of the people, it *was* the nation.[15]

Sieyès (chosen to represent the Third Estate) was himself among the elected deputies who arrived in Versailles in the spring of 1789. After some delays, the Estates General opened on May 5, but within a few days, deliberations reached an impasse when the Third Estate refused to verify its credentials separately from the other orders. Five weeks of uncertainty passed before the Third Estate seized the momentum, voting at Sieyès's suggestion that it invite the other two orders to join it in a common verification of the representatives' credentials. This invitation was accepted by only a small number of priests. One week later (June 17), another, more momentous motion of Sieyès passed, as the Third Estate replaced the Estates General with the "National Assembly," and went ahead to prepare a constitution. Members of the other orders were encouraged to join the Third, which would enable the three estates to merge into a single body. Most clergymen came out in favor of this proposal, but the nobility and the bishop-deputies of the First Estate declined.

The pace of events reached a first climax on June 20, as the Third Estate was locked out of its chamber. It is not clear whether that was a sign of royal opprobrium. The representatives did not know, nor do we. Undaunted, the men of the Third Estate, having moved to a nearby tennis court, reaffirmed their right to form a national assembly and bound themselves to this decision in the Tennis Court Oath. Realizing that it was time for him to act now, Louis XVI made a number of concessions, promising the delegates freedom of the press, personal liberty, and the right to consent to taxes. It took him a few more days to order the noble and clerical deputies to join the National Assembly. But he stopped short of allowing the deputies to draw up a constitution.[16]

The revolution was still not bound to happen, even at this late stage, but the king gave the final blow to the Old Regime on July 11 by dismissing his reformist ministers, including Necker, the popular politician who had returned to the government in August of the previous year. Necker, a foreigner after all, was even banned from the kingdom. To make it clear where he stood, Louis formed a new government made up entirely of hard-liners. With all middle ground gone and the battle lines drawn between government and Assembly, other groups now intervened. The four hundred electors of Paris created an urban militia and declared themselves the city's government. The latter example was followed in Paris's districts. Crowds began to gather as well, some in support of these measures, others to loot customs posts and gunsmiths' shops. Soldiers sent to stop them joined the plunderers. People searched every nook and cranny for guns, gunpowder, and ammunition, anticipating correctly that the guardians of the status quo would not sit by idly as their position was undermined. Urban violence was not unique to Paris, but throughout the revolution it would be more effective than elsewhere in influencing politics, simply because the government resided there. In the morning of July 14, a crowd of thousands—including large numbers of artisans and shopkeepers—gathered to invade the Bastille, the old royal prison visible for miles around that was associated with arbitrary rule. In addition, it was known that large amounts of gunpowder had arrived there in recent days. As the crowd moved into the prison's central courtyard, the defenders opened fire, killing dozens of Parisians. The attackers did not lose heart and captured the Bastille before murdering seven defenders. They reserved a special treatment for the man who had been in command of the prison, beheading him and parading his head on a pike to the Royal Palace.[17]

The capture of the Bastille was followed by its thorough demolition in the subsequent months. Led by the monied entrepreneur Pierre-François Palloy, eight hundred men worked their way down to the ground until, by late November, they had removed almost the entire structure.[18] Like in Berlin two hundred years later, citizens then came in droves to see for themselves the tangible remains of a finished regime.

The Death of Feudalism

Although the economic and financial plight of countless Frenchmen had deteriorated in the previous two years, the government had continued to pass on its financial troubles to the taxpayers. Many of these could hardly afford to pay anymore. As storms and floods destroyed part of the harvest in 1787 and 1788, grain became scarce and speculation rampant. Wages did not keep up with the prices of some foodstuffs, which further harmed the peasants and exacerbated the urban malaise. In 1786, an industrial recession had set in, caused in part by the newly gained freedom to import British products. Industry after industry laid off workers, as textiles, clocks, gauzes, and other products found fewer consumers than before. Royal troops broke up a strike in Lyon, hanging three strikers. The severe winter of 1788–1789 then added insult to injury. Poor peasants and urban workers, neither group able to store or sell grain yet both consumers of bread, were often reduced to hunger and despondency, anxiously awaiting the new harvest.[19] Three months before the violence erupted that lost the king the Bastille, a combination of wage cuts and soaring bread prices had provoked episodes of violence and looting in the capital. All over the country, bread riots broke out that spring, frequently accompanied, as during riots in earlier decades, by "popular taxation": crowds would search out merchants, millers, and others suspected of hoarding grain, and proceed to impose a "just price," invariably far beneath the market value. Violence was much more widespread still in the countryside, where the inhabitants directed their anger at the lords.[20] Peasant revolts spread in the early summer, breaking out in the second half of July in Normandy, Franche-Comté, Alsace, Hainault, and the Mâconnais (Burgundy). Hearsay usually moved men and women to action. Rumors about a vast aristocratic plot bent on reversing the policies recently adopted in Paris were circulating in many different parts of rural France from December 1788 until March 1790. The lords were said to be planning to destroy the common people by starving them or putting them to the sword. They had engaged brigands, it was believed, who had been spotted in the area by the hundreds or thousands, eager to despoil the crops. The reports were not contradicted by village priests, who added to the prevailing uncertainty by ringing the bells to warn the population of imminent danger.[21] Rural France stood in dread of the imaginary brigands, who had allegedly been recruited from among the growing army of vagabonds or foreigners who were spreading death and destruction in the name of the landlord. Covering vast distances, the panic spread from hamlet to hamlet. Georges Lefebvre, the phenomenon's first historian, dubbed the fear of destruction,

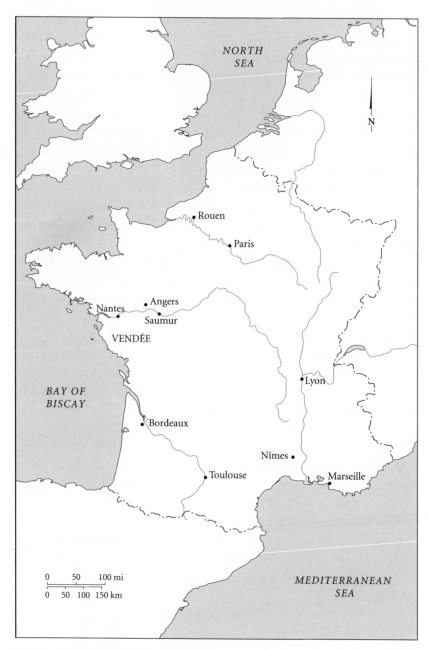

NORTH
SEA

N

Rouen

Paris

Angers
Nantes
Saumur
VENDÉE

BAY OF
BISCAY

Lyon

Bordeaux

Nîmes

Toulouse

Marseille

MEDITERRANEAN
SEA

0   50   100 mi
0   50   100 150 km

Map 3.1. France during the revolution.

whether by hunger or a revengeful lord, the "Great Fear." The fear of such groups, although they were imaginary, was not far-fetched. A deteriorating standard of living in the two decades preceding the revolution had led in the Auvergne, for instance, to the creation of a vast "army" of beggars made up of former day laborers as well as elderly and handicapped people.[22] Roaming beggars had become a normal sight long before the revolution, and rural gangs stepped up their activities as the economic crisis deepened.

Anxiety bred delusion, as Lefebvre writes: "Now when an assembly, an army or an entire population sits waiting for the arrival of some enemy, it would be very unusual if this enemy were not actually sighted at some time or other. . . . A suspicious character, a cloud of dust, less than this even: a sound, a light, a shadow is enough to start an alarm."[23] And when nothing happened after days or weeks of waiting for the brigands, the peasants vented their fury on the lords' mansions. The perpetrators were convinced that they acted only according to the king's wishes, since he had ordered that justice be done to the people in a decree that was kept from the public by plotting aristocrats.[24]

Many people in the capital shared the idea that a conspiracy had been organized to defeat the revolution. As late as January 1790, Assembly members believed that their project could not be carried out while conspiracies were still being planned. But, although panics occurred in three-quarters of all bailiwicks (areas with local royal courts), the Great Fear was not the sole manifestation of rural discontent. Other forms of protest manifested as land conflicts, subsistence rebellions, and anti-tax movements, although the foremost category of resistance consisted of actions against the lord's power.[25] Agitation was most widespread in regions where feudal dues had been unusually burdensome and nobles oppressive. Lords were usually spared, but the symbols of lordship were favorite targets of angry attackers. Seigneurial property was damaged or desecrated and land registers, in which the peasants' dues were recorded, burned.[26]

Small provocations could have serious consequences, as they did in the small village of Igé in the Mâconnais, where the wine growers, having lost a trial against their seigneur ten years before, had been forced to relinquish their communal woods. The dispute continued and came to a head over a fountain in the château's park. On July 21, as the seigneur left the church, some villagers requested permission to use the water for themselves and their animals, in view of the prolonged period of drought. The seigneur turned them down, pretending the water was needed for irrigating the meadows of the seigneurial domain. The following Sunday, peasants armed with clubs, pitchforks, and some old rifles forced their way into the château. When peasants from a neighboring parish, complaining about their own seigneur, joined the insurgents in Igé, the floodgates of rebellion opened. Within two days, attacks on feudal signs and emblems spread in all directions, as peasants fell upon dovecotes, weathervanes, and barns, and burned archives and surveys of the contractual obligations between landlords and peasants.[27]

By early August, disturbing news arrived in Paris about looting in all quarters of France. Châteaux and convents were burned in a movement that appeared unstoppable. These excesses helped bring about what one historian has recently called the Great Demarcation: the abolition of feudalism by the National Assembly on Tuesday, August 4.[28] This was by all standards an extraordinary piece of legislation, perhaps the most significant of the entire revolution. In one fell swoop, the new law dismantled the two pillars of the old regime's system of property. One was the private ownership of public and judicial positions. Thousands of men, including notaries, guild masters, and wealthy bourgeois, had bought their offices, which they could sell or transmit to the next generation. Even more numerous were the *seigneuries*, the feudal domains that entailed the right to exercise criminal and civil justice in a certain area. The other pillar was the system of multiple ownership of virtually all real estate, structured by a hierarchical relationship. Rural (and urban) tenants occupied their land, but did not fully own it, subordinate as they were to their lords, who themselves were dependents of higher lords.

The destruction of this entire complex had far-reaching consequences in all sections of society. It ended not only the right of the lords to exercise criminal and civil justice in their fief. More generally, the abolition of "feudalism" meant the termination of a property system that had guaranteed the maintenance of the traditional social hierarchy. Besides, a clear distinction was for the first time introduced between a public realm and a private one.[29] When the meeting on August 4 concluded, all privilege had been abolished and civil equality had been created for every Frenchman. Justice was to be free, fiscal privileges were to vanish, and citizens were to have equal opportunities to land a position. In short, all citizens were henceforth equal before the law. Deliberations and debates continued for another week. On August 11, a final decree was issued that began with the words: "The National Assembly completely destroys the feudal regime."[30]

An unforeseen consequence of the abolition of hunting monopolies was the large-scale massacre that took place among wildlife in the southern region of the Corbières. Equally disconcerting was the rapid and massive clearing of forests on the area's hillsides by poor and landless peasants, which brought in its wake environmental disaster. Legal equality, the revolutionaries learned, came at a price.[31] Meanwhile, the Assembly found no definitive solution for the tithes and the venality of offices, but it would be only a matter of months before both finally met their end. While offices could be redeemed and compensation was offered for most eradicated seigneurial rights, the Roman Catholic Church was not compensated for its losses. In November 1789, a more comprehensive offensive followed against the Catholic Church, as the religious orders were dissolved and all Church property was seized. Peasants were not the main beneficiaries of the confiscation, most of the land being sold to urban middle groups. Nor did the legislation relieve the plight of the poor and downtrodden. As much as the revolutionaries maligned the Church, its relief for the poor had fulfilled an important social function, and the state turned out to be an inadequate successor. In other ways as well, a rift opened between the deputies, who eschewed bishops and monks because of their alleged hypocrisy, and the French people. First, on April 12, 1790, the politicians refused to declare Catholicism the national religion. Three months later (July 12), they adopted a law with far-reaching unintended consequences. The Civil Constitution of the Clergy forcibly retired three-fifths of all male and female clergy, made the remaining clergymen salaried state officials, gave Protestants and Jews equal rights, and effectively ended France's ties with the papacy. On November 27, frustrated with the bishops' attitudes vis-à-vis the revolution, the Assembly made all bishops, parish clergymen, and clerical teachers swear an oath on the Civil Constitution of the Clergy.[32]

During the ancien régime, the *parlements* had led the drive for church reform, although the clergy itself pushed hard to introduce reforms, criticizing, for example, certain confraternities and numerous popular feast-day celebrations, often centered on apocryphal saints. Parish priests, heavily influenced by the Enlightenment, had long opposed the traditional church hierarchy, singling out the power of bishops. Yet if parish priests had supported the revolution in large numbers, often out of resentment of the power of bishops, they now firmly opposed the Civil Constitution. Many went underground or kept quiet only to stir up their flock. "Constitutional priests," who sided with the regime and were often outsiders, were frequently threatened and targeted by angry crowds. Some were even stoned to death.[33] Still, most priests seem to have been in tune with the sentiments of their parishioners, whom revolutionary laws alienated especially in areas where the language of communication was not French, but Basque, Breton, Catalan, Flemish, or German. The priests there were almost all refractory, as they were in parishes with a history of confrontations with nearby Lutheran or Calvinist populations.[34]

Not surprisingly, more than 30,000 priests fled abroad. In the course of the revolution, clergymen made up from one-fifth to one-quarter of all emigrants, a proportion much larger than their share of the population. The nobility were not far behind—one in six emigrants. As may seem obvious, the emigration of both groups was larger in border regions and near the Atlantic coast than it was in central France. The overall number of emigrants, half of whom belonged to the Third Estate, was around 150,000 or 160,000. Equaling only five- or six-tenths of 1 percent, emigration was hardly a significant phenomenon. Nonetheless, some newspapers blamed the *émigrés* for the economic downswing, accusing them of capital flight.[35] Yet the overwhelming majority of noblemen (at least 93 percent) remained on French soil. Many retreated from public life, while others sympathized with the revolution, supporting the constitutional project. The revolutionary leadership included Mirabeau, Lafayette, and more than a few other noblemen who were not rebuffed but received with open arms by insurgents of common backgrounds. Indeed, the proposal to abolish the feudal system came from the *vicomte* de Noailles, who had earlier taken part in the War of American Independence, along with his brother-in-law Lafayette. George Washington designated him as the officer to receive for the French the sword of Cornwallis at the British surrender. The revolution pressed Noailles hard, as it did other noblemen. A few years later, his estates were confiscated and he was condemned to death, but he managed to escape to Britain. Noailles then lived in the United States, returned to France to serve under Napoleon, and was killed in a naval encounter off Havana.[36]

Equality and Property

After August 4, the revolution continued at breakneck pace. On August 26, a most remarkable document was adopted: the Declaration of the Rights of Man and Citizen. Enacted provisionally by the National Assembly, this preamble to the yet to be prepared constitution was said to be based on rights that were to be discovered, not invented.[37] The document was a list of rights that the National Assembly recognized, beginning with a statement inspired by the opening sentence of Rousseau's *Social Contract* ("Man is born free, but he is everywhere in chains"): "Men are born free and remain equal in rights. Social distinctions can be based only on public utility." Language apart, the Declaration owed more to its American example than to French Enlightenment thought.

The example of the young republic had inspired several French protagonists to draft a similar document. Among them was Lafayette, who asked the U.S. ambassador in Paris, Thomas Jefferson, for advice. The American text also had its opponents. One member of the Assembly argued that in North American society, composed as it was entirely of property owners, propagating equality could do no harm, but in France, a country built on relations of dependency, it would be perilous to praise man's natural liberty. Another declared that there was an enormous difference between a young people severing its ties with a distant government and an ancient people overthrowing its own government. He might have added that the difficulty was to eliminate the social hierarchy without destabilizing the balance of power, in which the monarchy still played a role.[38]

Equality was nonetheless embedded as a principle in the Declaration's sixth article: "Law is the expression of the general will. . . . All citizens, being equal in its eyes, are equally eligible to all public dignities, places and employments." These promises, well-intentioned as they were, could not be fulfilled. It was not clear, first of all, how the general will could be implemented. Rousseau had portrayed it as indivisible and unrepresentable. In a city-state such as ancient Athens, democracy could thrive, but in a large nation like France it would be impossible. One member of the Assembly argued that the people, not the delegates, made the laws, even if the people were present only in spirit. Other constituents were not troubled that practice deviated from principle, since property qualifications would guarantee proper elections. The propertied man, having fulfilled his private passions, dedicates himself more easily to the public cause, as an independent citizen. Through his real estate, he is linked organically to the nation. Property is thus a system of collective security.[39]

Unlike equality, property had been included among the self-evident rights listed in Article 2 of the Declaration: "The aim of every political association is the preservation of the natural and imprescriptible rights of man. These rights are liberty, property, security, and resistance to oppression." The seventeenth and last article added that property was a sacred and inviolable right. In other words, the revolution combated inequality of birth, but did not want to touch inequality of wealth.[40] An element of fairness was, however, built into the Declaration. Article 13 mentions a general tax that should be "equally apportioned among all citizens according to their means." It took a few years before that actually happened. From the summer of 1789, tax collection was almost impossible given the widespread rural unrest. Hardly any direct or indirect tax contributed to the national treasury. Accordingly, progressive taxation had to wait until 1793.[41]

Equality did not extend to everybody in the French Empire. Although one delegate brought up the issue of slavery on the night of August 4, support was lacking for any measure to effect its abolition.[42] More than four years passed before action was taken, but when it did, it was momentous. In February 1794, the French eliminated slavery, in part under influence of events in its Caribbean colonies (see chapter 4). What would not happen in the United States for several generations after the revolution had been secured was thus legislated in France in the midst of the revolution.

Opponents of slavery had certainly existed in France in the early days of the revolution. Among them was Olympe de Gouges (1748–1793), a butcher's daughter from the southern town of Montauban, who wrote a play condemning the slave system. She also exposed another gigantic omission: women were conspicuously absent from the Declaration.

As a remedy, de Gouges rewrote all seventeen articles and renamed the document "Declaration of the Rights of Woman and Citizen." In her version, the first article starts with the words: "Woman is born free and lives equal to man in her rights."[43] Olympe de Gouges, who would die under the guillotine, was not alone in her quest for equality. In the fall of 1789, a group of women authored a pamphlet that addressed the National Assembly, asking rhetorically whether, exclusively for women, the Iron Age still existed. You have declared the French a free people, the women argued, and yet thirteen million slaves shamefully carry the irons of thirteen million despots. Another document advocated full female participation in government. Women, it argued, would neutralize the private interests that rule men.[44]

Women claiming their rights were fighting an uphill battle. Many *cahiers* had opposed women's rights, and newspapers warned against women's opinion. But in the course of the revolution, new laws did help the cause of women. They shed their status as legal minors and were the beneficiaries of a new divorce law (September 22, 1792), which determined that marriage was a contract that could be dissolved by either party. Seventeen months earlier (April 8, 1791), a drastic reform of family law had occurred, eliminating primogeniture and establishing equal inheritances for all siblings irrespective of gender or birth order. All over France, sisters clamoring for their share of the patrimony defeated brothers in court, upsetting family strategies. Beyond these tangible changes, the nature of the family was questioned as a result of the revolution, albeit without solving the position of women in politics and the family.[45]

But women did not just, and not even in the first place, defend their own rights. They were an integral part of the revolutionary movement, voicing their opinion and taking action alongside men. Their most distinct revolutionary undertaking occurred in October 1789, their actions the result of hunger, rumors about an aristocratic conspiracy, and the king's refusal to recognize the abolition of privileges and the Declaration of the Rights of Man, which had both been adopted in August.[46]

On October 5, female peddlers and other women stood in front of Paris's city hall demanding bread. Six to seven thousand of them, accompanied by some men, first made their way into the building, then began a march to Versailles. The demonstrators proceeded to the National Assembly, whose members voted for an audience for the women with the king. Upon their arrival at his chateau, the monarch agreed to have available grain supplies released to Paris.

Aided by its advertisement through a newspaper campaign, a rally took place the next day that aimed to bring the king from Versailles, where it was believed he could not escape the strong hold of the court, to Paris, where he would be surrounded by his people. Protesters pushed their way into the royal palace, some of them looking for Queen Marie-Antoinette, who barely escaped unscathed. Two members of the royal guard were killed. Popular pressure, it was clear, could no longer be ignored, and that night the royal family left for Paris in the company of sixty thousand men and women. The Tuileries Palace was to be their new abode. The National Assembly could only follow suit and move along to the capital.

Ordinary women remained active throughout the revolution, sometimes in conjunction with men, at other times independently. Urban women of the middling sort congregated in their own revolutionary societies, not only in the larger cities but with striking frequency in the southwest of the country. At times these societies went out of their way to back the revolution, as they did by hunting down priests who refused to take the constitutional oath. In general, rural women seem to have had a more critical attitude vis-à-vis the revolution. After a brief honeymoon, their dissatisfaction over economic problems led to distrust or outright hostility.[47]

Many women taking part in the events of October 5 and 6 hailed from the suburb of Saint-Antoine, located east of the city, which had been added to Paris in 1702. Home to at least forty-two thousand inhabitants by the time of the revolution, Saint-Antoine had supplied the rank and file of the revolution on July 14. No fewer than 70 percent of those storming the Bastille lived in Saint-Antoine. Most workers there were employed in the glass, paper, and porcelain industries. There were also many artisans, who worked independently outside of the guild system.[48] Both groups had experienced the industrial crisis that set in after 1786: while in 1791 in Paris as a whole around one-fifth of the population received food aid, in Saint-Antoine more than one-third were recipients. Most of these were unemployed or workers with children, and the majority were furniture makers and metalworkers. But the industrial workers were not the real firebrands. Instead, small artisans excluded from political life led the way.[49]

Crowds such as the ones that sprang into action in the turbulent October days of 1789 had much in common with politically inclined crowds that had rebelled under the old regime as they gathered by tolling the bell and then expanded because of wild rumors and the conviction that they acted in the name of the king.[50] Like in the declining years of the old regime, the authorities were alarmed about free expression of opinion in gatherings of all sorts. The police eavesdropped on conversations in cafes, and policemen attended meetings of political clubs. There was much to record, more than ever before. When the Marquis de Ségur returned from Russia to France in early 1790, he noticed that people expressed themselves more freely than before: in town squares, groups of men were engaged in animated conversations, fear and circumspection had disappeared from their eyes, proud and direct was their gaze, "even among individuals of lower classes," and everywhere there was noise and exceptional liveliness.[51]

There was a difference between the public mobilization of 1789 and the gatherings of years past. Townspeople learned that they could actually influence politics by means of collective action, which changed their perception of government. Meeting every day, urban government was a different institution from what it had been before the summer of 1789. Committees to protect law and order, monitor food supplies, and take control of the moribund local militias sprung up in many towns. Artisans and shopkeepers volunteered for the militias, even if the initiative was commonly taken by property owners who served the militias as officers. The committees, whose members usually came from the liberal professions (lawyers, physicians)—although merchants predominated in cities with textile industries—often took the place of town councils. This grassroots democracy was not to last, however. By 1790, daily discussions between townsfolk and committees had faded.[52]

Elections also underscored the people's involvement in politics in the early years of the revolution. Voting was frequent and was held for a myriad of posts, including mayors, Assembly lawmakers, national guard officials, justices of the peace, civil court judges, public prosecutors, parish priests, and bishops. In later years, legislators even considered a plan to have parents elect their children's teachers. But how many citizens were authorized to vote? The Assembly distinguished between "active" and "passive" citizens. Contrary to those who saw the conquerors of the Bastille as "active" citizens, the latter were defined as independent—as we have seen, because of property—and having an interest in "the public establishment." Women, men under twenty-five years of age, domestic servants, and men who did not pay a minimal sum of direct taxes were thus excluded. Illiteracy, however, did not bar one from voting, but potential voters were disqualified if they failed to show up for National Guard duty or jury service. Yet, according to the Assembly's own reckoning, 4.3 million Frenchmen were enfranchised by 1791. A minority among them actually used their right to vote, their numbers decreasing over time, perhaps by virtue of the tedious electoral process. This tendency was reversed after the distinction between passive and active citizens disappeared in the late summer of 1792, when virtually every male over twenty-one apart from indigents and domestics was allowed to vote and be elected. In one of the many ironic twists and turns of the French Revolution, the men who came out to vote in July 1793 took part in the most democratic elections anywhere in the Atlantic world before the twentieth century, yet ended up creating a regime that forthwith suspended all elections.[53] It would therefore be wrong to attribute to the revolution either the advent of democracy or a giant leap forward in democracy, as R. R. Palmer has famously done. On the local level, as in Burgundy, popular participation in village government even declined after 1789.[54]

Social change, meanwhile, continued unabated. If cases of military insubordination had been isolated incidents under the old regime, widespread action against privilege and authority occurred in the army after July 1789, leaving the institution in a chaotic state by 1790.[55] Likewise, the new regime's successive abolition of remnants of privilege effected or accelerated changes. Theater had once been the pastime of nobles and other well-to-do citizens, but its audience changed in the last decades of the old regime, as a popular theater emerged alongside the official one. The change was consolidated by the decree (of January 13, 1791) eliminating "privileged" theaters. As anybody could now open a theater and any citizen could write for the stage, theater rapidly became daily entertainment for the urban population at large, especially as free performances "by and for the people" became increasingly common.[56]

From Varennes to the Execution: The End of the Monarchy

Ever since July 1789, France was ruled by both the National Assembly and the king. This dual power necessarily amounted to an awkward collaboration. How Louis himself conceived of his new position was not public knowledge at the time, but he clearly abhorred the rapid sequence of events that was derailing the old regime. Many suspected his wife, the singularly unpopular Marie-Antoinette, of scheming with the émigrés and her Austrian relatives—her brother was the emperor of Austria, Joseph II. On June 20, 1791, the royal couple, dressed respectively as a valet and the children's governess, attempted to escape along with their two children (and the king's sister and the children's real governess) from a country that they had gradually come to see as their prison. They had been stripped of the royal guards in Paris, but were "protected" by the National Guardsmen. Having shed their royal garb, the family traveled by coach in the direction of Montmédy, a small town in Lorraine near the border with Luxembourg. The king planned to issue a declaration there in which he dissolved the National Assembly, thus robbing the revolutionary government of all legitimacy. Alternatively, he would lead an army of French and Austrian troops (promised by the Austrian emperor) to Paris. However, little mishaps delayed their voyage. The postmaster of a small town, whose son had recognized Louis, rode to nearby Varennes to warn the National Guard, setting the scene for an ignominious return to Paris. The king tried to minimize the damage by contending that the party was on its way to a nobleman in the border area, but there was no disguising the fact that he had tried to flee after a memorandum he had left behind in Paris, in which he condemned the principles of the revolution, was discovered.[57]

Something snapped within the militant circles in Paris, which began to envisage the coming of a republic. Other Frenchmen wondered whether the king was indeed the father of the people. The Assembly, however, did not take any rash steps, temporarily suspending the king, but restoring him to the throne a few weeks later and forcing him to accept the constitution. None of that was arbitrary. Numerous members of the Assembly objected to a political arena without a royal figure, and the protection of property was a key element of their revolution and the constitution that was nearing completion. If the king were permanently removed, radicalism could gain the upper hand. Apart from that, maintaining the king would guarantee domestic peace in some form. Since the king still had many supporters at home and with Austria and exiles ready to intervene, a civil war had to be averted.[58] Republican elements could not be silenced. In the days after the restoration, fifty thousand Parisians gathered at the Champ de Mars, pressing for a trial of the king. The National Guard, a civil militia formed in the July days of 1789 to protect the revolution from its enemies, fired on the masses, killing fifty and wounding many others. Although it would seem clear that breaches were appearing in the cross-class alliance that drove the revolution along, both the municipal authorities and the radicals failed to draw that conclusion after the massacre at the Champ de Mars. The demonstrators viewed their "aristocratic" adversaries not as social enemies but as immoral ones, while the authorities preferred to believe that outside elements—brigands, foreigners—were at work, stirring up the masses.[59]

In reality, of course, Varennes and its aftermath "exploded the unity of the Revolution."[60] The king's flight and arrest prompted more noblemen to abandon French soil than any other event in these years. Despite a law adopted the day after the king's arrest that made it illegal to leave the kingdom, thousands of army officers left their posts and sought refuge abroad. Only one-quarter stuck to their posts by year's end. A series of subsequent laws discouraged emigration even more, starting with the sale of properties of émigrés from August 1792, and continuing with the death sentence of exiles on October 25, mitigated only slightly by the grace period of two weeks announced in mid-November for those willing to return.[61]

The failed royal escape also put a damper on the joy about the constitution that was being prepared and would be adopted in September. This was a momentous document that espoused the decisions made on August 4, 1789, the night "feudalism" was toppled. The constitution granted the right to vote to all taxpaying males of at least twenty-five years of age, except for servants, debtors, felons, those indicted for crimes, and the insane.[62] All Protestants and Jews were given civil equality, which did not happen without controversy. The outbreak of the revolution in the summer of 1789 had "reawakened old memories of the Wars of Religion" in towns with large Protestant minorities.[63] Nationally, Jews were a small minority, but they faced bitter opposition in Alsace and Lorraine, where many villagers suggested in their *cahiers* to force Jews to engage in physical labor or expel them from the country. Nor was complete equality espoused by all Jews, many of whom wanted to preserve their communal autonomy.[64] Blacks in France also received equal rights, which contrasted favorably with the two laws adopted by the old regime that allowed a limited type of slavery on French soil.[65]

The adoption of the constitution closed an important chapter in the history of the revolution. Having done its job, the Constituent Assembly dissolved itself and made way for an elected Legislative Assembly. In many ways, this new body differed from its predecessor. Few nobles and clerics remained, far fewer lawyers were chosen, and the average age dropped dramatically: whereas the men elected in 1789 had an average age of about forty-five, half of the new deputies were in their twenties. Having been elected in the wake of Varennes, they were also much more radical in their views.[66] The youngsters had to share power with the restored king. The constitution maintained the king, who was given the power of veto and the right to suspend for three years laws that did not pertain to the constitution or fiscal matters. Louis used his veto in November 1791 against a decree that denounced émigrés and in June of the following year against a law that targeted refractory priests.

It was also in the fall of 1791 that the advance of Jacobinism began. All over the country, popular societies sprang up modeled on the Jacobin club of Paris, which had been founded in May 1789. In the fall of that year it moved into new premises inside an old Jacobin convent, which gave the movement its name. With a membership overwhelmingly drawn from the Third Estate, the Jacobin club in Paris offered members with seats in the Assembly the opportunity to make themselves known to their colleagues and thereby obtain posts on important Assembly committees. In all, six thousand Jacobin clubs were set up with one million Frenchmen as members, generally relatively well-to-do urban dwellers who were thus introduced to the world of politics. They were all offered, within the confines of the meeting, an opportunity to speak up. Still, membership was not open to everybody; in some cities, only members of the National Guard could join.[67] The clubs constantly corresponded with the original club in Paris that functioned as the supreme organ of Jacobinism. Disagreement was rare. Many clubs, for example, prohibited any discussion of republicanism after Louis's restoration in the summer of 1791, arguing that public opinion had spoken. Yet one year later, the Jacobins had come to see themselves as the interpreters of public opinion, by virtue of which they felt they had the right to share France's sovereignty with the Legislative Assembly.[68] As more and more politicians were members of both bodies, some of the main decisions were first taken in the old convent. Jacobins thus determined the course of the revolution.

Another group that carried the revolution forward in the second phase was the sans-culottes. In the famous contemporary definition, a sans-culotte "always travels on foot and lives very simply with his wife and children, if he has any, on the fifth or sixth floor." The sans-culotte was also typically male and a Parisian. He usually made a living as an artisan, a shopkeeper, or a journeyman. He wore long trousers, not the *culottes* or knee breeches worn by aristocrats, and often went out in public with the red Phrygian Cap, associated with classical freedom, which was the most conspicuous part of the Jacobin outfit.[69] A sans-culotte did not desire equality of ownership, but he favored an equal distribution of wealth. The prices of supplies, he found, had to be fixed. Collective liberties meant more to him than individual ones. He was convinced of his right to take part in legislation, which he actually did in times of crisis by gathering along with his fellow sans-culottes, although the extent of their impact depended on the degree to which they were armed. The main difference with the Jacobins was that they did the talking, while the sans-culottes were men of action. But both groups usually supported the same policies, at least until the spring of 1794.[70]

Jacobins and sans-culottes grew increasingly critical of their king. Louis XVI might have been officially restored in July 1791, but his popularity plummeted after his aborted flight. His vacillating behavior and his vetoes had only hastened the decline of his reputation. As political associations raised a hue and cry over a king who failed to acknowledge the general will, tensions boiled over in the weeks after the celebrations of the third birthday of the storming of the Bastille. Militant Parisians began meeting per section, that is to say in their own administrative division, of which there were forty-eight. The news that the Duke of Brunswick had crossed the border with a Prussian army and was en route to the capital made the feathers fly among the sections as well the Assembly, which declared the nation in danger, summoning a hundred thousand National Guardsmen to the capital. A manifesto that Bruns-wick issued added fuel to the fire. His message was that Paris would suffer for any harm done to the king. The sections now demanded that the king be deposed, and when the Assembly did not comply with their wish, they took action themselves by forming a commune of their own, independent of the existing municipal council, chasing that body literally from city hall in the night of August 9–10.[71]

At daybreak the sections, accompanied by National Guardsmen from Paris and elsewhere, marched in two columns on the royal palace in the Tuileries. Just in time, Louis and his family took refuge in the Assembly, where a bloodbath ensued. Six hundred of the nine hundred Swiss guards posted outside to protect the king were killed, as were 180 members of the National Guard on the other side. Having surrounded the Assembly building, the rebel Commune was able to impose its will on the legislature, which was forced to suspend the king. This was, in hindsight, a watershed moment. A period of eight hundred years of Capetian monarchical rule came to an end on August 10.[72] Beyond that, the events also meant that the revolution was no longer primarily a movement to introduce reforms in a legal fashion. The revolution existed now mainly as an end in itself,[73] as the Assembly carried out another demand of the Commune by dissolving itself in elections and making way for a Convention that was to write a new constitution. The triumph of the Commune was complete when the Assembly added to a new government one of the great leaders of the sections: Georges Danton. A thirty-three-year-old lawyer from a family of minor court officials, Danton had emerged as leader of the sans-culottes, a theatrical personality who had been vociferous in the drive to suspend the king.

The workers from the sections were not done yet. Nervous because of the approach of the Prussian army, they began to arrest priests and other reputed enemies on orders from their sectional assemblies. Their imprisonment did not last long. After the announcement on September 2 that the Prussians had seized Verdun, the last stronghold en route to Paris, an unprecedented massacre ensued in the Parisian prisons. Although most inmates were common criminals, mobs of men, convinced that all prisoners were counterrevolutionaries, killed more than eleven hundred of them. Among these were two hundred refractory priests and the three hundred Swiss Guards who had escaped with life and limb on August 10.

The Jacobin-dominated Convention was in tune with the demands of the Parisian sections. Although they embraced possessive individualism, or at least saw the inequality of property as a necessary evil, there was much about capitalism that the Jacobins abhorred. Hoarding and speculation were seen in the first place as antisocial activities.[74] Social engagement was one of the pillars of Jacobin ideology, exemplified by France's first progressive taxation introduced on March 18, 1793. Eighty-two government agents, so-called Representatives-on-Mission, introduced this tax in many parts of the country, while raising occasional forced loans to feed the hungry and equip the recruits. The Representatives had unlimited powers, which they used to influence local opinion and revamp political institutions. These measures were legitimized with reference to the extraordinary circumstances in which the country, threatened by war, found itself. The Representatives were strongly influenced in their decisions by local militants, who used them to defeat their political rivals.[75]

The less affluent part of the nation benefited not only from fiscal legislation. Another law was adopted after sans-culottes, who refused to pay more than in 1790, invaded grocers' shops in almost every Paris neighborhood in February 1793. The Assembly authorized local authorities in the country to control the price and supply of bread and flour, a measure that eventually took shape in the Law of the Maximum (September 3, 1793). Yet another law, adopted on May 11, 1794, provided elderly, sick, or disabled country dwellers with small allowances and housing if needed. And finally, attempts were made to stay on top of the food situation by erecting granaries in each district and by granting a national food committee the power to confiscate food and control distribution. Saint-Antoine, the Paris neighborhood that had made a name for itself in the early days of the revolution, gained significantly from these laws. By April 1796, almost all its residents received government relief in the form of bread and meat. Sixteen thousand persons alone were allotted three-quarters of a pound of free bread per day and a free pound of meat every ten days.[76]

But the revolution also had a negative impact on the needy French. The campaign against women's religious orders put an end to the crucial role that many of the fifty-five thousand female religious (more than twice the number of their male counterparts) fulfilled, who provided better nursing services in hospitals and asylums than anywhere in Europe. The poor, the sick, and foundlings suffered the most. The infant mortality rate in the town of Rouen climbed to almost 100 percent in the next few years.[77]

At the time of the September Massacres in 1792, the future of the revolution looked dismal. Prussian troops were unstoppable in their march to Paris. The Prussian commander, however, refused to go all-out in an artillery duel on September 20, which was then advertised as a French victory, although the majority of the victims were French. The encounter nonetheless did block the advance of the Prussians, who withdrew to the Rhine. The news of the "victory" was received with relish in the capital, where the recently elected Convention was about to be inaugurated. The new legislators did not waste time, abolishing the monarchy once and for all, but stopping short of taking action against the king. His later fate was no foregone conclusion. It was only after the discovery in the Tuileries palace of Louis's secret correspondence, mainly with his wife's family in Austria, that a trial became unavoidable. But what was the indictment? The Convention first grappled with the issue of inviolability. The king was not to be judged as the personification of the ancien régime, but as the constitutional king who had been "created" in September 1791. His inviolability could be rescinded only by three offenses: leaving the country, commanding a foreign army, or refusing the constitutional oath. And although his correspondence showed that he had pondered all three, Louis's guilt could not be proven. A thirty-four-year-old deputy, the former lawyer Maximilien Robespierre, argued that the whole matter was flawed. If the king could be brought to trial and therefore presumed innocent by a court, it could follow that the revolution was guilty. That same day, however, it was decided that Louis XVI *would* stand trial and that the Convention was to turn itself into a court of law. In the weeks that followed, the king and the lawyers assigned to him tried in vain to plead their cause. Given the mood in the country, he simply could not escape a guilty verdict. But even now it was still uncertain whether the death penalty would be the outcome. The deputies were divided on the matter, but at the second vote the supporters of capital punishment outnumbered those in favor of clemency. That decided the argument. On January 21, 1793, Louis XVI, now referred to by his ancestors' civilian name of Capet, was executed before a joyful crowd of twenty thousand Parisians.[78]

The king's death was a watershed, at least in the eyes of the Conventionnels, who set out to make a clean sweep. As Saint-Just (see below) explained, "everything that is not new in a time of innovation is pernicious."[79] A few months earlier, on its second day in session, the Convention had decreed that official documents had to be dated the "First Year of Liberty." One year later, they introduced the revolutionary calendar, in which August 10, 1792 (the day of the palace invasion) was day 1 of Year I of equality. At the same time, it was resolved that September 22, 1792 (the day of the Convention's inaugural meeting) was henceforth the first day of Year I on a new calendar that all Frenchmen were told to adopt. Calendar reform was only the beginning of a thorough reform program. With the units of measure gram and meter serving as standards, for the first time in history the metric system was brought into operation. The decimal system was deemed superior to all other systems because it was rooted in nature: after all, everybody had ten fingers. The calendar year was also subjected to the decimal system by dividing the year into ten months and the week into ten days—each month had three weeks and there were five or six leap days; most new festivals (celebrating youth, marriage, old age, agriculture, or French military success) were to be held on the tenth day. The ten new months were given names such as Pluviôse (derived from the Latin *pluviosus* or rainy) and Messidor (from the Latin *messis* or harvest) that reflected the weather or agricultural activities typical for those months. The revolutionary calendar made much sense to the legislators, who were happy to outlaw many holidays, as well as "Saint Monday"—the day that many workers idled—by designating only one weekday as a day of rest. But the calendar never caught on with the average Frenchman, mostly because it lacked any genuine advantages.[80] Outside of the official channels, the calendar suffered neglect until it was put out of its misery in 1806.

Parts of the population did, however, share the neophilia. In Year II, about twenty-five hundred priests who had tried to combine a calling as priest and a commitment to the revolution resigned their positions spontaneously and enthusiastically, in hopes that a civic regeneration might be accomplished. They wished to destroy the symbols, relics, and representations of everything that was considered part of "fanaticism."[81] The priests fought side by side with members of the Jacobin clubs, among whom a minority happily participated in a movement of cultural destruction. Statues of saints and monarchs were toppled and destroyed in several towns, libraries were confiscated, and the Jacobin club in Fontainebleau publicly burned royal portraits, including a painting by Leonardo da Vinci.

The tabula rasa that occurred disgusted many citizens and found a formidable opponent in the eloquent abbé Grégoire, constitutional bishop and member of the Convention. To describe the destructive fury he denounced, Grégoire coined the term "vandalism." He held the old regime, which had allegedly trained people in infamy, responsible for this conduct.[82] Clearly, French legislators had not taken the initiative. In 1790, a group of artisans had requested the National Assembly that the king destroy all monuments created during the old regime. The Assembly did not respond on that occasion, springing into action only after the fall of the monarchy in August 1792 had precipitated a spontaneous whirlwind destruction of statues of former kings. The Assembly then ordered the communes of France to remove all statues, bas-reliefs, and inscriptions from public monuments. The law added that the bronze thus obtained could be cast into cannons and used to defend the fatherland.[83]

If this rupture with the past manifested itself fully in 1792, the tendency had been visible since the revolution's first stages. As early as 1790, the conservative British politician Edmund Burke had chastised the French revolutionaries for their lack of respect for tradition. It was myopic, he wrote, to break completely with the past and then build a new commonwealth. Old polities are time-honored, because "they are the results of various necessities and expediences. They are not often constructed after any theory; theories are rather drawn from them."[84]

The initial response to the revolution had not been negative in the outside world. British Prime Minister William Pitt expressed the hope that the events would lead to the establishment of a constitutional monarchy. Other Englishmen were unconditionally devoted to the revolution. The storming of the Bastille was immediately reenacted in at least three London plays, while the Theatre Royal in Dublin staged "Gallic Freedom or the Destruction of the Bastille."[85] In Germany, the revolution had ardent supporters in the academic world. Freedom was festively celebrated along with victories of French armies, and the republican calendar was adopted. The German Jacobins included men such as Matthias Metternich, who made it the prime objective of his journal *Der*

Bürgerfreund to inform his fellow citizens about the true human rights. But the mood changed completely after the September Massacres of 1792 and Louis XVI's execution. Friedrich Schiller, whom the National Assembly had made an honorary French citizen, even considered writing an apologia for the king.[86] Elsewhere, the prison massacres in September 1792 lost the revolution many foreign supporters. The Russian ambassador to France, Ivan Simolin, who had considered the Champ de Mars massacre of July 17, 1791, "the only means of restoring peace and tranquility in the capital," now wrote: "The history of tigers and anthropophagi [man-eaters] did not record such barbarous and wild scenes, and the vengeance of these monsters demands retaliation on behalf of all Europe, and a war of extermination in order to spare the rest of the human race from similar insanity."[87]

Nationalizing French Life

British historian J. M. Roberts has summed up the activities of the Jacobins during their heyday as "the biggest attempt yet seen to nationalize the life of a whole state, to regulate it in all its aspects from a central source of impulse and to make all Frenchmen and Frenchwomen feel the reality of nationhood."[88] The line separating the public and private realms became blurred through public pressure and legislation. All over France, people started wearing the cockade not out of devotion to the Jacobin cause, but to hide their true feelings. Soon, there was no alternative anymore, as men (July 8, 1792) and women (September 21, 1793) were obliged by law to wear the cockade. Artist Jacques-Louis David even worked on a civic uniform, one that would, however, never be worn.[89]

Unity became the main objective of French politics. The Jacobins first purged their own ranks, suppressing minority opinion to preserve unanimity. In the Convention, one group of Jacobins, the Montagnards, led by Robespierre, ousted another one, the moderate republicans called Girondins. The latter feared the sections and the extremism that seemed to propel the revolution forward. They were, however, late converts to a political practice based on legality, having themselves encouraged the events of August 10. To the Montagnards, unity demanded the fusion of the three powers (executive, legislative, and judicial). A two-chamber assembly was deemed incompatible with revolutionary unity. Robespierre, therefore, would have none of the British Parliament. There was, after all, just one general will. Nor did unity leave room for intermediate social bodies such as the Church. It was because of the principle that everyone be required to toe the same line that priests had to swear an oath to the constitution.[90]

Using it with great frequency to suggest an imaginary public opinion, deputies manufactured the term "general will" as they saw fit. They certainly did not consult with their constituents,[91] nor had they done so at an earlier stage of the revolution. There was no mandate, for example, to write the constitution. The Jacobins justified their freedom to voice public opinion by presenting themselves as a vanguard that expressed the ideas of an idealized French people. Legitimacy resided not in numbers of votes, but in the virtue of the revolution's leaders. And the leaders saw their virtue recognized by the actions of sans-culottes who kept the flame of the revolution burning.[92]

Accordingly, relations with foreign countries changed drastically. The revolutionaries' initial cosmopolitanism had served to temper their nationalism,[93] but as the French Revolution became a European question in the wake of Varennes, the outlook of the members of the Assembly began to change. By 1793, they had started to worry about the outside world, facing as they did enemies all around, from Spain in the south via Venice, Rome, and Naples, to the Dutch Republic and England, as well as Austria, Prussia, and Russia. These countries feared France for two reasons: the danger that French principles and politics would catch on at home, and the possibility of sudden aggression from the French army, not unlikely given the unpredictability of the revolution. The French invasion of the Austrian Netherlands (Belgium) in the spring of 1792 seemed to confirm this fear. Convinced of their own invincibility vis-à-vis kings and tyrants, the French embarked on an adventure that soon turned into a nightmare. While they caught the Austrians by surprise, their armies barely advanced and were repelled or disintegrated due to lack of discipline. The invasion into France by a Prussian army, however, turned the tide, restoring the morale of the troops and the French nation. The stage was thus set for the annexation of Nice, Savoy, Belgium, and the Rhineland. The most salient aspect of these wars is that, at least on the French side, they lacked any ideological content. They were not waged to support the principles on which the revolution was erected.

What is more, once the nation was at war, the members of the Assembly turned out to be great admirers of the man they had despised as the incarnation of the old regime: Louis XIV. To them, the Sun King's foreign policy seemed worthy of imitation.[94]

The common man was less enthusiastic. If the revolutionaries had initially counted on volunteers to man the armies, after the setbacks in Belgium another approach was needed. There was no going back to the old regime's foreign mercenaries and press gangs. Instead, for every community, a quota was set of men, and ballots were used to select the young men who would go off to war. Many more soldiers than before the revolution were peasants, whose proportion in the army rose by more than 10 percent, while that of artisans declined commensurately between 1789 and 1793. The foreign threat, perceived or real, also made cosmopolitanism melt quickly. England and Austria had initially been portrayed as the main enemies, but soon it was dangerous not only for Englishmen and Austrians but for all foreigners to move about in Paris. Each one of them was in principle a suspect among a people betrayed by the whole world, said Louis Antoine de Saint-Just, the young firebrand (born in 1767). Not that these strangers could affect the French, the Jacobins thought, save by spoiling them. Virtue—the sacrifice of ordinary Frenchmen for and dedication to the nation—was, indeed, the republic's professed foundation.[95]

The wars did not simply divert attention from domestic matters. Long-term projects such as proposals to revamp the national education system were shelved, since the wars took precedence.[96] In a law adopted on August 23, 1793, all men aged eighteen through twenty-five were to register themselves for military service, although only single men were to be drafted. Measured by the number of recruits incorporated into the French army, 750,000 by 1794, conscription was a resounding success. Not just young unmarried men were obliged to service by this law. In fact, the whole nation was mobilized for war: the young men had to go to battle, married men forge arms and transport provisions, women stitch tents and uniforms and serve in hospitals, children turn old linen into lint, and old men go to the public places and preach the unity of the republic and the hatred of kings.[97] The law would be known as the *levée en masse*. Mass conscription inspired great enthusiasm to join and defend the fatherland. Many soldiers would die for their country in foreign wars: approximately 530,000 fell in the period 1792 to 1799, most of them before April 1797.[98]

But war was not just declared against the outside world. The list of domestic enemies increased the longer the Jacobins held sway. Enemies were important to the revolution, since their exclusion worked in practice as its permanent motor.[99] These perceived enemies were labeled as outlaws and thereby guilty of breaking natural law and the law of nations, just as Louis XVI had allegedly done. This accusation enabled the Convention to bypass civil prosecution and start a comprehensive new stage of the revolution: the Terror.[100] The first step was the enactment of a series of decrees in September 1793 that determined that all suspect persons would be arrested, that surveillance committees (filled, of course, with sans-culottes) were to prepare lists of suspects in their own districts and to issue warrants against them. Public authorities were to carry out the arrests. Suspects soon included the indifferent and "egoists."[101] All citizens were made to carry a certificate of civic virtue, a proof of good behavior that rapidly became a political passport. At first, the police, elected officials, or surveillance committees had been charged with giving out the certificates, but individual Jacobins came to absorb the responsibility. In September 1793, it was resolved that citizens unable to produce a certificate could be arrested instantly.[102] The Committee of General Security, which was responsible for police and internal security, tried the detainees. It was the second state organ, subordinate only to the Committee of Public Safety, whose functions were to initiate legislation, control foreign policy, appoint generals, and purge local politics. Robespierre, now nicknamed "the Incorruptible," emerged as the committee's undisputed leader, who increasingly bent the Convention to his will.[103]

With the exception of a small minority—including Queen Marie-Antoinette, who was executed on October 16, 1793—most victims had initially welcomed the revolution. Discontent may have been taken as resistance to the revolution; but very few Frenchmen would have wanted to return to the old regime. The revolution's self-proclaimed guardians disagreed. They legitimized their rule by presenting their actions as necessary for the revolution's survival. Robespierre explained in a speech: "The government of the revolution is the despotism of liberty against tyranny." "Terror," he added, "is nothing more than prompt, severe inflexible justice."[104] Indeed, said Saint-Just, the arrests made in Paris were for the safety of the people and the government. Soon, in the climate of paranoia that seized France, execution followed imprisonment as a matter of course. In revolutionary justice, the accused was presumed guilty, and evidence against opponents was no longer needed.[105] The scale of persecution was unheard of. Half a million men were arrested, twenty thousand of whom were executed, often under the guillotine. This new instrument was recommended, although not designed, by Dr. Joseph Guillotin, deputy in the original National Assembly, as a humane means of death. It was in reality a device that would fill the French—and foreigners—with dread. Goethe's mother even abhorred the toy guillotines that were sold at the time, refusing to follow her son's suggestion to present "such an infamous murder machine" as a gift to her grandson.[106]

The polarization between Jacobins and others was repeated in many cities, its specific form depending on local circumstances.[107] In Lyon, France's second city, a veritable class struggle played itself out in the days of the revolution. For more than a century, two groups with different interests had faced off. As the eighteenth century advanced, the city's highly skilled weavers, of whom there were five to seven thousand by the time of the revolution, faced increasing competition from a group of merchant entrepreneurs. The merchants "secured commissions in bulk, signed contracts with selected weavers, and sold finished fabric on a wholesale basis." They used to their advantage a series of local government measures that made it increasingly difficult for weavers to sell their own products. While the weavers felt that they were the mainstay of the textile industry, the merchants came to act increasingly as their employers who preferred to negotiate separately with every artisan about prices. Foreign competition and the loss of domestic markets heightened the tensions after the mid-eighteenth century, but in the fall of 1789 the tide finally seemed to turn for the weavers. The king lent a ready ear to the weavers, approving a scale of rates they had suggested. The weavers' political activism, beginning with their enrollment in Lyon's first political club, must be seen as an attempt to maintain and perhaps expand what had been achieved. Weavers also backed the town's republicans who were active from August 1792, and even received support from the local Jacobins, who denounced men of substance and suggested taxing them mercilessly.[108]

Jacobin activities led to a successful rebellion of moderate elements in the city and supporters of the monarchy. They seized power on May 29, 1793, incurring the wrath of the Montagnards in Paris. Representatives-on-Mission were sent from the capital with an army that restored order and showed no mercy. The capture of the town on October 9 was followed by the destruction of the houses of the wealthy and the killing of seventeen hundred suspects. Finally, Lyon was renamed Ville-Affranchie ("Emancipated City"). Lyon had not been alone in resisting the Montagnards' takeover. Other provincial towns like Nîmes, Toulouse, and Marseille also no longer recognized the authority of the Convention in 1793, condemning the Jacobin assumption of power and the arrest of twenty-nine legislators, predominantly Girondins. The other towns awaited a similar fate as Lyon. The politicians who had governed Marseille were overthrown after an invasion by regular army units. Four hundred men were executed and several buildings were razed to the ground. Marseille was henceforth called "The City without a Name."[109] Nor was such massive retribution necessarily the regime's reaction to municipal insubordination. In Nantes, local authorities teamed up with the Representative-on-Mission, tying groups of non-refractory priests to a barge that was sunk on successive occasions in the Loire River. Others who had resisted Jacobin Paris, as well as common criminals, died in the same way. The men and women who were drowned or guillotined numbered in the thousands, forcing a dozen new cemeteries to be opened between January and August 1794.[110]

In parts of rural France, especially in the west and the south, the population tended to turn against the revolution, which was uncommon in the cities. After the summer of 1789, the French countryside remained turbulent, in part because the economic recession continued unabated. The rural population sometimes protested townspeople who bought their lands without consulting them. In other cases, the peasants turned against the state, once they discovered, for example, that the old feudal dues had indeed been abolished, but that national taxes, on the other hand, had risen. Yet others merely wanted to be left alone. In the west of the country, peasants turned against Paris with a vengeance. In 1791, their resistance assumed the form of guerrilla warfare in the entire area north of the Loire. Regular army troops put down this movement in the last days of 1793.

Active resistance seldom reared its head thereafter.[111] More successful in its defiance were the Vendée and three adjacent departments, collectively known as the "military Vendée."[112] In the spring and summer of 1793, armed resistance caused by the forced recruitment of unprecedented numbers of youths spread rapidly. Genuine armies sprang up that were several hundred thousand strong by mid-1793 and measured up to regular French troops. Brittany and other parts of western France fell, including the cities of Saumur and Angers, but the conquest of Nantes failed, leaving the insurgents without the seaport that could have served as a bridgehead for British soldiers and émigrés. The failure also enabled the regular army to regroup so that by October, the revolt had lost its momentum. In the wake of the rebels' defeat in December, the army took drastic action, destroying entire villages, seizing crops, and killing anyone who stood in their way.[113] As both sides refused to yield, the human toll was enormously high. Many tens of thousands of soldiers died in the "military Vendée," while the local population lost perhaps a quarter million men, women, and children, a demographic decline of more than one-fifth (and maybe as high as one-third).[114]

The rift between the west and Paris did not predate the revolution. The *cahiers* drawn up in the west were certainly not less critical about the seigneurial regime than they were elsewhere in the country. Like other parts of rural France, the west had hardly been given a voice in the Estates General of 1789 or the Legislative Assembly that came into being two years later. Bills unpopular with peasants were thus adopted as a matter of course. Conscription was an important source of rural discontent, occurring on an unprecedented scale and creating large numbers of draft dodgers who contracted hastily arranged fraudulent marriages, paid substitutes, or went into hiding. Whatever the case, everyday life was disrupted, in particular because so many men had suddenly withdrawn from economic pursuits. Often, however, conscription merely provided a lightning rod, channeling discontent about the Civil Constitution or anger among tenant farmers who had a bone to pick with their landlords.[115]

In Paris, meanwhile, the spring of 1794 saw the apotheosis of the Terror, as the revolution devoured its own leaders. On April 5, it was the turn of Danton, the influential journalist Camille Desmoulins, and their partisans. Danton was accused of bribery and corruption, charges that as usual were completely unfounded. Even Robespierre, for so long the undisputed spokesman for both the Jacobins and the Convention, did not escape the Terror himself. Disparate groups of deputies to the Assembly decided to act in unison in order to save their own lives. On 9 Thermidor, Year II (July 27, 1794), they shouted "Down with the tyrant!" as he tried to speak in the Convention, and ordered his arrest. The next day, Robespierre was silenced for good, when he ended up under the guillotine along with Saint-Just and over one hundred other sympathizers.[116]

Now the revolution could finally settle down, although initially there was no sign of change. Blatant lies, used so often in the previous years by authorities to steer the revolution in the preferred direction, were again invoked in order to legitimize Robespierre's fall. The Committees of Public Safety and General Security deliberately spread the false news that "the Incorruptible" had harbored royalist designs. There was said to be a mountain of evidence that he had planned to crown himself. This rumor had numerous variations, but in most he had even courted Louis XVI's daughter, suggesting Robespierre's links with a regime that the revolution had vanquished.[117]

Dismantling the Terror

In the remaining months of 1794 and the first of 1795, the Terror was dismantled step by step. Jacobin clubs were closed, surveillance committees were outlawed, the influence of sans-culottes was curbed, thousands of prisoners were released, Girondins were readmitted to the Convention, and "Terrorists" were expelled. In January 1795 émigré workers were authorized to return, and in August all political clubs were closed. In the southeast, especially the cities of Marseille and Lyon, which had seen such brutal oppression, the end of the Terror signaled the start of massive anti-Jacobin actions. In what has been called the "White Terror," mobs butchered hundreds of Jacobin prisoners in Lyon, Nîmes, Aix-en-Provence, and Marseille, while officials turned a blind eye to the slaughter. Other Jacobins were killed as they fled to the countryside. Private scores were sometimes settled under the guise of political revenge, which almost spiraled out of control in Lyon. The attackers there did not give up their arms and surrendered only when after more than four months of visceral counterterror an army arrived from the capital.[118]

The politicians of 1795 viewed the revolutionary past from a critical distance. Likening Robespierre's "dictatorship" to the power wielded by absolute kings in earlier decades, they implemented the Anglo-Saxon parliamentary system by introducing a two-chamber assembly. Under the new regime, dubbed "Directory," the lower council was called the Five Hundred, whose minimum age was thirty. These men voted on resolutions, which the Ancients (250 deputies of at least forty years of age) then transformed into laws. The executive power was in the hands of five directors, who were elected by the two councils and who decided on matters of war, diplomacy, police, and administration. In theory, the legislative power was divided and the executive strengthened. The French let themselves be openly inspired by their American forebears, especially in the concept of the separation of powers. The committee of eleven that designed the constitution of 1795 cited with approval John Adams's *Defence of the Constitutions of Government of the United States* (1787, translated in 1792), even if one member confused the author with Samuel Adams. In practice, though, sovereignty was still indivisible and political pluralism abhorred.

There were other signs of continuity. The same parliamentary majority that had first supported the Girondins and then the Montagnards, and next turned against Robespierre and consorts, formed the leadership of the Directory. The calendar was not thrown out, the urban middling sort continued to benefit from the revolution, buying more than 90 percent of the land sold after 1795, and the old Catholic Church was forced to remain in hiding until the laws against refractory priests were revoked in August 1797.[119] Likewise, once French troops began to overrun foreign countries, the lessons of the insurgency in the Vendée were obviously lost on the French authorities. As in the Vendée, religious alienation in neighboring countries combined with resistance to conscription to form a powerful mix. In the Southern Netherlands, which had been annexed in October 1795, the French abolished regular orders and monasteries in September 1796 and thus made ten thousand clergymen homeless. Adding insult to injury, priests were required to swear allegiance to the laws and an oath of hatred of monarchy and anarchy.

Virtually all priests rejected these demands and were deported. A peasant revolt finally broke out against French rule in eastern Flanders, Brabant, and German Luxemburg in October 1798. The result of the French invasions, therefore, was to make many more enemies rather than to win over people to the republican cause. The military superiority that had enabled the sister revolutions to succeed also prevented genuine democracy from taking root. Instead, French arms unwittingly provoked the emergence of a phenomenon that everywhere united the enemies of revolutionary politics: nationalism.[120]

Although political life remained volatile, French society returned to some form of normalcy. Civic peace was restored, as people began to freely air their opinions again, assisted by the press that returned aboveground. Plays that used to be popular before the revolution were in demand again. Foreign troops evacuated French territory and workers and artisans went back to work.[121] The new climate allowed the Convention to turn to the issue of education. A law of November 17, 1794, obliged the government to provide a schoolmaster and schoolmistress for primary schools in every municipality that had over one thousand inhabitants. Numerous obstacles prevented implementation of the law: the dearth of teachers, their poor qualifications, but most of all the economic woes that plagued the country, hitting urban workers especially. Lawmakers gave up on universal and free public education by 1795.[122]

Political turmoil in previous years had contributed to a serious economic recession. The extraordinary events that rocked Lyon, for example, slowed down the city's silk cloth production. The severe winter of 1794–1795, the coldest on record since 1709, did not help matters. Many Frenchmen took to eating unhealthy food like unripe corn, rotten fish, and moldy vegetables. Grain, obviously, was in short supply almost everywhere, and where it was not, its price was astronomic. Every night, long lines formed outside Paris's bakeries in hopes of obtaining half a pound of poor bread after a five- or six-hour wait. As famine became more widespread, overall mortality increased significantly, while the birth rate plummeted. The abolition of price controls exacerbated the French plight, as inflation began to rise at once.[123] Not everyone suffered under these conditions. Some *nouveaux riches* emerged, who made fortunes by provisioning the armies and by speculating in treasury bonds and church property sold by the state.[124] But the living standard of most Frenchmen declined.

Hungry men and women staged an open insurrection on May 20, 1795, invading the Convention premises. Their failure to topple the government enabled the authorities to call in troops that restored order. The Directory had to fight off various other challenges. One potentially dangerous opponent was the Count of Provence, brother of the executed king, who held court in Verona, Italy. After the death in prison of his brother's young son in June 1795, Provence proclaimed himself Louis XVIII. He issued a statement that anticipated the return of the society of orders, were he to become king. Provence was no real threat, though. More serious was the landing in Brittany in the summer of the same year of émigré troops, who had been financed and transported by Britain. But the plan to have western rebels and émigrés join forces and form a counterrevolutionary army was nipped in the bud when the troops were routed immediately after landing. All 748 émigrés were shot as traitors.

The next challenge came from a conspiracy that was thwarted in May 1796. The mastermind, François-Noël or "Gracchus" Babeuf (1760–1797), had proclaimed that the revolution had betrayed its own principles. Noblemen might no longer rule, he argued, but equality, the chief goal of the revolution, had been trampled. What is more, the revolution had turned against the people. By late 1794, Babeuf denounced the hostilities in the Vendée as a war of extermination waged by the government to reduce the population.[125] Babeuf's ideal, propagated in his newspaper *Le Tribun du Peuple* and in the Club du Panthéon—a new patriotic society in Paris—was the abolition of private property, which would free up all land for everybody; the land's produce would be equally shared. If equality was a panacea in Babeuf's plan, the state was also given a key role in the social revolution that he planned. The state would assign citizens to economic tasks and would make sure that all goods were equally distributed among the French. But his vision, elaborated during his many imprisonments, lacked any reflection on economic development, and the "Conspiracy of Equals," his organization for overthrowing the government, seriously overestimated the number of potential followers, counting on seventeen thousand men to spread the insurrection in Paris, including six thousand disgruntled policemen. When push came to shove, the most conspicuous inaction came from the sans-culottes, whose role was played out by now.[126]

Royalists, on the other hand, returned to politics, surprisingly winning the national elections of May 1797 by a landslide. On the advice of the five directors, General Pierre Augereau then staged a coup on September 4 with the troops of Paris under his command, paving the way, at least temporarily, for more radical policies. One hundred sixty émigrés who had illegally returned to France were shot. Two directors, fifty-three lawmakers, and many journalists were deported to French Guiana, where they would await a sure but slow death; in practice only nine deputies, however, faced that plight. Eighteen hundred priests were arrested and electors were forced to swear an oath of "hatred towards royalty and anarchy."[127]

In the first months of 1799, the ascendant Neo-Jacobins gained important posts in the government, reinforcing fears of an impending new Terror in the summer of the same year. Abbé Sieyès, who had survived all purges of the 1790s, was in a position to respond, having been elected director in May. He closed down the meeting hall where the Jacobins had recently gathered and pondered a new leadership to replace the Directory. Another coup d'état was needed. The man to help him was Napoleon Bonaparte, the Corsican-born general widely known for his military successes abroad. Lacking support among the deputies, Napoleon needed Sieyès just as much as Sieyès needed him. When backing from bankers had been secured, Sieyès stepped down (as did two other directors) on November 9, 1799, to make way for a coup scheduled to take place that day. According to the plan, Napoleon, just anointed as the new commander of troops in Paris, went to the Saint Cloud palace where the Council of Five Hundred was meeting to convince the deputies of a Jacobin plot, which in reality did not exist. Shouted down, Napoleon left the palace, but was saved by his brother Lucien, whose position, conveniently, was that of president of the legislative body. Lucien exclaimed to the soldiers of the Paris garrison waiting outside that the palace was full of assassins who were after his brother's life. Lucien's action produced the desired result, as troops stormed the palace, clearing it of any opposing deputies. The revolution thus effectively ended November 9–10, 1799, or 18–19 Brumaire of the Year VIII on the revolutionary calendar.

The French Revolution was not an isolated series of events, but took place in a continent where privilege came increasingly under fire as the eighteenth century advanced. The Genevans and the Dutch experienced revolts of their own before 1789. Nor was the French Revolution simply the result of domestic developments. International affairs exacerbated tensions that had existed for a long time under the old regime. A succession of costly wars made tax increases necessary, but without solving the financial malaise of the French state. The tax system was badly organized, relying excessively on the agricultural sector and on the practice of selling offices, which led to the strengthening and spreading of privilege. After a string of ministers had failed to cure the fiscal headache, King Louis XVI decided to convene a meeting of the representatives of the three estates, who would advise him about ways to escape from this quagmire. It was this decision that unintentionally set in motion a chain of events that resulted in the French Revolution. The election of representatives of the estates and the compilation of the lists of grievances that they were to bring to the Estates General served to empower the Third Estate, which used the printing press and other public venues to promote the portrayal of French society as one divided between those who worked and those who enjoyed privilege.

Public opinion was on the side of the deputies of the Third Estate who arrived in Paris in the spring of 1789, enabling them to force those representing the other orders to join them in a single assembly. A reform-minded government might still have saved the old regime, but as the king opted for a hard line, the middle ground disappeared. Anticipating a violent reaction from the privileged groups, ordinary Parisians, prepared to arm themselves, searched everywhere for arms and ammunition, even storming the Bastille, where they expected to find stores of gunpowder. The successful and bloody capture of this symbol of an unfair society marks the start of the revolution. It also stands at the beginning of a string of popular interventions in French political life.

The members of the assemblies that ruled the country in the next few years set about outlawing various forms of privilege and introducing a panoply of freedoms. But they stopped short of giving each man the vote, except in 1792–1793, when virtually every adult male could go to the polls. Indeed, although a partnership of the relatively well-to-do city dwellers called Jacobins and the less affluent sans-culottes made

France appear democratic, genuine democracy did not take root. When new wars erupted, the participation of ordinary citizens in political life was jeopardized and the path to political pluralism cut off. Individuals, towns, and entire regions that disagreed with the Jacobin line were labeled as enemies and eliminated in a ruthless civil war. Not even the end of the Terror brought an appreciation of pluralism.

Nor did the men who were in charge of the revolution by the mid-1790s learn from the opposition that the revolution had generated domestically. When French troops marched into neighboring countries that espoused the very ideals that had driven the French Revolution, earlier mistakes were repeated. Significant parts of the populations of these sister republics experienced French liberation as occupation. Just like international warfare had induced the French to adopt an emphasis on the virtue of serving the nation, French intervention elsewhere provoked a nationalist backlash that was at odds with the principles that had inspired the revolutions in the first place.

4

From Prize Colony to Black Independence

The Revolution in Haiti

When Frenchmen referred to Saint-Domingue in the 1780s as the wealthiest colony in the world, they did not exaggerate. The value of the crops transported to Europe exceeded that of all merchandise reaching Spain from her colonies. Forty percent of all the sugar cultivated worldwide and half of all the coffee was grown in the western third of the island of Hispaniola. Founded by buccaneers in the middle of the seventeenth century and formally incorporated into the French Empire in 1697, Saint-Domingue was divided into three parts. By 1789, the north was most intensively cultivated, numbering 2,009 coffee, 443 indigo, 288 sugar, 66 cotton, and 7 cacao plantations. The west boasted 1,804 indigo, 811 coffee, 541 cotton, 314 sugar, and 7 cacao plantations, and the south, finally, had 903 indigo, 297 coffee, 191 sugar, 182 cotton, and 40 cacao plantations.[1]

In the eighteenth century, France's Atlantic ports grew along with Saint-Domingue's remarkable economic expansion, their commerce and associated manufactures flourishing, especially in Bordeaux, which dominated colonial trade, and Nantes, which sent countless indentured servants and African slaves to the prize colony.[2] The value of the commodities that Bordeaux and Nantes shipped to Saint-Domingue in 1786 and 1787 was, respectively, three and six times that of their exports to the other Caribbean colonies of Martinique, Guadeloupe, and Cayenne.[3] In return, both ports obtained massive amounts of colonial produce. Other French ports also came to depend on trade with the prize colony. By 1791, half of the ships entering and leaving the small harbor of La Rochelle came from or went to Saint-Domingue.[4] Nor were the colonial ties confined to the towns that fitted out colonial expeditions and their hinterlands. Dauphiné in the east of France may seem to have had little to do with the colonies, but in reality maintained close links with

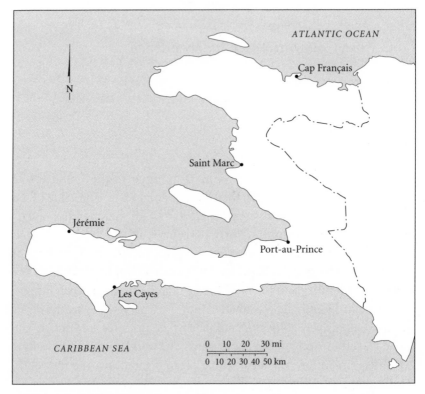

Map 4.1. Saint-Domingue in 1791.

Saint-Domingue. Local industrial products that found a market there included cloth, gloves, and paper. Merchants, officers, and royal officials from Grenoble and its hinterland moved to the booming colony in large numbers, many of them buying a plantation.[5]

Much of the wealth remained on the island. The northern capital of Cap Français ranked as the most prosperous town in the overseas French Empire. Home to more than one hundred jewelers, it was transformed every Sunday into a marketplace without equal.[6] Although the wealth was based on returns from trade with the mother country, it was an artificial wealth, since virtually all planters were up to their ears in debt. But debt was not a cause for concern, because foreclosure was impossible. However far the planters fell behind in payments, there was no legal means to seize their plantations, their land, or their slaves. Saint-Domingue—like Guadeloupe and Martinique—was a debtor's paradise, and the creditors were usually merchants in France, who had no choice in the matter. If they refused to act as bankers, they could lose valuable business partners, who would approach other merchants willing to provide credit. As a consequence, the merchants of Nantes had holdings of almost eighty million livres in the colonies by the late 1780s.[7]

Yet this fortunate position was not enough for the planter elite, which aspired to complete commercial autonomy, for which it was willing to fight with France. Relations with the mother country had never been harmonious, but became strained after the Seven Years' War. When France's Minister of the Navy required the colonial population to pay for the island's defense costs, the colonists declined. They received support from the *conseils supérieurs* (the colonial equivalent of France's *parlements*) of Cap Français and the colonial capital of Port-au-Prince.[8] The disastrous outcomes of the war also led to new policies in other areas. A new administrative team arrived in April 1764 with the task of rooting out trade with North America and, if possible, all other foreign commerce. Soon, however, these administrators themselves were forced to disregard the new rules and allow for trade with the North Americans.[9]

Trade with foreigners was as old as the colony itself. In the early years, the ubiquitous Dutch had rendered every commercial assistance, and in the eighteenth century, settlers of the British colonies in the Caribbean and North America proved eager to establish and extend commercial relations, especially with the west and south of Saint-Domingue. Planters in the colony's southern province, abandoned by metropolitan French merchants in part because it was dangerously close to Jamaica (a liability in wartime), exchanged indigo, not so much sugar, for slaves, provisions, and dry goods sent from this British neighbor, while New England became the main customer of molasses, importing as many as twenty-one thousand barrels by 1767. With every barrel weighing a thousand pounds, the shipments totaled over twenty million pounds.[10]

Commercial autonomy had three advantages for the planters: it would lower the cost of living, raise the price of coffee and sugar, and halt the export of specie. Rum and molasses were ideal for export abroad. Their supplies were abundant, there was no market in France, and in the British colonies they could be traded for wood, salt provisions, and flour, all in high demand.[11] The desire for foreign trade coincided with the development of a nativist sentiment. Planters, whether French-born or creole, came to resent the phenomenon of absenteeism, especially in the years after 1763, which saw the establishment of many small and medium-sized coffee plantations exploited directly by their owners. They considered themselves to be the true "inhabitants, the only ones apt to direct colonial politics," blaming the absentee planters for all of Saint-Domingue's maladies: marronage, social instability, the absence of a public spirit, and weak resistance to the mother country's alleged selfishness. In 1768–1769, this nativism came to the surface, when planters, helped by merchants and poor whites and mulattoes in Cap Français and Port-au-Prince, defied the French administrators by staging a revolt.[12] The revolt was the first occasion on which the ideal of self-rule was publicly expressed, an ideal whose realization was deemed possible only by means of British intervention. Southern residents offered their submission to British overlordship in a letter to the governor of Jamaica, before spreading the lie that the arrival of a British squadron carrying ten thousand men was imminent. By becoming subjects of King George, the settlers hoped to enjoy both self-rule and a larger measure of commercial freedom.[13]

Whites, Free People of Color, and Slaves

These ideas flowed out of the pens of the *grands blancs*, the well-to-do whites who as planters and merchants formed the colony's economic elite. There were a few noblemen among them, but the vast majority had common roots. Not only did these whites live the good life, they were also eager to show off their wealth. One contemporary author noted that a rich man had four times more domestic slaves than he needed; his wife surrounded herself with female slaves wherever she went. Such conspicuous consumption was not unique in the colonial Americas. The same phenomenon has been noted for Brazil. The difference was that the attendance of Mass offered an ideal occasion for wealthy Brazilian whites to parade their domestic slaves, whereas public religion was almost nonexistent in Saint-Domingue. Unlike in Martinique and Guadeloupe, Sunday Mass and Easter communion were not generally observed. Nor was marriage common, immigrants and creole Frenchmen alike preferring concubinage with white or black women.[14]

Apart from the grands blancs, massive numbers of *petits blancs* arrived in the colony after the Seven Years' War. Although the demand for indentured servants had disappeared, their tasks having been assumed by free people of color, many French natives tried their luck in the colonies at a time when French America had shrunk dramatically. Saint-Domingue was their preferred destination, receiving about a thousand new immigrants each year, almost invariably young men without families and not a few fleeing the law in France, especially army deserters. They were bound to compete for jobs with the free people of color, finding temporary employment on plantations as carpenters or masons, or working permanently as tutors or butlers, or otherwise as domestic servants. Other men who did not work joined the army of vagabonds, while many women became prostitutes.[15] More prominent petits blancs had the ambition to become planters, strike it rich, and then return to France. That would still have been possible before the Seven Years' War, but credit and know-how had become much more important, and the people of color had by now obtained from their white relatives or from the government vast tracts of land that they transformed into coffee plantations.[16]

Since they were sojourners rather than settlers, bound to return as soon as they had made it, it is not surprising that many scores of petits blancs participated in the rebellion of 1768–1769. They were not attached to Saint-Domingue and therefore resisted attempts to be forced into militia duty.[17] There was also a social dimension to their attitude. The petits blancs demanded consideration in a society that did not respect the hierarchies that characterized life in France. Moreover, their whiteness made them stand out as members of the social elite. To serve in the militias would be a step down, since soldiering was associated in the colony with the indentured servants of old. The petits blancs knew that in the eyes of the slaves, they would descend to the rank of "white negroes."[18]

In the 1770s and 1780s, the petits blancs faced increasing competition from the free people of color, who grew in number from 210 (1681) to 1,500 (1715), 3,000 (1745), 6,036 (1774), and finally 27,548 (1789). They thus approached the white population, which had grown from 20,247 to 30,826 in the fifteen years before 1789. In the south and west, free people of color even made up 48 percent of the free population by this time.[19] Females of color were skilled as shopkeepers, retail traders, and peddlers, worked as *ménagères*, for example, managing the plantation of their white male companions, or were involved in buying and selling urban real estate. Numerous free coloreds—women and men—owned slaves, even those who were not wealthy and made a living as provision farmers. Many urban colored males competed with whites as coopers, carpenters, and masons, often settling down in the countryside after marriage. Their rural activities were also successful, in particular in the coffee sector, which did not require the same initial investments as the sugar industry.[20]

Such achievements were almost exclusively the privilege of free mulattoes, whose blood lines had often enabled them to acquire rural property. Free blacks, on the other hand, who made up at least one-third of the free people of color, had a hard time obtaining land and thus passed their days in the cities. The presumption of slavery, by virtue of their skin color and the custom of white and mulatto slaveholders to free their offspring, prevented them from climbing the social ladder.[21] Still, free blacks, like free mulattoes, were very important to the colony militarily, serving in the militias and the *maréchausée* (the rural police force). Along with other free men of color, they made up one-third of the Chasseurs-Volontaires de Saint-Domingue, who sailed to Savannah, Georgia, in 1779 in order to relieve the town and remove the British occupiers. The 941 freedmen distinguished themselves during this episode of the American Revolution.[22]

When the free people of color began to actively pursue equal rights with the whites in 1769, their armed service formed their main argument.[23] Their struggle became urgent when a strict separation between whites and nonwhites was introduced in the years following the Seven Years' War. While King Louis XIV had mentioned only free people and slaves in his Code Noir—the decree of 1685 that specified the rights of these two groups—the 1720s had seen the first legislation to identify free people of color as a distinct social group. But not until the 1760s and 1770s was their separate legal status stressed, and in a way more rigid than anywhere in the New World. They were forbidden to ride in coaches, to be surgeons or midwives, to have certain types of household furniture, and to adopt the dress, hairstyles, or bearing of whites. They were to be rigorously punished for hitting a white person, even if they had been hit first. If the Code Noir mentioned only the singular respect owed by the individual freedperson vis-à-vis his former master, the new legislation demanded that every free colored person owed respect to every white.[24]

Some even wanted to extend the racial segregation to the metropolis, where an increasing number of blacks had arrived with their masters in the middle decades of the century. One radical solution was to entirely forbid blacks from arriving on French soil. A high-ranking official, the *procureur du roi* (the king's representative to the Admiralty court), argued that otherwise the French nation would soon be "disfigured." A metropolitan merchant with experience in colonial trade added that race mixture might as yet be nonexistent, but that everything should be done to preserve the purity and beauty of the nation.[25]

An important source of inspiration for the free people of color was *Histoire philosophique et politique des deux Indes* by abbé Raynal (1713–1796), although the passages in the third edition that may have appealed came from the pen of Denis Diderot. All humans, Diderot wrote, inside and outside Europe, deserved to be treated with dignity.[26] A French metropolitan report of 1779 about the country's Windward Islands in the Caribbean asserted that the free people of color "know abbé Raynal by heart." Raynal was reputed to be an ardent defender of the principle of equality, even though in reality he did not advocate the abolition of slavery. Nor did he campaign for granting equal rights to free blacks and mulattoes. Despite his sympathy for their plight, he wanted them to remain subordinate, while demanding that they should be given more rights.[27]

The intellectuals and lawyers responsible for the racist laws rationalized the complete separation of black and white by stressing that the respect blacks owed to their masters was the logical counterpart to the brutal force associated with slavery. Separation enabled domination. One influential author argued that separation was impossible without a buffer between the two principal classes in the form of a separate class of free mulattoes. The intermediate class had to be absolutely distinct from that of the slaves. One had to start by marrying all free blacks in the colony to female mulattoes and all male mulattoes to free female blacks.[28] Historian John Garrigus has shown how the colony's white ideologists, building on the paradigm elaborated by the philosophes Buffon and de Pauw, helped create a new racial stereotype by presenting men and women of mixed blood as weak, degenerate, and "unnaturally feminine." By contrast, they depicted colonial whites as vigorous and therefore not in need of strong government by metropolitan institutions. The message was that they could rule themselves without interference from the people of color.[29]

By the close of the seventeenth century, African slaves must have already formed the majority of Saint-Domingue's population. Their numbers continued to grow during the eighteenth century, reaching 108,854 in 1740 and finally 465,429 in 1788, thus constituting by far the largest slave population of the Caribbean.[30] Slaves from Central Africa, especially Kongo, predominated without forming a majority. They tended to work more on coffee plantations than did those of other nations, while Africans born in the Bight of Benin, in particular from Allada (the Ewe-Fon) and Nago (the Yoruba), who were seen as stronger and harder workers, labored on sugar rather than coffee estates. Men and women from Senegambia, the Ivory Coast, the Bight of Biafra, and the Gold Coast were represented in much smaller numbers.[31]

Slaves formed the main form of investment in Saint-Domingue. By the end of the colonial regime, their combined value was more than three times that of all the colony's lands and buildings.[32] Most slaves worked on the numerous estates, subjected to a labor regime that instilled great fear in them. The worst conditions prevailed on the sugar plantations, where slaves performed a variety of tasks from sunrise to dawn, interrupted only by a lunch break. They were allowed to work in their small gardens to supplement their diet, but only during their rare free moments and on Sundays. The field slaves usually lived in their own village, set apart from the other houses on the estate, where they were left to their own devices. Many a slave was dressed in rags, malnourished, and punished in the most brutal ways, often by fellow black overseers.[33] Such abuse was more common on absentee plantations, where neglect and exploitation were rampant and no free workers cared about the slaves' proper nourishment, lodging, and hygiene.[34] And yet, many masters convinced themselves that the lives their slaves led were better than those of the peasants in France. One wrote in a letter that the peasants, weighed down by corvées and taxes, starving from hunger and dying from cold in the winter months, and sleeping on two straws, would eagerly accept servitude in Saint-Domingue.[35]

African-born slaves outnumbered creoles on the average estate, although the two groups balanced each other out on sugar plantations.[36] Their relationship was often tense, as creoles looked down upon newly arriving Africans, with whom they felt no affinity. The annual baptismal ceremony of slaves who had come in the previous year was an occasion that brought out the creole sense of superiority.[37] For both creoles and Africans, protest was part of everyday life, expressed in words, songs, gestures, or a lackluster attitude. Slaveholders, of course, were more afraid of violent protest and lived in constant fear of physical harm.[38] Apart from a few very small-scale uprisings, four conspiracies were organized in Saint-Domingue that were aimed at exterminating the whites, all planned in the early days of the colony, between 1679 and 1704. The absence of subsequent conspiracies may be explained by the ethnic diversity of the slave population, even if that was offset by various possession cults, often referred to as vodou, that were practiced at secret meetings on the plantations.[39]

The tradition of marronage (slaves absconding for longer or shorter periods of time) went back to the start of slavery. Slaves hid in a vast area in the south, stretching eastward, frequently moving their settlements and surviving in spite of the expeditions sent against them. Fugitives were usually under the age of thirty-five and mostly male, but women were not absent from their communities, since maroons stole female slaves during their plantation raids. The Code Noir had determined the punishments for running away: those absconding for one month had their ears cut off and were branded on one shoulder. Repeat offenders had their hamstring cut and were branded on the other shoulder. A third escape was castigated with execution.[40] The multiplication of coffee estates in the second half of the eighteenth century significantly reduced the area to which slaves could escape. It might offer one explanation for the slave revolt that would break out in 1791.[41]

Revolution in the Metropolis

When the Estates General were convened in 1788, no invitations to elect representatives were extended to the colonies. But in Saint-Domingue, elections still took place, albeit in a way that differed profoundly from the mother country, where those without a voice had been allowed to

make themselves heard. The only voters in Saint-Domingue were proprietors; men making their living as merchants or in other professions
could vote only if they owned lands. Elections were organized in every
parish in the first months of 1789, first in the north, then the west, and
finally the south.[42] Embarking for France, the delegates all maintained
that Saint-Domingue was not a colony. A colony, one of them said, is
formed by immigrants from the metropolis who are sent to a deserted
area or a land conquered by the state. Saint-Domingue, however, had
not been formed by migration or conquest. It was therefore not a colony,
but a Franco-American province. Another added proudly that Saint-
Domingue had been very valuable for France. "We have not been able
to avoid disaster, but we did prodigiously retard it."[43] What the words
of the planter elite, undoubtedly under the influence of the American
Revolution, also convey is that the whites should be allowed to keep
their administrative liberties because Saint-Domingue had voluntarily
placed herself under French rule. They refused to be governed by laws
other than those conceived and drawn up in the colony itself (and subsequently sanctioned by the king), and tried to strictly limit the powers
of the governor and intendant, outsiders who sojourned in the colony
for only three or four years.[44]

An issue dear to the planters was commercial autonomy. Foreign trade
had in the past been absolutely prohibited until Môle Saint-Nicolas was
established as a free port in 1763. When it proved unable to handle the
growing flow of goods, the French government designated three ports
(Cap Français, Port-au-Prince, and Les Cayes) as the new free ports in
1784, authorized to export molasses and rum. Some foreign products,
such as tobacco, beer, and whale oil, could be imported, but the massive
flour shipments from the United States were never legalized, leading to
a feud between colony and mother country at the start of the French
Revolution. The settlers argued that in 1788 and 1789 France had hardly
been able to feed itself, and that the *parlement* of Bordeaux even for-
bade the export of wheat to the colonies. Over time, the planters agreed
on one simple commercial goal: unrestricted imports and exports. That
was, of course, demanding the impossible. The metropolitan stance was
that relaxing the rules ran the risk of losing the colonies, which might
break away or attach themselves to another empire. One had to be very
cautious about permitting colonials to send goods to foreign places.[45]

In the first months of the French Revolution, the issue of free trade came to a head over the food supplies imported by the colony. In view of the disastrous position of France and the cessation of metropolitan flour exports to the colonies, the Marquis du Chilleau, governor general of Saint-Domingue, issued a provisional ordinance authorizing the United States to export flour to the colony. However, the Chevalier de la Luzerne, minister of the navy, annulled that ordinance and recalled the governor. Saint-Domingue's six deputies to the National Assembly, who had been admitted as full members, made much of the danger of an inevitable famine. Each year, one of them asserted, hunger killed ten to twelve thousand blacks. A metropolitan committee that studied the colonists' request to authorize trade with the United States countered that whatever shortage of flour there was hardly affected the black population. Only sick slaves were given bread in the countryside, while urban blacks did eat bread, but in small quantities. They had therefore not suffered during the wars, nor was there an extraordinary mortality among slaves in Saint-Domingue. The whites just had to pay higher prices.[46]

News about the French Revolution did not lead to immediate turmoil in any French colony, east or west, except for Chandernagor in western Bengal, near Calcutta, where all royally appointed officials were deposed and the commander fled.[47] In Saint-Domingue, only the intendant was chased out. Rather than opposing the revolution, the colonial elite viewed it as an opportunity to lend force to their goal of autonomy. At the same time, the elite feared the revolution, especially since the position of the free people of color in the colony might come up for discussion. A group of prominent absentee planters residing in Paris in the Hôtel Massiac and hence called the Massiac Club asked the chambers of commerce of the western French ports in late August 1789 for their collaboration in blocking the return to the colonies of colored men who might, they feared, introduce the germs of subversion. The idea that colonial insurrection might be incited by nonwhites returning from France and infected by Enlightenment principles was in itself not new. In 1777, the minister of the marine had demanded a complete prohibition on slaves entering France, which happened when their masters took them along on a visit to the metropolis. Upon their return to the colonies, the slaves might "carry with them the spirit of liberty, of independence and of equality that they communicate to the others."[48] Indeed, the news about the storming of the Bastille and the following chain of events had at first been kept from the colonies. Slaves arriving in France from Saint-Domingue were sent back before they were able to hear about the revolution. Captains of ships leaving France in the opposite direction had to leave the letter bags behind. Once news did arrive in the colonies, one of Saint-Domingue's delegates in Versailles proposed that no law adopted by the National Assembly would bear on the colonies. The Declaration of the Rights of Man was seen as a particularly dangerous document.[49]

The issue of the rights of the free people of color refused to go away, in part because of the presence in Paris of free colored artisans and domestics, whose spokesman was Étienne-Louis Hector de Joly, a white barrister and member of the municipal government of Paris. They protested that they had been barred from taking part in the assemblies that named Saint-Domingue's deputies to the National Assembly, and campaigned to be admitted to that legislature. They called on the deputies to end the humiliating distinction between one free citizen of Saint-Domingue and another, and desired that blacks and colored creoles be admitted to honorable functions of civil government and military service. It was an injustice, a certain "J.M.C., American, mixed-blood" argued in a pamphlet, to confuse them with blacks. All mixed-race persons should be declared free at birth.[50]

At the end of 1789 and in the early months of 1790, the Society of the Friends of the Blacks took up the cause of the free people of color. Founded in February 1788, this organization had a moderate program, striving for the abolition of the excesses of slavery, not the institution itself. Her main complaint was the considerable subsidies the state lavished on the slave trade.[51] Like the members of this Society, abbé Henri Grégoire argued strongly in favor of free colored integration, decrying that the Declaration of the Rights of Man apparently applied only to whites. In a pamphlet published in October 1790, Grégoire exposed a contradiction in the white settlers' line of reasoning. The whites opposed a decree granting equal status to mulattoes, since that would mean whites were going to be killed. By whom, asked Grégoire? By the blacks? Are you really afraid of these people that you portray as so happy under your regime that their fate is infinitely preferable to that of the villagers of France?[52]

The debate about the rights of the free colored was tied in with that about the abolition of slavery and the slave trade. The apologists for slavery maintained that the institution benefited both France and the blacks themselves. A colonist from Cap Français residing in Paris explained that the blacks were born into slavery and therefore accustomed to it. They lived happy lives, because they had been removed from their own land where their masters had been men without principles, and placed with more humane, more reasonable masters, interested in their well-being. Others argued that—as one of them put it—only the hands of the Africans could fertilize the soil of the tropics. Removing slaves from plantation agriculture was the same as taking away the agricultural implements from a peasant. Moreover, abolition spelled disaster for France. The wine culture of Provence, Guyenne, and Saintonge would be cut in half, grass would grow in the cities of Marseille, Bordeaux, La Rochelle, Nantes, Le Hâvre, and Rouen, and more than five million men dependent on colonial trade and related industries would be reduced to the utmost misery. They might start a bloody revolution.[53] Abolition, others argued, would also play into the hands of Great Britain, which had little to lose from eliminating slavery in its empire. All her American colonies had reached the highest grade of cultivation, could not grow further, and showed a tendency to decline. Britain was leading the campaign against the African slave trade only to incite a civil war in France and sow discord in other European countries, enabling her to remain the sole great power.[54] The famed orator Antoine Barnave and other members of the Assembly who defended the interests of the colonial elite maintained that mulatto emancipation would inevitably lead to the abolition of slavery. Worse, abolition would ultimately result in the loss of the colonies.[55] The Society of the Friends of the Blacks, by contrast, aimed its venom at the barbarities committed in the colonies. Alleviating the plight of the slave was impossible, the Society maintained, without the abolition of the slave trade, which would make it harder for the master to replace a slave. Four mulattoes in Paris went a step further, suggesting a gradual abolition of slavery based on both economic grounds and the very principles of the revolution.[56]

The National Assembly did not side completely with either party. She did wait on Saint-Domingue's white elite hand and foot by deciding in June 1791 that the French legislature could modify constitutional laws of the colony only at the request of the colonial assembly. Settlers were thus freed from ministerial decrees. On the other hand, the absentee colonists suffered a huge blow when a new decree was adopted on May 15, 1791, which allowed all taxpaying adult males born of free parents to vote. This meant in practice that some mulattoes were enfranchised, although not a majority—more likely one in four or five free colored men in Saint-Domingue. Julien Raimond, a native of Saint-Domingue born a free mulatto, was partly responsible for this modest victory of the people of color. He had stressed that very few free residents of the colony had been slaves themselves. This was especially true for the mulattoes. The planters' repeated allegation that the colored men owed their freedom to whites was therefore not true.[57] The decree was also based on the Code Noir, which stipulated that manumitted people of color were to enjoy the same rights as whites. Mulattoes would therefore, so the reasoning went, not be granted *new* rights.[58]

However watered down, the decree was deemed so dangerous that merchants in all major French ports were paralyzed with fear. Authorities in the department of the Gironde temporarily suspended the departure of merchantmen to the colonies to prevent them from carrying "incendiary letters." But once again, the news could not be stopped. White colonists rose in protest, defending the status quo and proclaiming that the whites' best protection had always been the mutual hatred between slaves and men of color. The colonies, Saint-Domingue's Provincial Assembly of the North wrote in a letter to the Assembly, need a class in between the whites and the black slaves, which would drive home to the slaves how vast the gap was that separated them from their masters.[59]

Four months after May 15, on September 12, Jacques-Pierre Brissot, founder of the Society of the Friends of the Blacks, stood before the Assembly. The opponents of the decree, he said, are afraid that the blacks in the islands, aware of the rank to which the mulattoes have been elevated, will break their irons in order to elevate themselves. That fear, Brissot thought, was a fantasy.[60] He could not have been more wrong. Just three weeks before, unbeknownst to him, a slave revolt had broken out in the north of Saint-Domingue, and the rebels seemed unstoppable. The planters' fear seemed to have been justified.

The two previous years had been marked by unrest in the colony. In April 1790, whites, including more than a few who had been involved in the rebellion of 1768–1769, formed a "General" Assembly in the town of Saint Marc, which ignored colonial administrators and declared itself a sovereign power. The Assembly held the demands of the free people of color in contempt and excluded whites married to nonwhite women from full citizenship. These statements created an atmosphere of civil war.[61] A large part of the settlers, government, and army remained loyal to the central government and did not follow the Assembly in all its actions. When the Assembly men decided to open the colony's ports to foreign merchants and declared their unwillingness to share power with mulattoes, the governor and the commander of the regiment at Port-au-Prince intervened. Aided by troops from Cap Français, white soldiers and free-colored militiamen from the capital marched to Saint Marc, where violence claimed victims on both sides. Many members of the Assembly had retired to their estates, but eighty-five radicals embarked on a ship taken over by mutinying sailors that was conveniently waiting in port. They sailed to France to present their case to the National Assembly.[62]

The white planters were not the only ones to be upset. Some free mulattoes also began to lose their patience. One of them, Vincent Ogé, a fabulously wealthy native of Saint-Domingue, had resided in Paris since 1788 and was a member of the group that urged the National Assembly to grant free people of color equal rights. Realizing that this campaign had come to nothing, he boarded a ship for Saint-Domingue in July 1790, planning to seize power in the colony. His attempt to do so with an army of barely three hundred men was, however, ill-conceived, not in the least because Ogé refused to recruit slaves. The white authorities, who saw this revolt as a sign of the smoldering hatred among the free men of color, executed twenty rebels and disarmed all free people of color in the north.[63]

The Slaves Revolt

Slaves also rebelled, starting in the other French Caribbean colonies of Martinique and Guadeloupe. The activities of the Society of the Friends of the Blacks had not gone unnoticed in slave circles, in part because of the fear that the abolitionists instilled in the slaves' masters. In particular, a letter the Society sent to all French *bailliages* (bailiwicks) responsible for the election of deputies in 1789, asking the Estates General to occupy themselves with the freedom of slaves, may have been instrumental in making the slaves of Martinique think that slavery had been abolished in France.[64] The Society also influenced public opinion in France itself, as is borne out by the forty-nine (out of six hundred) *cahiers de doléances* that proposed reform of the slave trade or gradual emancipation of the slaves. White sailors, disembarking in the colonies, probably helped spread news about the French Revolution. As this news coincided with tales about the growing power of the society, some slaves were led to believe that the king and his advisors had proclaimed emancipation, but that it was withheld by local authorities who connived with the planters. When slaves in Martinique brought the matter up with the authorities, they were told that they were mistaken, upon which they wrote two petitions, but to no avail. They expected that emancipation would be proclaimed on Sunday, August 30. When this failed to materialize, slaves began to gather by the hundreds. Three hundred fled to the mountains, only to return within a few days.[65] In Guadeloupe, domestic slaves persuaded field hands on seventeen plantations that since the French had dethroned their king, they were free to throw off their yoke. Their rebellion was to start in the night of April 11–12, 1790, by slaves setting fire to one plantation, to be followed by the assassination of slave owners, but heavy rains preempted this scenario. After the plan leaked out, five slaves were publicly hanged.[66]

Another rumor was spread by slaves at meetings that took place in the central parts of Saint-Domingue's northern province. For weeks in the summer of 1791, slaves from many plantations gathered on Sundays to prepare a general insurrection. When the day had come to decide on a date, one man read a statement that the king and the Assembly in France had issued a decree for the benefit of the slaves. They were no longer to be whipped and would have three free days per week, a decree local authorities allegedly ignored. This rumor may have been based on the 1784 royal regulations that were intended to mitigate slavery but that were never implemented in the colonies. Alternatively, the decree of May 15, 1791, may have set off the rumor. Whatever the case, the rumor was as powerful in Saint-Domingue as the Great Fear had been in motivating peasants in France.[67]

The vast majority of American slave revolts had been betrayed at the last moment by one of the conspirators. All remained tight-lipped now, so that in the evening of August 22, 1791, the largest slave uprising in the history of the New World could start. It took a few hours for the whites in Cap Français to find out about the events taking place in the countryside. A hatless man on horseback, riding a horse with no saddle, brought the news. "To arms," he shouted, galloping through the streets, "all slaves on the northern plain are killing our brothers and burning our possessions." The man was initially taken for a fool, but soon people realized that he was speaking the truth. While the whites hatched a plan to halt the revolt, local slaves responded to the situation by demanding "the rights of man."[68]

The revolt, which had been organized by elite slaves, perhaps all leaders of slave gangs, on as many as 100 sugar plantations, spread like a heath fire. By the end of September, more than one thousand Frenchmen were dead, 161 sugar and 1,200 coffee plantations had been burned down, and damages were estimated at six hundred million livres. The effects were soon felt in France as well. News of the slave revolt caused the price of colonial produce to triple. The merchants in Bordeaux advised the planters with whom they traded to make use of the circumstances by liquidating their debts. Some, especially sugar producers, followed this advice. Ports were hard hit, like La Rochelle, half of whose ships had sailed back and forth to Saint-Domingue. Five of the main merchants went bankrupt as the town slid into poverty.[69]

The slaves were led by a number of skilled leaders. Jean-François (d. 1820) was probably a slave before the revolt and may have been a maroon. He seems not to have shared the desire of his troops to exterminate the whites, aspiring to the more modest goal of chasing the plantation managers from the island. Together with Georges Biassou (d. 1801), he transformed the rebellious slaves, many of whom had fought in wars in Kongo, into disciplined armies that preferred guerrilla warfare over pitched battles.[70]

Free men of color often collaborated with whites in the fight against the slaves, but the groups went their separate ways after news arrived of a decree adopted in the National Assembly on September 24, 1791, annulling that of May 15. While both free groups in Saint-Domingue began to enlist slaves against each other, the Friends of the Blacks in Paris increasingly made their influence felt both in Jacobin clubs and in the National Assembly, especially after the election of Brissot and

Figure 4.1. View of Cap Français in 1791. Courtesy of the John Carter Brown Library at Brown University.

Condorcet to that body. As a consequence, a new law was adopted on April 4, 1792, reversing the one of September 24 and giving all free men of color full civil rights. The bill also stipulated that seven civil commissioners were to go to the colonies, including three to Saint-Domingue: Légér Félicité Sonthonax (1763–1813), Étienne Polverel, and Jean Antoine Ailhaud.

These men were armed with sweeping powers, free to dissolve colonial assemblies and use force to pursue the execution of their orders.[71] In the years immediately prior to the French Revolution, Sonthonax had worked as a lawyer at the Paris *parlement*, the country's highest appeal court. He supported the revolution from the outset, first as a journalist, then as a Jacobin. Polverel followed the same trajectory: lawyer–journalist–Jacobin. Like Sonthonax, he abhorred slavery. They sailed in July 1792 along with the new governor general, seventy-two-year-old Jean-Jacques d'Esparbès, and six thousand troops.[72]

Upon arrival, sensing that their reputation as abolitionists had preceded them, Sonthonax defended slavery in order to placate the suspicious whites. These did not form a solid block but were divided into royalists and radicals who stealthily pursued independence. D'Esparbès, meanwhile, did little more than obstruct the work of the commissioners. He became the darling of the royalists. In Paris, meanwhile, the Assembly had given the civil commissioners unlimited powers soon after August 10, leading to the dismissal of d'Esparbès, who was ordered to return to France. In late 1792, Sonthonax and Polvorel split, the first taking charge of the north and the second of the west and the south, where Ailhaud was supposed to have moved, but he returned to France.[73] Since free men of color were not represented, the commissioners dissolved the existing assemblies and everywhere reassigned administrative posts to mulattoes, who ended up with a virtual monopoly of public office. They arrested hundreds of radical whites and deported them to France. Meanwhile, the ever-swelling stream of voluntary emigrants preferred the United States, Jamaica, and Cuba to France. Deportation and voluntary emigration helped Sonthonax and Polverel establish their authority, although they needed to subdue Port-au-Prince with the help of a naval force. Ashore, the main fighting occurred between the French troops and rebelling slaves on the plain outside Cap Français, where the slaves were first defeated before recapturing the area.[74]

François Thomas Galbaud, born in Port-au-Prince, was named d'Esparbès's successor, receiving more powers than his predecessor, although still subordinate to the commissioners. They did not see eye to eye. One bone of contention was the proclamation the commissioners had issued protecting slaves from being overburdened and enabling them to bring complaints against their masters and overseers to local authorities. Eventually, the commissioners had Galbaud arrested and confined to a ship in the harbor. Other ships anchored there happened to have scores of fellow political prisoners on board, with whom Galbaud made common cause. They persuaded two thousand sailors to make an armed landing, and after the national guard joined them, these rebel troops attacked Cap Français. After a period of heavy street fighting against colored soldiers, they captured the city on June 20, 1793, Sonthonax and Polverel barely escaping with their lives. In the chaos that ensued, slaves were freed from jails, some of whom took up arms against Galbaud's men. It is unknown who started them, but fires broke out that lasted for two weeks, reducing most of Cap Français to ashes.[75]

After blacks resident in the town and many others from the neighboring plain and mountains offered their services to recapture the burning town, the commissioners announced on June 21 that all blacks fighting for the French republic would be given their freedom and would enjoy the rights of other French citizens. They took this bold step without consulting the metropolis. The proclamation helped a group of over three thousand slaves to side with the commissioners and rapidly oust Galbaud's troops, forcing thousands of whites, including Galbaud himself, to flee by ship. Escaping to the United States, they would never see Saint-Domingue again.[76]

Abolition

Two months later, on August 29, Sonthonax went a step further, declaring general liberty in the north, a measure that took Polverel off guard, having embarked on a path toward gradual emancipation in the west. But he followed suit on October 31. Sonthonax's proclamation was not simply the decision of a benevolent abolitionist. In the two weeks prior to it, slaves as well as free men in Cap Français made known their wish for slavery to end. A petition signed by 842 free men demanded that the rights of man be extended to the slaves, in the name of whom they spoke. The petitioners were accompanied by a crowd of ten thousand slaves to the house of Sonthonax, who told them he would yield to their demand. Four days later, he published the proclamation in French and Creole, sparking scenes of joyful celebration across the north that lasted several days. The commissioners were careful to warn the former slaves that liberty did not mean that they could now do whatever they pleased. They were to remain on their plantations (although they could request to be transferred to another plantation), where they would receive wages. Whipping was outlawed and former slaves were punished only by withholding their wages. Polverel allowed the plantation workers to select their own managers and designed a system in which the former head slaves formed a council that represented the workers and determined work schedules, as well as how to run the plantation and how to spend revenues.[77]

The abolition of slavery still lacked the stamp of approval of the Convention in Paris, but the climate in the Convention was soon ripe for the final, momentous, step. On February 4, 1794, Louis Dufay (1753–1815), a Parisian Jacobin who had embraced abolitionist ideas by 1789 and moved to Saint-Domingue in 1791, gave a speech. Elected white deputy for the north province after Sonthonax proclaimed abolition, he had arrived in France, along with two other delegates, just weeks before.[78] Presenting an account of the recent developments in the colony, Dufay demanded that the Assembly ratify Sonthonax's abolition decree. Dufay's speech was remarkable because he cited slaves themselves. All male slaves, he argued, were willing to fight for France and had to be compensated with freedom. They are asking us a favor: could we emancipate their wives and children as well? "Is it the fault of our women, they say, that they have not been able to arm themselves for France? Should one punish the weakness of their sex? After all, they share our feelings. What is more, they will inspire our children and work to feed the warriors. As for our children, they are our possessions, our blood."[79]

Some delegates tried to shelve the issue or undermine the decree by proposing that the word "slavery" not be mentioned. Freedom was, after all, a natural right. Then one representative stood up and remarked that a discussion that went on too long about this topic would dishonor the Convention. The decree, he said, must be introduced immediately.

Thereupon the whole Convention rose up and the matter was settled.[80] Slavery was abolished in all French colonies, which meant that seven hundred thousand men, women, and children were to be freed immediately. Two and a half years after ending "feudalism," French parliament thus obliterated slavery, once again with support from the Parisian population, which had embraced the sans-culottes' ideas about the redistribution of wealth and the creation of a free, brotherly, and virtuous middle class. When the Convention elaborated the law in this same spirit, she decided not to indemnify the colonial proprietors, a move so radical that it would never be repeated in other slaveholding societies.[81]

In Saint-Domingue, meanwhile, the war became increasingly complex. The authorities in the Spanish part of the island had already been in touch with the slave armies for some time, when the government in Madrid ordered Santo Domingo's government to contact Saint-Domingue's blacks and mulattoes in order to wrest the colony from the French. Many slave columns began to fight for the Spanish, who provided them, at least initially, with uniforms and weapons. It soon emerged, however, that they were of more use to the Spanish than vice versa. By April 1794, a considerable part of Saint-Domingue may have been formally under Spanish control; the Spanish troops—many of them originating in Cuba—were entirely dependent on the blacks and mulattoes.[82]

Some black allies, such as those commanded by Pierrot and Macaya, abandoned the Spanish cause as early as June 1793, responding to Sonthonax's call for help in recapturing Cap Français. But the commissioners failed to persuade Jean-François and Biassou, who served in the Spanish army as lieutenants-general. Both had tied their fate to that of the Spanish of Santo Domingo because the French had showed no support for their struggle for rights. In addition, their cause was the royal cause, defending the Bourbons. Jean François later intimated that he would not believe the slogans of freedom and equality until the French administrators married their daughters off to black men.[83]

It was an inferior of Biassou who would epitomize the Haitian Revolution. Toussaint Louverture was born in 1743 on a sugar plantation near Cap Français as the son of Gaou-Guinou, who had been enslaved in Africa, sold to the French on the coast of Benin, shipped to Saint-Domingue.[84] Born a slave, Toussaint was freed when he was about age thirty, accumulated property, owned slaves, but never betrayed his father's Allada background. He was equally at home among African-born blacks and free people of color.[85] Toussaint did not rise to fame in the early stages of the revolt, but gradually worked himself up from the post of Biassou's secretary to aide-de-camp and then his first officer.

To Toussaint, the commissioners were opportunists acting in bad faith, first ill-disposed to the slaves and then proclaiming liberty in order to attract them to their cause.[86] Toussaint's attitude was shared by most insurgents, who ignored the commissioners' measures and spread the revolt in the summer of 1793. In the south, freedom extended to armed slaves was conditional upon them fighting devotedly for France, while the other ex-slaves had to return to their plantations and work. Many blacks, upset at their own leaders, did not acquiesce and took their frustration out on the plantations, pillaging and ransacking. On some plantations, the former slaves expanded the subsistence grounds. On others, where the owner or manager was present, they demanded a five-day work week. And everywhere, slaves were found who refused to work, sometimes collectively. All the same, most slaves had still not left their plantations by 1793, apart from the central north where the rebellion had started. They stayed put out of loyalty, fear, or other reasons. Many warned their masters about impending slave attacks, and if they did take up arms it was often to defend their owners rather than fight them.[87]

Toussaint and the other blacks fighting under leaders like Jean-François and Biassou were very successful in the war with the colony's French authorities on which Spain openly embarked. Toussaint's army surged from a few hundred to a few thousand men, who achieved resounding victories against both the French and the free mulattoes. At the start of 1794, only Cap Français and the area of Port-au-Prince, where the new French commander-in-chief Étienne Laveaux was active, remained in French hands. In 1793, Britain had also become involved in the war, like the French and the Spanish trying to lure the slaves to their side. In September of that year, at the request of the French planters of the Grande Anse, an area opposite Jamaica, the British governor Adam Williamson landed troops at Jérémie and Môle St. Nicolas.[88]

In the south, support for British protection came from some mulatto artisans and from large sections of the white population. Other mulattoes, led by André Rigaud (1761–1811), had taken up arms for republican France. A goldsmith born of a white father and black mother, Rigaud was a talented army chief, yet he could not halt the British invaders from Jamaica. Within eight months, one-third of Saint-Domingue was under British occupation,[89] while another British army sent from England captured Martinique, Guadeloupe, St. Lucia, and Tobago from the French. The British intervention was part of a wider war with France, although the fear that the slave revolt would spread to British colonies also played a role. In the years ahead, the British government continued to send soldiers, tens of thousands in all, who often died like flies—in the year 1796 alone, more than fourteen thousand were lost. Three out of five soldiers in the British service were victims of yellow fever and malaria.[90]

Having been hailed as liberators, the British rapidly lost their reputation by confiscating property from white settlers and discriminating against mulattoes, who lost their posts in the *maréchaussée* (mounted militia) to whites and saw their wish to obtain equal civil rights ignored. Many mulattoes who had initially allied with Britain now changed sides and joined slave bands.[91] This left the British army with no choice. She had to court the slaves as well, holding out the promise of liberty in exchange for military service. Royalist planters helped Williamson to raise thirty-four hundred slave soldiers, which enabled the British to withstand Toussaint's troops, who were also fighting Spanish troops in the east.[92]

Toussaint and his four thousand troops had changed sides in May 1794, when he chose to ally himself with republican France and end his alliance with Spain. Traveling with him as officers were the former slave Jean-Jacques Dessalines (1758–1806) and Henri Christophe (1767–1820), a free man of color who was born on Grenada but ended up in Saint-Domingue as a young boy. At age eleven, he was slightly wounded at the siege of Savannah.[93] Toussaint's about-face was undoubtedly inspired in part by the clash with Jean-François and Biassou, who had sold women and children as slaves to the Spanish. Toussaint had been making overtures to the French for about a year, but to no avail. When he finally made the switch, there was no direct connection with Sonthonax's proclamation—too much time had passed—or the decree of February 4—a copy of which had still not arrived. But his reversal did form part of a more general uprising on the part of slaves and people of color against the Spanish invaders. In 1794, fresh troops had arrived from Cuba, Puerto Rico, and Venezuela, which turned the tide for the

French planters and enabled the restoration of the plantation regime. There was nothing the commissioners could do to halt the Spanish advance. They surrendered in May and were shipped back to France.[94]

Laveaux's decision to copy Sonthonax's policy of relying not on mulattoes but on blacks yielded dividends when Toussaint, with his trademark tactical brilliance, recaptured most of the north in late 1794 from Jean-François and the Spanish. One year later, Toussaint came to the rescue of the French commander, when whites and people of color in Cap Français revolted against his authority. A new rebellion, four months later (March 20, 1796), turned into a coup d'état when a mob burst into the government building in Cap Français, casting Laveaux and three other senior officials in jail. Only when nearby black commanders were informed of the events and demanded immediate release of the prisoners did Laveaux regain his freedom. Six days later, Toussaint came to show his support for the Frenchman with two infantry battalions and an imposing cavalry.[95]

In the five years since the start of the slave revolt, Saint-Domingue had changed dramatically. But the past was not effaced. Production of cash crops had not stopped, although customs revenues had declined by perhaps three-quarters. The most consequential change was the loss of power of French whites. The colony was now divided into a mulatto-dominated south, a west ruled by the British, and a black-controlled north and northwest. No longer ruling anything, the French whites were now overwhelmingly recent immigrants, who were very unpopular with the old settlers. Many petits blancs, especially the mariners, had lost their jobs after the revolution and had turned to piracy and privateering or entered the criminal circuit.

Having been left in control of the south by the civil commissioners upon their departure, Rigaud built up a virtual state. In the commissioners' spirit, he confined black workers to the plantations, while redistributing abandoned white property to free colored men. And he was the only man able to restore calm after former slaves under mulatto command had created a bloodbath among white landowners in August 1796.[96] Rigaud's army developed into a force to be reckoned with, although the ten thousand men under his command in 1798 formed a squad only half the size of the army of Toussaint, his ally since 1794. One British officer was deeply impressed by Toussaint's soldiers: "Indeed, such complete subordination prevailed, so much promptness and dexterity, as must astonish an European who had known any thing of their previous situation."[97] In tandem with Rigaud's troops, Toussaint's army ended up wearing out the British troops, who were gradually withdrawn until, by the close of 1798, no British soldier remained on the island.[98]

Meanwhile, the slave population had been drastically reduced. Many slaves had fallen as rebels or by fighting rebels, while thousands of others had emigrated with their owners. The blacks who remained after 1796 rejected any return to white rule or slavery. Many distrusted Toussaint, suspecting that he planned to restore slavery. But what he actually pursued was a restoration of the plantation regime without slavery. He welcomed back planters and introduced the labor regime for which Sonthonax and Polverel had once been responsible.[99]

Leclerc's Expedition

Toussaint nonetheless embroiled himself with Sonthonax after the latter's return in 1796 at the head of a five-man civil commission. Distrusting the abolitionist, Toussaint made it appear as if Sonthonax had incited him to declare independence and put innumerable white inhabitants to the sword. Sonthonax soon left for France, where he had to defend himself against this imputation. He denied the allegation, retaliating by calling Toussaint one of the chiefs of Saint-Domingue's Vendée. Ironically, the next representative of the French Directory sent to Saint-Domingue had earned his reputation as "pacifier" of the French Vendée. Restoring order in the colony was too tall an order, however, for Gabriel d'Hédouville. He alienated the black majority by attempting to implement a transitional apprenticeship for agricultural laborers before they could embrace full freedom, and antagonized the black army when he tried to arrest the well-liked General Moïse. A popular uprising forced d'Hédouville to pack his bags after only six months.[100]

With the mutual French enemy gone, collaboration between Toussaint and Rigaud rapidly gave way to enmity. And enmity bred civil war, in which the northern army, commanded by Dessalines, emerged triumphant in 1800, aided by British and U.S. ships blockading southern ports. In the aftermath of the fighting, Rigaud and the other leaders were forced to go into exile, while Dessalines had 350 soldiers of Rigaud's former army shot, most of them officers. Some sources accuse Dessalines of killing many civilians as well.[101]

Toussaint was now virtually the absolute ruler of Saint-Domingue, rarely consulting with France and personally signing treaties with Britain and the United States. He derived inspiration from the example of his black brothers in Jamaica, who as maroons had filled the local British government with despair. Flirting with independence, Toussaint convened an assembly that was to prepare a constitution. That document, promulgated in July 1801 and clearly based on French revolutionary constitutionalism, made Saint-Domingue a self-ruling colony of France. It abolished slavery for good, established an egalitarian society, introduced commercial freedom, and declared Catholicism the only public religion. The ink was barely dry when Toussaint invaded the Spanish part of the island and annexed Santo Domingo, spiking the guns of a future French expedition force.[102] But in doing so, he overplayed his hand, because his independent course angered Napoleon. In an attempt to make quick work of Toussaint's regime, the first consul sent a force under the command of his brother-in-law, General Charles Victor Emmanuel Leclerc (1772–1802), which made landfall in February 1802 with twenty-two thousand soldiers. Another sixty thousand were sent in the following months, among them André Rigaud and Alexandre Pétion (1770–1818), the son of a white man and a mulatto woman, who had defected from Toussaint's army to Rigaud during the civil war in 1799.[103]

Leclerc was to restore slavery in the formerly Spanish part of the island, but to leave the forced labor regime in the French part as it was. Remarkably, his men faced little opposition as they traversed the colony. Several of Toussaint's generals surrendered immediately, perhaps eager to prevent the destruction of the plantations that they now owned themselves. "The superior order," a British officer would later reminisce, "had attained a sumptuousness of life. . . . The interior of their houses was, in many instances, furnished with a luxe beyond that of the most voluptuous European, while no want of transatlantic elegance appeared."[104] Leclerc was able to capture Cap Français, but to no avail, since Christophe burned down the town. Christophe, Dessalines, and Toussaint were all forced to retreat to the mountains, where they continued to fight.[105]

But when Christophe unexpectedly surrendered to Leclerc, the other two had no choice but to do the same, cut off as they were from arms and ammunition. In May 1802, Toussaint signed a treaty, in which he buried the hatchet with the French. His soldiers were to fight for France, joining Christophe and Dessalines, but Toussaint himself remained skeptical of the French, despite Leclerc's assurance that he had come to guarantee freedom. Toussaint's distrust proved justified when Leclerc arrested him just weeks later, the French general accusing him of continuing to foment actions against the French and planning for independence. Toussaint and his family were sent to France and imprisoned high up in the Jura Mountains. That is where the "first of the blacks," as he once called himself in a letter to Napoleon, passed away in April 1803.[106]

It had gradually become clear that the French were aiming to return to the old plantation regime. In July 1802, news arrived in Saint-Domingue that the French government had reintroduced slavery in the colonies and taken away the equal rights once granted to the mulattoes. If the news—which was welcomed by white settlers—needed confirmation, it was not long in coming. A French general dispatched by Napoleon to Guadeloupe began to reanimate the old plantations in 1802. Everywhere in Saint-Domingue, autonomous insurgent guerrillas now sprang up, led by men born in Africa, assuming the form of a general insurrection in the north. Any resistance was ruthlessly suppressed, and ten thousand men and women were executed. Leclerc began to disarm the nonwhite population and eliminate black and mulatto generals, but disarmament was successful only in the cities. As the insurgency waxed and Pétion, Dessalines, and Christophe turned against him, Leclerc wrote to Napoleon that all people of color over twelve years of age had to be killed. A British officer noted that the French slaughters of black troops "daily took place in the vicinity of Cape Français, that the air became tainted by the putrefaction of the bodies." Blacks as well as mulattoes were killed at the drop of a hat—drowned, hung, shot, or devoured by bloodhounds especially imported from Cuba for this purpose.[107]

Nothing changed in French policies after Leclerc fell victim to yellow fever on November 1, 1802. His successor was Donatien-Marie-Joseph Rochambeau, son of the French general who helped the United States gain independence. The younger Rochambeau executed or drowned a total of twenty thousand blacks and mulattoes between November 1802 and March 1803, inviting reprisals from his enemies. Toussaint had al-

ways refrained from perpetrating massacres, but Christophe and especially Dessalines were every bit as murderous as the French.[108] Through
it all, the south defeated the French on its own; no help from Dessalines
or Pétion was needed.[109] But the south did recognize the overall leadership of Dessalines, who was slowly driving the French into a corner,
eventually settling the war in late November 1803. Rochambeau and his
soldiers returned to France, but forty to fifty thousand men in French
service never went back. They had succumbed to bullets and diseases,
and there was nothing to show for their efforts.[110]

After Toussaint's arrest, the *Times* of London had written: "Europe
will, of course, recover in that quarter the ascendancy and dominion
which it justly claims from the superior wisdom and talent of its inhabitants, and whatever measures of kindness and benevolence may be
extended to the Blacks, they will at least know, that all their physical
force, however exerted, cannot succeed in a contest with experienced
Generals and disciplined troops."[111] The European powers underestimated the resilience of the black rebels. No Western observer thought
it possible that the former slaves would defeat the whites.[112] And when
the blacks proved formidable opponents, members of Leclerc's expedition proceeded to engage in acts of mass murder. If slaves had spared
the lives of many masters in the course of the revolt, large numbers of
former slaves and free people of color were now summarily shot. Of
course, the war had seen many atrocities on both sides, but the French
took the initiative to perform especially egregious acts reminiscent of
the war in the Vendée.[113]

A New Start

On January 1, 1804, the victors proclaimed their independence and
announced the birth of a new country. Its name was Haiti, as the Taino
inhabitants reportedly had called their island before Columbus's arrival.
When he stood before the new nation, addressing the citizens of the new
country, Jean-Jacques Dessalines warned of the spirit of proselytism that
could destroy the whole enterprise. Let us leave our neighbors alone, let
them live under their own laws. We should not set ourselves up as legislators of the Antilles. But Dessalines was not ready yet to bury the arms,

exclaiming: "Let us frighten all those would dare to steal our freedom; let us start with the French!" Anybody born a Frenchman who sets foot in our territory will be killed.[114]

This was no bluff, as the next months were to prove. Everywhere, soldiers rounded up whites and killed them, often after extensive tortures. In some cases, soldiers asked white victims to be paid in gold in exchange for the promise not to arrest the innocent or to liberate prisoners, only to kill them anyway. Women were spared if they agreed to marry blacks, which very few did. In the town of Jérémie, a British ship captain reported, Dessalines drew up a list of the white inhabitants remaining. Of the almost 450 men, women, and children, 308 were executed in the course of three days, staining the streets with their blood. In Port-au-Prince, 800 were killed within eight days, and in Cap Français, nine out of every ten Frenchmen lost their lives in a single day. Some whites escaped this slaughter, hidden away by Haitians. Christophe persuaded Dessalines to spare the lives of non-French whites in Cap Français and those Frenchmen who had been honest with blacks and who had served with them (especially priests and surgeons). Scottish merchant Duncan McIntosh spent a fortune to obtain the release of 2,400 Frenchmen. Revenge for white massacres of blacks is one explanation for Dessalines's actions, the dehumanization of the enemy that had accompanied the war another. But self-enrichment must also count as a cause of the elimination of the remaining French, among whom were owners of large plantations.[115]

When the bloodletting was done, Dessalines stated: "We have repaid these cannibals war for war, crime for crime, outrage for outrage. Yes, I have saved my country, I have avenged America!"[116] His ego inflated, he was eager to match Napoleon when the news reached him that the senate in Paris had offered the Corsican the title of Emperor. Upon his own suggestion to his generals that he should be named Emperor of Haiti, Dessalines was proclaimed Jean-Jacques the First, Emperor of Haiti. The coronation ceremony took place on October 8, seven weeks before that of Napoleon. In the two years that followed, Dessalines delegated even less than Napoleon, making himself the sole ruler. He refused to respect individual rights, shrugged at the suggestion to separate the powers, and never stopped victimizing anybody, of whatever ethnicity, who dared to cross him. It was no surprise that he accepted a challenge from the eastern part of the island, whose governor, Louis Ferrand, threatened to seize Haitians and sell them into slavery. But Dessalines's attack of Santo Domingo, defended by a garrison under Ferrand, in March 1805 failed miserably, forcing Jean-Jacques the First to withdraw his troops. On the way back to Haiti, thousands of rural dwellers were taken prisoner and put to work on fortifications in Dessalines's state or incorporated into his army.[117]

In October 1806, Dessalines's brief rule came to a violent end. Having alienated mulatto landowners and foreign merchants, the emperor misbehaved again during a tour of the south and began to review the legal titles to estates confiscated in the last stage of the revolution. He was doomed when a revolt spread from Les Cayes to Port-au-Prince and many officers and soldiers—upset about overdue debts—joined the rebels. The army leader was killed by his own troops and his corpse mutilated, dragged through the streets of Port-au-Prince and exposed in the parade ground. The dictator was dead.[118]

Although Dessalines's reign extended the rule of fear and violence for another two years after independence, 1804 was in many ways a new beginning. Within two weeks, blacks and mulattoes who had left the colony during the revolution were told they could return. All those arriving from the United States on North American ships were promised forty *gourdes*. Dessalines also tried to increase his population by welcoming blacks from Africa. He offered to open Haitian ports to British slave ships, but the Jamaican slavers turned down his plan to give them the exclusive right to sell enslaved Africans in the black nation. Nor did Dessalines's successor Henri Christophe shy away from buying Africans in order to give them their freedom in Haiti.[119]

In an attempt to forge unity, the constitution of May 1805 stipulated that "all citizens of Haiti will henceforth be known under the generic denomination of blacks." Haitian historian Beaubrun Ardouin (1796–1865) commented that this was contrived, given the presence of naturalized Poles, Germans, and Frenchmen. It would have been more appropriate to call the citizens Haitians. The French lieutenant-general Pamphile de Lacroix, who had arrived with the expedition of Leclerc, had found that the terms "negro" and "mulatto" were experienced as hurtful by Haitians, who shared a hatred of "the old days, the old slavery." Nonetheless, old habits did not fade away overnight. An English visitor noted a continued display of deference toward whites.[120] Or was it simply courtesy that made Haitians salute foreigners in a friendly and respectful way?

Linguistic equality of all inhabitants could not extinguish the feud between blacks and mulattoes. Four months after Dessalines's death, the two camps elected their own presidents. The black Christophe was to rule the "state of Haiti" in the north and west, the mulatto Pétion was the president of the "republic of Haiti" in the south. The two states would continue to fight each other off and on for the next fourteen years. The difference in mentality was expressed in foreign relations. Although both regimes courted British merchants, Christophe aimed at a complete break with France, even in matters of culture. Himself a native of Grenada, he invited British teachers and architects to his state, flirted with Protestantism, and toyed with the idea of making English the official language of his state. Remaining closer to France, the mulattoes glorified the French language, which enabled them—or so they thought—to maintain a certain cultural superiority over the former slaves.[121]

Confrontation between Christophe and France came to a head in October 1814. After Napoleon's defeat at the hands of the Allies in April, an international diplomatic conference had adopted the Treaty of Paris. The treaty allowed France's continued involvement in the African slave trade for another five years and a secret clause enabled her to hold on to her colonies, including what was still referred to as Saint-Domingue. The monarchy restored in France, King Louis XVIII sent as his envoy to Haiti Jean-Joseph Dauxion Lavaysse, a former member of the Committee of Public Safety. His message to Christophe, written from Kingston, Jamaica, announcing the end of the era of Napoleon, contained a barely veiled threat: Haiti was to recognize Louis as her king, and if not, France would not hesitate to train enslaved Africans as soldiers, who would replace the current Haitian population, which the French would overwhelm. While Pétion entered into negotiations with Lavaysse, Christophe's state council refused to submit to French domination. Haiti, it declared, will triumph, shielded by Great Britain, the world's great liberator.[122] Lavaysse was wise enough not to enter Haitian soil, but sent the diplomat Agostino Franco de Medina, who entered Haiti from the Spanish part of the island. Upon crossing the border, he was arrested with papers in his possession that revealed the real reason for the French mission: slavery was to be restored in Haiti. Christophe capitalized on this mistake by having Medina attend his own funeral before sparing the man's life.[123]

Eleven years later, it was the French who triumphed. Having abandoned the hope of returning Haiti to a colony of slaves, France sent a naval squadron of twelve warships that succeeded in persuading the Haitian government to pay an indemnity for the war expenses France had incurred in exchange for recognition of Haitian independence. The indemnity of 150 million francs, to be paid in five annual installments, led to heavy protests among black Haitians. Only because of French recognition did Great Britain follow suit, recognizing Haiti as an independent state three years after it had recognized the independence of the much younger nations of Mexico and Gran Colombia.[124]

For all the differences that Haitian historians have identified between Christophe's state and that of Pétion, the similarities abounded.[125] Both regimes consciously emulated European polities, systematically banning vodou—as Toussaint had done before them—while endorsing Roman Catholicism, although Rome withheld its support (and Christophe, as we have seen, also considered Protestantism). Autocracy was another hallmark of both Haitian states.[126] Christophe was the more outrageous of the two, urging the state council to adopt a law that made the patron days of Saint-Henry and Sainte Louise—his and his wife's patron saints—national holidays. He also changed the name of Cap Français to Cap-Henry. The constitution of 1811 crowned his efforts of self-aggrandizement by making his state a kingdom with Christophe as King Henry I. In a statement addressing the people, attached to the constitution, an explanation was offered for why the federative model of the United States did not suit Haiti. Although we are also a new people, the statement read, our needs, morals, virtues, and vices are those of the peoples of Antiquity. We recognize therefore, with the great Montesquieu, the excellence of paternal monarchical government.[127]

The same constitution, which also abolished divorce, provided for the creation of a court society reminiscent of Louis XIV's Versailles, with former slaves elevated to princes, dukes, counts, and chevaliers.[128] A foreign observer noted: "All those to whom he could trace any degree of relationship, whether by his own side, or that of the Queen, he appointed to the highest offices in the state, and enriched with some of the best plantations in the Island. . . . In selecting the rest of his nobility, Christophe was careful to guard against those individuals, however few, who either opposed his measures, or evinced a disposition to create discontent among the people; and whatever their abilities or services, he excluded them from all offices of importance, and deprived them of the influence they had previously acquired."[129] For the duration of his reign, Christophe ruled with an iron fist, although he was not guilty of the atrocities typical of his former chief Dessalines. Pétion never came close to committing barbarities, but often ignored the senate and overstepped his constitutional rights, directing, for instance, the state's financial affairs as he saw fit, and dissolving the senate in order to carry out land reform.[130]

The main problem in Haitian politics after independence was the legacy of the plantation economy. Like Toussaint before them, Dessalines and Christophe were keen on keeping the plantations intact and having them worked by forced laborers. Dessalines divided the population into soldiers and workers. Those Haitians who did not bear arms or practice an urban craft or trade were forced to work the land. At the same time, Dessalines wanted to annul the landed property that many mulattoes (now called *anciens libres*) had acquired in 1802–1803 when French planters had left in great haste. His insistence on verifying property titles contributed to his assassination.

When Pétion began his reign, he tried to secure support by enabling the new elite of military leaders, senior officials, and prominent *anciens libres* to obtain (more) land. After 1812, Pétion broke new ground by parceling out land, thereby destroying the plantation regime in the south. From the more than one hundred thousand hectares distributed during his rule, numerous small tracts of land were made available to the black majority, although the mulatto elite was still the chief beneficiary of this reform. Christophe's polity, in which forced labor was maintained, benefited even more from a state-led economy. Soldiers, who were in fact the successors of the old overseers, guaranteed continued production, despite the massive flight of rural laborers to the cities and to Pétion's republic, lured by the prospect of owning land.[131]

The dictator Christophe began to lose the support of the army in 1820. The generals of his own army began to conspire against him and the garrison in Saint Marc submitted voluntarily to the republic, where Jean Pierre Boyer had succeeded Pétion as president after the latter's natural death two years before. Boyer sent his entire army to Saint-Marc, while insurgent soldiers in Cap-Henry headed for the citadel where Christophe resided. The king decided to take the honorable way out and committed suicide. Boyer used the situation to his advantage and that of Haitian unity. He addressed his people by calling for unity, exclaiming, "The past is forgotten!"[132]

As in British North America, the Seven Years' War was followed in Saint-Domingue by growing tension between the colony's white elite and the metropolis, which found its expression in a revolt in 1768–1769. This feud was complicated by the arrival on the political scene of free mulattoes and enslaved blacks in the aftermath of the French Revolution. The revolt that started in August 1791 was by no means a simple battle between black slaves and white masters. Blacks could side with the Spanish or French troops, mulattoes with invading British soldiers, and many fell victim in the brutal war between blacks and mulattoes. The hostilities thus constituted both a civil and an international war. The eventual outcome was hard to predict until the very end. As Toussaint passed into French custody, it seemed impossible that Saint-Domingue would soon be lost to the French Empire. If Napoleon had played his cards right, the war in Saint-Domingue would have featured among his many successful campaigns. But when it became obvious that the French had come to their West Indian islands in 1802 to restore slavery, something snapped in black circles. It was only then that independence became possible.

5

Multiple Routes to Sovereignty

The Spanish American Revolutions

The empire that Spain created in the Americas was in its time unrivaled in size, population, and resources. Governing such an empire was a formidable task, which required the adoption of a vast array of laws, offices, agencies, and correspondences. The Spanish Empire was ruled not by an emperor, but by a king, whose territories in the Old World and the New made up the so-called Spanish monarchy. In ruling the American colonies, the king was assisted by the Council of the Indies. No king ever traveled across the Atlantic to behold the western lands with his own eyes. Instead, viceroys and audiencias acted as the chief royal agents. The viceroy was usually a scion of a leading Spanish noble family. As the highest civil and military authority, he was concerned with defense and royal revenues. He also had the right to appoint ecclesiastical officials. The viceroy's power was checked by the audiencias, which combined the functions of an administrative body, advisory board, and court of law. The audiencia lacked the competence to promulgate laws, which remained the king's prerogative.[1] The viceroy's realm was the viceroyalty, four of which were founded in the course of three centuries. New Spain (with its capital, Mexico City) was established in 1535, Peru (Lima) in 1543, New Granada (Santa Fé de Bogotá) in 1717 and again in 1739, and Río de la Plata (Buenos Aires) in 1776. Each viceroyalty was subdivided into a few audiencias. The senior officers in the provinces were *alcaldes mayores* and *corregidores*, who proclaimed the orders of the Crown, directed the collection of revenue, and could intervene in town government. *Corregidores de indios* were provincial magistrates appointed in Indian towns to oversee local justice, taxation, and commerce with Spaniards. At the town level, finally, the *cabildo* ruled. This municipal council, initially made up of conquistadores, soon became the mouthpiece of the local economic elite. As councilors, these landowners, mine operators, and merchants, but also lawyers and clergymen, oversaw taxation, the distribution of land, and other matters.

New Spain was easily the most populous viceroyalty with 6.1 million inhabitants in 1813. The other old viceroyalty of Peru had 1.2 million in the same year, far fewer than New Granada, including Venezuela, which counted a population of approximately 2.2 million around 1800, and Río de la Plata, which had approximately 1.6 million. The Caribbean colonies of Cuba, Puerto Rico, and Santo Domingo added another 0.9 million.[2]

The societies and institutions in the viceroyalties were as diverse as the Americas' climate zones. Indians were the overwhelming majority in some colonies (Guatemala, Quito, Lower and Upper Peru, Paraguay, and southern Chile), while natives had almost died out in others (Venezuela and parts of the Río de la Plata). Blacks were an important presence in Venezuela, coastal New Granada, and parts of Peru, but virtually absent in Paraguay and sections of Central America. Whites were usually a minority, but not necessarily privileged. Many made a living as artisans, small landowners, petty officials, or soldiers, and some led the unsettled life of vagabonds. Economic staples also differentiated Spain's colonies, some of which revolved around mining (Upper Peru, Mexico), others cattle breeding (northern Mexico, Argentina), and again others cash crops such as indigo, cacao, or tobacco (Guatemala, Quito, Venezuela, Cuba). In non-mining areas, the hacienda was often the main economic institution, one by which the landowner enjoyed vast powers over his workers, slave or free. However, his position cannot be compared to that of the European nobleman, who enjoyed a variety of legal privileges.[3]

The preeminent group in these hierarchically structured societies was the predominantly creole (locally born white) aristocracy, some of whose members could trace back their ancestry to the conquistadores, while other families had amassed wealth and noble titles through mining, planting, or other forms of entrepreneurship. They preserved their family fortunes preferably by creating entail, the consolidation of property that could not be divided and thus passed entirely from generation to generation.[4] Creoles shared the elite status with *peninsulares*—Spanish-born officeholders, merchants, and military officers whose careers had brought them to the Americas and whose children were frequently creoles. On top of the hierarchy sat the monarch, universally seen as a benevolent ruler and the source of all justice, whose role it was to arbitrate disputes.[5]

Map 5.1. Spanish America around 1800.

Whether noble or commoner, creole or *peninsular*, whites found themselves at the apex of societies that were organized according to racial hierarchies.[6] From the very first, Indian communities were to be separated from Spanish towns, and even though Spaniards and mestizos began to settle in highland native communities in early colonial times, such migration remained prohibited until the mid-eighteenth century. Conversely, innumerable Indians escaped from tribute and labor obligations to make a living in Spanish cities and haciendas. Only under King Charles III (1759–1788) were the segregative laws annulled, as the authorities took away Indian common lands in areas with prized farmland, forcibly removing Indians from their ancestral lands. No fundamental changes occurred for people of African birth and descent. Throughout the colonial period, black slaves were by law relegated to a miserable existence, and free blacks and mulattoes—unlike mestizos—encountered numerous obstacles because of their ascribed vices, all purportedly rooted in their slave origins. They paid a special royal tribute, were not allowed to live on their own, could not become clergymen, scribes, or notaries, and could not have Indian servants, and females were forbidden to wear gold, silk, or pearls. They did not even have the right to walk side by side with whites in the streets, nor were they to be given a chair in white houses.[7]

Creoles viewed the rights, privileges, and political offices reserved for them as royal rewards for the descent that they could claim from the conquistadors and their purity of blood. In their quest for purity, they could cite the Real Pragmática, a decree of 1776 in which King Charles III announced that no marriages were accepted that were marked by "notable" inequality between the partners. Any union between whites and Indians, mulattoes, or blacks, or even whites with an admixture of nonwhite blood, was thus outlawed.[8] But at the end of the century, the Crown ostensibly allowed breaches to be made in the walls separating black and white by giving *pardos* (free people of African descent) the right to purchase the legal status of whiteness. The white elites then sprang into action. In a revealing document, the cabildo of Caracas argued that white honor was valuable only if inequality were maintained. If pardos were going to fill positions of dignity, whites would abandon these posts, dooming various institutions to obscurity. The reason, they went on, why so few whites make a living as artisans is that they shun the mechanical professions, which employ many free people of color. It is time, the cabildo argued, to return to ethnic distinctions, by forcing pardos to work the land and by dissolving their militias. Their place was to be below that of the plebeian whites.[9] The cabildo of Buenos Aires also insisted on clarity by suggesting in 1789 that all nonwhites, except Indians, should be excluded from guild offices and separated physically from whites at meetings, religious observances, and public processions. At the end of the eighteenth century, it seems, a critical point had been reached in urban America, where mulattoes were occupying posts formerly reserved for whites. Some were priests, others military officers, and in Lima, mulattoes even made up the majority of the surgeons and medical doctors.[10]

Another issue that troubled the white elites was the degree of *mestizaje* (race mixture) reached in the colonies, not only between whites and nonwhites but in other combinations as well. By the late eighteenth century, the number of people of mixed descent was rising dramatically. In some areas, the majority of nonwhites were officially designated as "Spanish" (white), but by no means was this the case everywhere.[11] Whites sought to distinguish themselves from nonwhites by underscoring the impure blood of the latter. Just like converts to Christianity could never aspire to the same respect that those whose families had always been good Catholics enjoyed, people with an Indian or African heritage were not deemed honorable. Many a person who could not claim noble birth derived a sense of honor from establishing his purity of blood in a court of law. To combat *mestizaje*, separation of blacks and Indians was to be strictly enforced, authorities in Lima opined. After a long and very bloody revolt in the 1780s, they feared that those two groups were a potential threat to the colonial state, especially if they joined forces. Their mixture was therefore forbidden by law and condemned in various publications.[12]

Appeals by colonial elites to the Spanish Crown often went unheeded. Imperial communication between Spain and Spanish America left much to be desired and disputes between government agencies multiplied over time, but the resulting benign metropolitan neglect had, on balance, a salutary effect.[13] American societies gradually established their own identities and American economies developed increasingly independent of the mother country.[14] The Crown unintentionally encouraged this process in the mid-seventeenth century when it started selling colonial offices on a large scale. Until then, the sale of offices had been limited to those functions without any judicial or administrative duties, posts such as clerks and scribes. But pressed for money, the Crown put higher offices up for sale as well, both at home and in the colonies.[15] The sale of appointments to audiencias from 1687 through 1750 accelerated a process in which the American colonies grew more autonomous, since it enabled creoles—American-born Spaniards—to buy their way into the courts. By 1750, fifty-one out of ninety-three judges in the audiencias were born in the Americas, as creoles with close ties to the landowning elites dominated the courts in Lima, Santiago de Chile, and Mexico City. Royal power was weakened accordingly.[16]

Cash-hungry Spanish-born officials frequently allied themselves with local elites, thus promoting economic interests that did not always coincide with those of the mother country. After all, officials did not operate in a social vacuum. Whether they had obtained posts in the colonial administrations by appointment, election, or purchase, they wanted to be accepted by the local elites. In Spanish America, "high officials were quickly incorporated through alliance or cooptation into an informal structure that created the conditions for a loyalty divided between the metropolitan authorities and local interest groups."[17] In order to maintain good relations, they chose to occasionally disregard official regulations or ask for their modification.

Another problem rooted in the seventeenth century was that the Crown had stopped paying salaries to the *alcaldes mayores* and *corregidores*. With capital advanced by merchants, these district officers compelled the Indians to accept cash and equipment in order to produce an export crop or to consume commodities. This was the *repartimiento*, which forced the Indians into dependence and diminished imperial control before it was abolished in 1787.

Imperial control over colonial trade had long since been lost. In part due to the inflexibility of monopoly trade and excessive taxation, smuggling with foreigners thrived in most parts of the New World, especially on the northern littoral of South America (Colombia, Venezuela), on the east coast of Central America, and in Cuba, Puerto Rico, and the Río de la Plata. These places constituted important markets for many producers in Northern Europe, while forming a prominent source of pesos, cacao, indigo, tobacco, and hides for the Old World. The risk that contraband trade carried for the English, Dutch, and French traders sailing to Spanish America from their island bases in the Caribbean was offset by the potential profits reaped.

The Bourbon Reforms

A new generation of officials declared war on the institutional mayhem that characterized Spain and its empire. They resolved to thoroughly reform existing structures and make the empire more efficient and manageable, in order for the monarchy to regain its former power and prosperity. The main obstacle they identified was the corporate bodies that possessed a special franchise in the state. Reforms commenced under the first Bourbon monarchs, Philip V and Ferdinand VI, but accelerated under the university-educated ministers appointed by Charles III. These sons of the lower nobility were deeply influenced by the Enlightenment, which they saw as an almost magic potion that could cure Spain's empire.

What the Bourbon policymakers took from the Enlightenment was, first and foremost, a lack of respect for existing traditions and institutions. The empire's political structures they believed to be irrational, bungled work kept together by compromise and custom. In their ambition, optimism, and narrow-mindedness, the Bourbon bureaucrats were much like modern technocrats. They sought to dispassionately organize society with the aid of rational scientific ideas. Although they were only moderately successful, they never questioned the accuracy of their assumptions and labeled their critics ignoramuses. For example, despite proof to the contrary, officials in the Río de la Plata continued to base their policies on the mistaken belief that they were dealing with one single people. The viceroyalty's ethnic and cultural variety was completely overlooked.[18]

The Bourbon planners had no scruples about targeting religious institutions. To them, the church epitomized the odious principle of privilege. "Its wealth," one historian has written, "was measured not only in terms of tithes, real estate and liens on property, but also by its enormous capital, amassed through donations of the faithful, capital which made the Church the largest spender and lender in Spanish America."[19]

Perhaps the most spectacular act of the Bourbon monarchy was its declaration of war on the powerful Jesuit order. In 1767, a decree banned the Jesuits from all of Spanish America, after they had previously been exiled from Portugal and Brazil (1759) and rendered illegal in France (1764). In the Spanish colonies, Jesuits had been dominant in urban education, overseeing 120 colleges and missionary activity among Indians in the Río de la Plata. In Paraguay, they monitored a network of missions that at one point housed a hundred thousand natives. Enjoying administrative autonomy in these communities, the Jesuits taught the natives farming techniques and provided religious instruction. The reasons for the order's expulsion were never disclosed, but several reasons can be adduced. Most important, the Jesuits formed a state within a state, controlling education and possessing large amounts of real estate in both rural and urban areas. Their subordination to the pope, their alleged exploitation of Indians, and the role they supposedly played in instigating riots in Spain in 1766 also made the Jesuits numerous enemies. When the expulsion order was put into effect, some twenty-six hundred priests and friars were forced to leave Spain, and a similar number departed from America to Italy, many of them creoles.[20] Their migration unexpectedly made it possible for enlightened ideas to make new inroads into the colonies, as curricula were revised and forbidden authors suddenly became fashionable.[21]

The Bourbon reforms gained momentum during the Seven Years' War, which had made it painfully clear how far Spain had sunk as an international power. In 1762, shortly after Spain's entry into the war, the British navy, with incredible ease, captured the strategically important ports of Manila and Havana. British merchants used the occupation to flood the market with cheap and high-grade British manufactures, whetting the appetite of local residents. Even where there was no clang of arms, the war made Spanish officials face the sobering facts. As the viceroy of Peru, Manuel de Amat y Junient, prepared Peru for war with Great Britain, he discovered that everything from gunpowder and weapons to uniforms and discipline was in short supply.[22]

The military was just one area of postwar reform. Another concerned the gradual reversal of the policy to name Americans to audiencia posts. While no *oidor* was fired, most vacancies were henceforth filled with *peninsulares*. The effects of this sea change were already visible by 1777, when no audiencia except for the one in Lima maintained an American majority.[23] Lima's pivotal place in the empire had by then been diminished by the creation, in 1776, of the new viceroyalty of Río de la Plata. Made up of the territories of today's countries of Argentina, Bolivia, Paraguay, and Uruguay, this southernmost viceroyalty was founded both to withstand a feared British invasion and to legalize the large flow of Northern European merchandise that had entered Buenos Aires surreptitiously for many generations.

Beginning with Cuba and Louisiana (1763), New Spain (1765), and Peru (1777), *visitas* (inspections) were held in a series of colonies, which opened the door to sweeping changes, such as the inauguration of a hierarchical order that replaced *alcaldes mayores* and *corregidores* by subdelegates, who were accountable not to distant Spain but to their immediate superior. Since officials were now also paid a fixed salary, the system left little room for compromises with local elites.[24] A resolution adopted to inaugurate a new commercial regime was the abolition in 1765 of Cádiz's monopoly of navigation with Spanish America. "Free trade" allowed Cuba, Santo Domingo, Puerto Rico, Trinidad, and Margarita to open shipping lanes with nine ports in Spain. This privilege was later extended to the notorious smuggling centers of Louisiana (1768), Campeche, and the Yucatán (1770). In 1778, all of Spanish America was included in the new system of colonial traffic that came to replace the fleet system, with the exception of New Spain and Venezuela, which were kept out until 1789.[25]

Financing the reforms was not easy. Taxes were therefore increased and collected more rigorously than before, in particular the sales tax (*alcabala*), which had not been raised since the late sixteenth century. In addition, royal monopolies—provided with their own police force— were imposed on tobacco, salt, gunpowder, and spirituous liquor (*aguardiente*), yielding high profits.[26] The attempt to tap American financial sources was so successful that by 1810, according to a contemporary Spanish estimate, more than half of the government revenues derived from the American colonies.[27] Not only did war expenses in the 1790s lead to Spanish requests for "voluntary" gifts, the Spanish state repeatedly introduced new loans and taxes. The main target was New Spain, which was thus punished for its economic prosperity. Virtually all professions contributed to the never-ending flow of money to the mother country, and still, it was not enough. After a new war erupted with Britain in late 1804, a financial crisis set in. Remittances from the Americas dried up, an agrarian slump made it necessary to import grain from France, and the French emperor pressured King Charles IV to pay the annual war subsidy of 192 million reales, agreed upon in the previous year. The only way out of the financial conundrum for Spanish officials was to introduce amortization in New Spain and Peru, enabling the Spanish state to appropriate capital and sell landed properties belonging to Pious Foundations and Chantries, the main banking institutions in the colony.

Merchants, landowners, and mine operators on whose properties most ecclesiastical capital was invested in the form of annuities and chantry funds were hit hard. Others hurt in the process included parish priests reliant on income from chantries to supplement their meager salaries.[28] But in the end, it was the plebeians who bore the real burden of the Bourbon reforms.[29] Financial demands led to a tax increase for nonwhites, since the *alcabala* and the tribute paid by Indians and free blacks were regressive in nature and placed increased labor demands on workers. As real wages fell, living standards dropped, giving rise to crime and vagrancy, including marronage, on an unprecedented scale.[30] Before long, protest ensued. In various Mexican towns, such as Guanajuato and San Luis Potosí, the first rallies took place after fiscal demands and militia enlistment had raised concerns. The demonstrators gathered again when the viceroy and the visitor-general tried to implement the expulsion decree of the Jesuit order. The authorities had no mercy on the rebels, hanging 85 people and punishing 864 others with flogging, banishment, and imprisonment.[31] Both the causes of popular complaints in Mexico—military service and the unjust treatment of esteemed clergymen—and the harsh reaction of the authorities are reminiscent of the problems surrounding the introduction of the Civil Constitution of the Clergy in France.

Still, resistance to Crown policies was not as widespread as it had been during the war with Great Britain (1779–1783). The so-called *comuneros* revolt in New Granada (1781), involving thousands of protesters— creoles, mestizos, and Indians—stood up to the heavy-handed visitor-general who was responsible for raising the *alcabala*, reviving a tax on naval defense, and reorganizing the liquor and tobacco monopolies.[32] In terms of objectives, scale, and loss of human life, the *comuneros* rebellion was a minor affair compared to the Túpac Amaru revolt in Peru (1780–1783). In these years, an increasingly rebellious climate in the interior of that viceroyalty reached a climax, after the number of revolts had grown from five in the 1740s to eleven in the 1750s, twenty in the 1760s, and sixty-six in the 1770s.[33] Like other colonial uprisings, the Túpac Amaru revolt was sparked by fiscal measures. The doubling of the *alcabala* to 4 percent in 1772 and the subsequent increase to 6 percent in 1776 ended up pitting many men and women against Spanish officials. But there was more to the big revolt, whose leader, Túpac Amaru (b. 1742), a cacique from the Cuzco area, could base himself on a long tradition of Andean messianism.[34] Túpac called for the suppression of the repartimiento and the audiencia and aspired to breaking off all relations with the Spanish king, replacing the distant monarch with an Inca emperor. He also planned to introduce structural changes in the economy that Spain had created in Peru, such as the elimination of the *alcabala*, the *mita*, and large haciendas, and the implementation of free trade. Envisaging a nation in which creoles, mestizos, blacks, and Indians would live together in harmony, he appealed to the creoles to support this movement and declared war to the death against Spaniards.[35] Even if there were creoles who agreed with some of the rebellion's stated objectives, the overall movement was far too revolutionary for them to participate. Acting in concert, creoles and Spaniards therefore brutally suppressed the rebellion. By the time they had succeeded, as many as one hundred thousand Indians and ten thousand whites were reported dead.

These movements may have been provoked by the Bourbon reforms, but it is less clear what their connection was with the later struggles for independence. By and large, the eighteenth-century revolts did not call into question the legitimacy of monarchical rule or Spanish overlordship, although the frequent neglect of the traditional policy of accommodation eroded imperial authority in many parts of the empire. Prior to 1808, the outbreak of the independence movements would have been very difficult to predict. Even Alexander von Humboldt, the Prussian baron who traveled extensively across Spain's American provinces between 1799 and 1804, later acknowledged that he had underestimated the desire for independence in Venezuela, which as it turned out would become a hotbed of revolution.[36] It took an outside event to trigger the protracted independence process.

Napoleon's Intervention

The first fissures in the imperial construction indeed appeared as a consequence of events an ocean away. In 1807, Napoleon, now emperor of France and master of the larger part of Europe, invaded Portugal, inducing the Portuguese court to move from Lisbon to Rio de Janeiro. The flight of the king and ten thousand of his supporters to Brazil caused a remarkable change. Now Portugal became the colony, Brazil the metropolis. It would prove to be the first step toward Brazilian independence.[37]

One year after he invaded Portugal, Napoleon imprisoned the Spanish king, Ferdinand VII, and his father, Charles IV, and ordered his own brother Joseph to fill the vacant throne. Under Charles IV, Spain had in fact been ruled by the king's favorite, Manuel Godoy, Príncipe de la Paz. It was Godoy who involved Spain in France's warfare at the Treaty of San Ildefonso (1796). Both partners suffered in the end, as Britain established naval supremacy by destroying the combined fleets of France and Spain at the Battle of Trafalgar (1805). As a consequence, Spain could no longer defend her colonies. At home, Godoy's policies made him many enemies. The discontent contributed to the coup d'état of crown prince Ferdinand in March 1808, known as the Mutiny of Aranjuez, which led to the dismissal of Godoy and the abdication of Charles IV. This changing of the guards was not directly in France's interest, since Napoleon had previously sent many soldiers to Spain in an attempt to strengthen the Continental System, his grandiose plan to seal off the whole European continent from British ships and commerce.

Ostensibly to mediate in the affairs of the Bourbon family, the emperor next invited the old and the new king to Bayonne in the southwest of France, not far from the Spanish border. Once he arrived, Ferdinand was forced to abdicate in favor of his father, who in turn left the throne vacant for Napoleon. And Napoleon ordered his brother Joseph, King of Naples, to fill the throne. The emperor now made the mistake of believing that, as elsewhere in Europe, he could establish control over Spain by way of a few swift campaigns. He had not reckoned with the Spanish people, who rose in revolt, roused by the clergy against the "atheist"

French.[38] The insurgency began on May 2, when the French government tried to bring the remaining members of the royal family in a carriage to France. Eleven weeks later, the Spanish army crushed their French opponents, mostly second-rate soldiers, in the Battle of Bailén. The French were so hard-pressed that King Joseph was briefly forced to leave Madrid not long after his accession. But the French recovered and the central junta—originally appointed by Ferdinand before he departed for Bayonne—that coordinated Spanish resistance had to abandon its headquarters in Seville. The junta relocated to Cádiz, situated on a peninsula in the southwest, the only town that remained free territory. In the rest of the country, guerrillas kept the resistance alive, supported by English expedition troops. The Spanish army no longer played a role, having been defeated in a year and a half.

The English troops, commanded by Arthur Wellesley, the later Lord Wellington, had initially been raised for an expedition to Spanish America.[39] After the Bourbon family was deposed in Bayonne and Joseph Bonaparte was elevated to the Spanish Crown, London feared a scenario in which Spain's colonies chose the side of Napoleon.[40] It seemed opportune to send a "liberating" expedition. It is unlikely, however, that the British soldiers would have been received as liberators or protectors. The memories of the British invasions of Buenos Aires in 1806 and 1807 were still fresh. In June 1806, British expeditionary forces, returning from the Cape of Good Hope, where they had conquered the Dutch colony, sailed to Buenos Aires without authorization from the British government. They occupied the town without much resistance from the viceroy's troops, but were expelled by a local army that included a good number of volunteers. Tempted to recapture the city, London sent reinforcements to the Río de la Plata that proceeded to occupy Montevideo. The audiencia acted responsibly in the face of this new threat, deposing the viceroy and counting again on local militias, which once more defeated the British soldiers as they entered Buenos Aires.

In the spring of 1808, the British ministers did not envisage conquering all of Spanish America, but considered it realistic to occupy a string of strong points.[41] Napoleon could not let this happen. When messages and rumors from Northern Europe about the imminent departure of a British fleet to the Spanish colonies came to his attention, he urged the dispatch to America of scores of ships. They were to carry guns to help the inhabitants resist British troops.[42] By the time these plans reached fever pitch, events in the Iberian Peninsula intervened, making it impossible for the Franco-Spanish expedition to Spanish America or for the British fleet to sail. In early June, desertion among the Spanish troops who were supposed to protect the new king began to reach dramatic proportions. Entire regiments deserted, leaving only officers behind. Nor did popular opposition subside. Wellesley's expedition was therefore diverted to Spain, where the insurgents had called on Britain to form an alliance against the common enemy. Napoleon now also decided to concentrate on Spain, although he did not forget about Spanish America.

Napoleon chose to go on a diplomatic offensive in the Spanish colonies, dispersing at least three dozen agents, who spread propaganda, especially on the northern coast of South America and in the Caribbean colonies.[43] The target audience of senior officials, parish priests, and prelates was not swayed, however, nor was the population at large. The governor of Caracas was forced to provide the French envoys with an escort—it seems by Spanish soldiers in civilian clothes—to the seaside in order to prevent them from being killed.[44] Other Spanish officials had no mercy on such intruders. In Mexico, two of Napoleon's emissaries were arrested and executed.[45] In the end, Napoleon's plans were thwarted by the outbreak of Spanish America's independence wars, which he himself had unwittingly sparked.[46]

From Tradition to Revolution

The news about the events that transpired in Spain in 1808 caused confusion in the colonies. For many years Charles IV had been the king, France the ally, and Britain the enemy. Now Joseph was Spain's monarch, Britain the ally, and France the enemy.[47] All over Spanish America, the knee-jerk reaction to Napoleon's advances was to display allegiance to Ferdinand VII. In Chile, young creoles started wearing badges in their hats, bearing the king's portrait.[48] In Mexico, Ferdinand was hailed as the best monarch in Spanish history or even the best in the world, although the king had barely ruled for one month and the population was in the dark about his policy plans. The Mexican population also petitioned to organize festivities in the king's honor. Mexicans swore allegiance to the captive king on August 13, the anniversary of the conquest of Tenoch-titlán, the capital of the Aztec Empire.[49] In Lima, public rogations were held a few days after allegiance had been sworn to the new king. In the cathedral, the residents implored God for helping the Spanish armies, before they carried Our Lady of the Rosary in a solemn procession from her sanctuary to the metropolitan church. In the collective memory, this procession had been successful in defeating the epidemic diseases that plagued the city in 1759 and 1764.[50] If spiritual help was forthcoming, practical aid was not absent, New Spain distinguishing itself with numerous fund-raising drives. The donations of colonial peasants often came from community funds that were earmarked for the payment of religious services and the maintenance of local roads. Despite its poverty, Guatemala contributed 43,000 pesos, and Mexicans donated 68,892 pairs of shoes to the Spanish army.[51]

Yet continuous Atlantic warfare prevented a regular flow of colonial remittances to the Spanish coffers. Under the circumstances, Spain's government, stuck in Cádiz, came to rely largely on the financial resources of the city's merchants, who were hit with one exaction after another. The price for this dependence was that free trade, a desideratum of virtually every colonial elite, became nonnegotiable. Cádiz's merchants even demanded the restoration of their monopoly of colonial commerce.[52]

The connection between Spain and her colonies had meanwhile become very loose. Americans believed that not Spain, but the Spanish king held sway over the American provinces. The provinces were, in other words, not colonies but the king's patrimonial property. It followed that the Americans were left to their own devices now that the king was incapacitated. Sovereignty had reverted to the "people." This meant in practice that, in imitation of what had happened in Spain itself, town councils took the initiative to assume power in Ferdinand's name. Under the Bourbon kings, the cabildos had been regenerated and had in turn begun to ask for an extension of their powers.[53]

The autonomy enjoyed by Americans was affirmed by the five-man Regency that replaced the central junta in Spain in 1810. Addressing the Spanish Americans, the Regency asserted: "Your destinies no longer depend on ministers, viceroys, or governors: they are in your hands."[54] This statement was incorporated into a momentous decree, by which the Regency announced the convocation of the Cortes, the parliament of Spain that had not been summoned since 1789. The decree called for the election of American representatives to attend the Cortes, which was to be held in Spain on the island of León in Cádiz, still free from French occupation. The procedure was hardly democratic, because representation was a privilege enjoyed only by town councils of provincial capitals, and genuine elections were not held. By lot, three locally born men were appointed from a group of names selected by the town council. Since the American deputies were expected to arrive late in Cádiz, twenty-six names of Americans living in the peninsula were drawn. These substitute deputies were to represent America until the proprietary deputies arrived. As it turned out, the deputy from New Mexico did not join the Cortes until August 1812, almost two years after the opening of this parliament. Most Peruvians also arrived in 1812 (and one in 1813).[55]

All deputies agreed with an ideology, inherited from the Bourbon kings, that stressed imperial unity and a common religion, language, and culture. What is more, all deputies, except for a few *peninsulares*, agreed that the American territories had never been colonies in the judicial sense. But when push came to shove, one part of the empire proved to be more equal than the others. The American deputies insisted on parity in representation, criticizing the provisions, which allowed one deputy for each fifty thousand peninsular inhabitants, while the Americans were allowed one deputy for each hundred thousand inhabitants. The *peninsulares* put up a stubborn resistance, realizing that parity would not simply benefit the American territories but hand them a majority in the Cortes. After all, Spain's population stood at 10.5 million, while Humboldt's estimate of 15 to 16 million—although in reality too high—was accepted for Spanish America. Here was a dispute that resembled the feud that erupted in France in the late spring of 1789 about the relative weight of the deputies of the Third Estate. But whereas the Third Estate triumphed and all deputies ended up joining the National Assembly, the peninsular deputies in Cádiz did not give in.[56] They availed themselves of the old Bourbon family metaphors, which presented Spaniards and Americans as faithful vassals of a father king. But the family metaphor could also be used against colonial rule. America, its deputies insisted in the first months of 1811, had reached maturity and was well aware of its rights and dignity. The *peninsulares* replied that most children did not break off family ties or neglect reciprocal duties.[57] What the *peninsulares* did not state was that they had an agenda of their own, which aimed at revolutionizing the imperial societies, but that required a centralized regime. And Spain was to remain the center.

The opinions diverged especially when the respective numbers of deputies for the "two Spains" (the peninsula and America) came up for discussion. While neither side wanted black slaves to enter into the equation, the debate hinged on the question of whether the *castas*—free people with varying degrees of African admixture—were to be counted as Americans. The Spaniards resisted that proposal, arguing that only "natives" of Spain and America (including Indians) were considered citizens, and that the African roots of mulattoes were more important than their American birth. Their numbers should therefore not be taken into account in determining the size of the American delegation to the Cortes. In response, several Americans brought up the large degree of *mestizaje* in their countries and the difficulty in determining someone's race. Often, they said, one could only go by the person's reputation. The Americans' attempt to increase their population base failed in the end, because the majority of *peninsulares* did not budge an inch.[58]

Equal representation topped the list of demands presented by the American delegation in December 1810. Other issues included the freedom to produce all commodities that had previously been prohibited, freedom of trade, the suppression of monopolies, and the restoration of the Jesuit order. Apart from the freedom to plant and manufacture all goods, no demand was granted and many were shelved.[59] In other respects, the Cortes did accede to American demands, such as administrative reform. One outcome of the Cortes was that towns with at least a thousand inhabitants were granted a cabildo, but that was no more than a consolation prize. The Americans were left virtually empty-handed, since the decrees that they had welcomed were often not even introduced in the American colonies. The freedom of the press, decreed on November 10, 1810, was still not introduced by the viceroy of New Spain in 1812. His counterpart in Peru and the governor in Cuba had by then restricted the liberty of the press.[60]

Although some Spanish deputies sympathized with the creole cause, differences between the two sides of the Atlantic proved irreconcilable. The Americans who shared the revolutionary principles of the Spanish liberals did not see the need to remain united to Spain in order to introduce those principles in their own societies. And the loyal Americans defending the union with Spain were generally conservatives who rejected the ideas and political goals of metropolitan liberals.[61] Nonetheless, the deliberations in Cádiz did have a concrete outcome that all agreed on in the form of a constitution promulgated on March 19, 1812. It would be the blueprint for many American constitutions adopted in the years ahead. And a remarkable blueprint it was. The constitution abolished the Inquisition, Indian tribute, and forced labor. It limited the role of the king, created provincial deputations that were to serve as colonial legislatures, and set up a Council of State that was to be the Crown's only advisory body. The constitution also provided for biennial elections, which renewed the entire legislature. The first elections for the ordinary Cortes, which would succeed the extraordinary Cortes, were called immediately. They would inaugurate an electoral system based on the whole population, replacing the one emanating from the old corporate structure. The elections were indirect and took place in three stages. Men born in Spain or Spanish America residing in any part of the empire had the right to vote. Excluded were domestic servants, criminals, public debtors, members of the regular orders, and men of African extraction, but all other males, Indians and mestizos among them, were authorized to vote, provided they had a place of residence. Suddenly, then, day laborers, muleteers, and shepherds were part of the electorate. This meant that in Mexico City, 93 percent of the adult males were enfranchised.[62]

The ordinary Cortes went ahead as planned in October 1813, but many obstacles prevented the new American delegates from reaching Cádiz. Those who did arrive had a rude awakening in 1814, when Ferdinand VII returned to power, shortly after Napoleon's first defeat and exile. The old and new king dissolved the Cortes in May, abolished the constitution, and exiled or jailed perhaps twelve thousand "liberals," including many members of the Cortes, Americans and Spaniards alike.

The March of Revolution

In the American colonies, events had happened in quick succession during the years of Ferdinand's absence. On January 1, 1809, one faction of Buenos Aires's elite, made up of both *peninsulares* and creoles, had tried to set up a junta in imitation of the councils that had been formed in Spain. Its main objective was to oust Santiago de Liniers, a French-born naval officer who had led the resistance against the British invasions, for which he was rewarded with the post of interim viceroy. Although Liniers was able to survive due to support from the creole militia, his French background made him vulnerable, and it was only a matter of time before his position was under attack again. A visiting British merchant found in 1809 that the spirit of independence had pervaded every stratum except the peninsular merchants and senior civil servants. Apart from the bishops and two or three higher dignitaries, the clergy were also firm revolutionists.[63] It was the creole militia that made a decisive step in the direction of independence, establishing, after the arrival of a new viceroy had forced Liniers to step down, a junta on May 25, 1810, that did not include Liniers's successor.

In the years that followed, Buenos Aires was mired in political turmoil, returning to some calm only after a coup by two men who had won their spurs in the Peninsular War in Spain and had recently returned home. In October 1812, José de San Martín (1778–1850) and Carlos María de Alvear ousted one triumvirate and installed another. San Martín chose to play no further political role, preferring the military path to spread revolution in America. Apart from domestic strife, Buenos Aires had been at odds with other parts of the viceroyalty since 1809. Upper Peru and the other interior provinces of the Río de la Plata all had economic interests that diverged from Buenos Aires. The free trade championed by the *porteños*, as the residents of Buenos Aires were known, was anathema in areas where producers tried to protect their manufactures from foreign competition. In La Paz in the mining province of Upper Peru, rebels formed a junta in July 1809 that strived for autonomy from both Spain and Buenos Aires. The prominent place of mestizos in the junta alienated many creoles, who did not resist the forces sent from Lima and Buenos Aires against the revolution. By October, Upper Peru was therefore back in royalist hands, where it would remain for most of the ensuing years until 1825, in spite of three expeditions sent from Buenos Aires after May 1810 that met with different levels of success.[64]

Montevideo and, by extension, the entire Banda Oriental (east bank) of the Rio de la Plata also refused to do Buenos Aires's bidding. Montevideo's relation to Buenos Aires resembled that of Buenos Aires to Spain: a

Figure 5.1. Buenos Aires's largest marketplace in the early nineteenth century at the Plaza Mayor. Courtesy of the John Hay Library at Brown University.

port city that wanted to free itself from commercial tutelage and political subordination. The aftermath of the British incursions of 1806 and 1807 added to the tensions, as the *porteños* hurt the pride of their neighbors by downplaying Montevideo's contribution to the glorious defeat of the invaders. And if some in Montevideo may have hoped for Buenos Aires to grant the Banda Oriental autonomy in the May days of 1810, they were deceived. Buenos Aires's junta immediately claimed authority over the rest of the viceroyalty.[65] The man in power in Montevideo, first as governor and then (from 1811) as viceroy of the Río de la Plata, was the staunch royalist Francisco Javier Elío; his antagonist was José Artigas (1764–1850), an erstwhile smuggler turned officer in the local Spanish service, who epitomized the local desire for independence. As Montevideo remained loyal to Spain, Artigas deserted his army post in early 1811 and crossed the river to join the revolution in Buenos Aires. When his small army threatened to take Montevideo, Elío first turned to the Portuguese government in Brazil for help, but when the Portuguese sent an army that occupied the Banda Oriental—an area long since disputed by both Iberian powers—he appealed to Buenos Aires for aid. The armistice that was concluded was soon breached by the *porteños*, who began to lay siege to Montevideo. Realizing that the revolutionary leadership intended to incorporate the Banda Oriental into its own polity, Artigas now took his forces to the interior of the Banda Oriental, recently vacated by the Portuguese army, ensuring that Buenos Aires, which captured Montevideo in June 1814, would not control his native country. A long period followed in which Brazil and Buenos Aires asserted their respective rights to govern the east bank, only to cede independence to Uruguay in August 1828.[66]

Nor was Buenos Aires able to include Paraguay in its realm, as local forces prevailed twice over a *porteño* army under Manuel Belgrano in 1811. In the wake of these momentous feats, the creole elite seized power in Asunción and declared Paraguay's autonomy of Buenos Aires or any other power—they were especially afraid of Brazil, which had been invited by the Spanish intendant to intervene. With the creole lawyer Dr. José Gaspar Rodríguez de Francia (1766–1840) as the undisputed leader, Paraguay declared its independence on October 12, 1813. One year later, Dr. Francia was made dictator for five years, a tenure soon converted to perpetuity. Francia, helped by a few assistants, dispensed with a legislature, ruling Paraguay virtually single-handedly for the next quarter century. He passed away in 1840.[67]

On the other end of South America, the news from Bayonne and later Seville had also stirred creoles into action. In Caracas, the captain-general nipped in the bud a conspiracy organized in November 1808 by a few dozen men who almost openly planned to form a junta. The ringleaders included virtually all titled nobility, who were let off with light punishments on account of their status. This proved only a temporary reprieve for the royalists, since on April 19, 1810, a junta was installed after prominent creoles deposed the captain-general. Although the new leaders professed their loyalty to Ferdinand, some would later admit that the oaths of fealty had been tactical, and their prime concern had been not to alarm the people.

The examples of Spain and Caracas were rapidly imitated in other parts of Venezuela and all over New Granada, where numerous towns erected their own juntas.[68] With conservatives dominating the junta, a group of young, middle-class men seized the momentum in Caracas in the closing months of 1810, putting increasing pressure on the junta to adopt its suggested policies. A rising star among them was twenty-seven-year-old Simón Antonio José Bolívar (1783–1830), born into one of the wealthiest families of Venezuela. Bolívar's possessions included horse and cattle farms, copper mines, and extensive plantations where cacao and cotton were grown. After his young wife's death, Bolívar left for Europe, where he became convinced of the need to free the American colonies from Spanish rule.

Bolívar and others persuaded the junta in Caracas to allow native son Francisco Miranda to return home from London. Historians have aptly named Miranda (1750–1816) the Precursor. Decades before the wars erupted in Spanish America, Miranda sought to convince his interlocutors of the need for the Spanish colonies to become independent. And the seasoned traveler had interlocutors galore. Wherever he went in Europe and North America, he arrived with letters of recommendation and he always left with new ones. An engaging personality, he counted among his friends Catherine the Great, Alexander Hamilton, Joseph Haydn, and the philosophers James Mill and Jeremy Bentham, and he spent time with Edward Gibbon, Frederick the Great, the Marquis de Lafayette, Napoleon, Moses Mendelssohn, Thomas Paine, William Pitt the Younger, and George Washington.

Having served as an army captain in Spanish garrisons in North Africa and Andalusia, Miranda fought with Spanish troops in the American Revolution, taking part in the Battle of Pensacola. He quit service when he learned that he was about to be arrested on charges of spying for Great Britain. After moving to London in 1790, he sent one letter after another to the British government, recommending the emancipation of Spanish America, starting with Venezuela. After two years of fruitless attempts, his financial means had dwindled so much that Miranda sailed to France to sell his ideas there. In order to make a living, he had himself recruited in the French revolutionary army as field marshal, serving in the Army of the North in the Austrian Netherlands against Prussian and Austrian forces. Discredited by his military conduct, he was in and out of prison in the next years.[69] His unflagging zeal to free his fatherland finally resulted in an expedition in 1806, fitted out in New York City. The strange company that Miranda had gathered around him was surprised by a Spanish warship before it could even make landfall in

Venezuela. Many sailors were arrested and ten of them hanged in public. Miranda escaped and returned a few months later, going ashore in Coro, but accomplishing nothing. After only eleven days, afraid of being encircled by Spanish soldiers, the Precursor decided to reembark. Like the simultaneous British expedition to Buenos Aires, Miranda's attempt to liberate Venezuela had failed miserably.[70]

In 1810, Miranda was offered a chance to redeem himself. He accepted the invitation from the Venezuelan junta—or rather, Bolívar, who pretended to act on the junta's orders—to take over the Venezuelan government. Soon after he disembarked in Venezuela, elections were held based on property requirements. They produced an elite congress that quickly radicalized and declared independence on July 5, 1811. But this was a false start. The first Venezuelan republic lasted for just over one year. The new oligarchy first had to fight off the defiant city of Valencia, one hundred miles west of Caracas, which was vehemently opposed to independence. A force led by Miranda subdued Valencia, but another challenge soon appeared when the Spaniard Domingo Monteverde disembarked in Coro from Puerto Rico and his royalist troops recaptured western Venezuela for the royalists. A terrible earthquake on March 26 added to the travails of the brittle republic, killing perhaps ten thousand people in Caracas alone and reducing various cities and villages to ruin. After the city was returned to Spanish hands, Miranda, who had been made dictator, saw no other course than to surrender. But acting on his own authority, he incurred the wrath of his fellow leaders. Bolívar and two others handed him over to the Spanish, who sent him on to Cádiz. For four long years the veteran revolutionary, by then in his sixties, wasted away in a prison cell before he expired.[71]

In Caracas, meanwhile, the royalists could not sustain their regime either. Besieged by forces from the west and east, it collapsed after barely more than one year. Monteverde was partly to blame, since the Spanish army chief rapidly alienated pardos and *llaneros*—residents of Venezuela's interior grasslands who considered the cattle roaming there their own—who had initially sympathized with his troops. He also violated the treaty with the vanquished by arresting former rebels and confiscating their property. Many of them (including probably Bolívar) had turned their back on the revolution, but now took up arms again. Bolívar repaid Monteverde by proclaiming the war to the death on June

15, 1813: "Any Spaniard who does not work against tyranny in favor of the just cause, by the most active and effective means, shall be considered an enemy . . . and in consequence shall inevitably be shot." Native sons would, however, be spared, even if they had supported Spain. This decree was issued when Bolívar was in the middle of a remarkable campaign, capturing town after town in western Venezuela with Napoleonic speed. On August 6, he entered Caracas in triumph and was granted the title "The Liberator." Without any rivals to challenge his leadership, Bolívar established a military dictatorship that was especially harsh on the Spanish population. His most egregious decision came in February 1814, when he ordered more than one thousand Spanish prisoners of war, most of them noncombatants, to be shot summarily. Bolívar ordered the massacre after receiving word that the royalist army of Spanish-born José Tomás Boves had committed acts of shocking violence in the town of Ocumare, putting three hundred residents to the sword.

The second republic was also granted a short life. In July 1814, Bolívar and his army vacated Caracas even before an enormous Spanish army had landed on the coast. Field Marshal Pablo Morillo disembarked in April 1815 with 10,500 Spanish troops who were expected to swiftly restore order. Dispatching this army—the largest Spain had ever sent across the ocean—was one of Ferdinand's first decisions after returning to the throne. If he had originally considered Buenos Aires as the destination, Tierra Firme was ultimately deemed of greater strategic importance.[72]

After stopping at the island of Margarita, Morillo's troops headed for nearby Cumaná and sailed from there to Cartagena de Indias. Developments in New Granada had been similar to those in Venezuela. Various juntas had been proclaimed, of which the one in the capital had national pretensions. In March 1811, the region around Bogotá formed the republic of Cundinamarca, but failed to get the other provinces on its side. Most of these provinces joined forces in a federation, except for Cartagena and a few other towns that declared their independence, not just from Spain but also from Bogotá. The ensuing civil war was brought to a close by Bolívar, whose army managed to bring Bogotá in line with the federation.

Cartagena, which still remained on its own, was the first town in New Granada to contend with Morillo's army. A siege of a hundred days proved fatal for the proud city-state. When its leaders surrendered in December 1815, few within the city walls were still alive. The royalist army had squared accounts with the insurgents in a preposterous way. The viceroy himself estimated that seven thousand men were shot to death, "individuals from the principal families of the viceroyalty." Others who had fought on the rebel side were exiled, jailed, fined, and condemned to forced labor or military service.[73]

Although Morillo may have won the military battle, support for the royal cause suffered from his treatment of enemy combatants. Nor did he show any leniency in the period ahead, especially since the instructions from Madrid, which he now finally received, gave him unlimited faculties in his campaign. Those who survived vowed to fight to the bitter end. Many found shelter in Les Cayes, a port city in the Haitian republic, where Bolívar and his Venezuelan brothers-in-arms also regrouped. They were assisted in all possible ways by President Pétion, who offered hospitality, guns, ammunition, other war matériel, and a printing press. He also supported Bolívar when the latter's authority was called into question. Pétion insisted that he did not want to be paid back, but during their meeting in the National Palace in Port-au-Prince, adorned with portraits of abbé Raynal, abbé Grégoire, and British abolitionist William Wilberforce, Pétion asked Bolívar to abolish slavery in his country.

With Haitian support, Bolívar now attempted to make Tierra Firme independent again, but failed completely. The battered expedition returned to Pétion's state, setting up camp in the town of Jacmel.[74] Aided again by the Haitian president, Bolívar finally succeeded in entering Venezuela, but military victories were few and far between in the period that followed. Resistance to the royalist regime grew to large proportions in the interior of New Granada and in Casanare, from where autonomous bands of guerrillas moved westward across the eastern Andes in 1818, after Morillo had taken some of his forces to Venezuela. The next year, the tide was turning for the insurgents after Bolívar invaded New Granada, defeating his enemy at the Battle of Boyacá (August 7, 1819), which decided the plight of this Spanish colony. Three years later (May 24, 1822), Bolívar also laid the foundation for an independent Quito, as he beat the Spaniards at Mount Pichincha. In the interim, he worked hard to forge a permanent union between the countries that he had "liberated." A congress convened in Angostura in eastern Venezuela decided to create the Republic of Colombia, made up of Venezuela, New Granada, and Quito.[75] To distinguish it from its later and smaller namesake, historians have dubbed this new nation Gran Colombia. It would not last, breaking up into its constituent parts in 1830, the same year in which Bolívar died, consumed by fatigue and tuberculosis.

It was not only republican military prowess that overcame Spanish might. Once Morillo had failed to inflict a swift defeat on his enemies and had to prepare for a long war, resources became a problem. Like his opponents, he resorted to confiscations but lacked the advantage of local troops who engaged in guerrilla activity by living off the countryside. By late 1820, Morillo had had enough and returned to Spain. At that point, the fate of Spanish South America was all but a foregone conclusion.[76]

Mexican and Peruvian Counterpoints

Mexico and Peru did not follow the typical trajectory of other Spanish colonies, where autonomous councils took over the government within two years after Napoleon's intervention in Spain. Mexican viceroy José de Iturrigaray was well disposed toward the creole elite and liked the proposal of the cabildo of Mexico City that he should take direct control of the government and convoke an assembly of the viceroyalty's cities. But on September 16, 1808, a group of circa three hundred *peninsulares*, virtually all members of the local Consulado, arrested both the viceroy, who was sent back to Spain, and the plan's main supporters.[77] The *peninsulares* were still firmly in charge when in December 1809 a conspiracy headed by creoles was foiled in the city of Valladolid. Its aim had been to raise eighteen to twenty thousand Indian and mixed-race troops.

Another conspiracy was soon brewing in the Bajío, a region with marked class differences between wealthy mine owners and *hacendados*, and the mass of Indians, free blacks, and mulattoes. But it was a group of well-to-do creoles that included officers in the colonial militia that was behind the plot. Led by Ignacio Allende, the son of a peninsular merchant, they were united in their hatred of the Spanish.[78] Although the authorities learned about the group's plans, the rebels decided to go ahead with their conspiracy. A priest named Miguel Hidalgo (1753–1811) issued the so-called Cry of Dolores on September 16, 1810, a Sunday, when a conveniently large number of potential followers were present in the marketplace. Probably avoiding the word "independence," Hidalgo called on the present Indians and mestizos to prevent a turnover of Mexico to Napoleon's France, stressing that oppression had reached an end and that the cessation of tribute was near. Hidalgo had taught Latin and philosophy before becoming a parish priest, although he barely engaged in typically priestly activities, involving himself more in small-scale industries. Long known for his unorthodox views, he joined Allende's group at a late stage, but went on to become its natural leader, gaining a large following within a short amount of time. The original thousand men with whom he marched had swelled to twenty-five thousand the next Sunday and to no fewer than eighty thousand men by October. The destination of their march was the mining town of Guanajuato, where the Spaniards failed to gather the support of the population against the invaders. As the lower classes of the city joined the insurgents, the latter could only go along with the unplanned attack of a building in which the principal citizens had hid. Three hundred men inside were killed—Spaniards and creoles alike—while two thousand insurgents died. It was the beginning of unprecedented bloodshed. After capturing the city of Valladolid, the rebels headed for Mexico City but did not enter the capital. This constituted the turning point of the war. Mass desertions began to plague Hidalgo's troops, perhaps due to an effective royal propaganda campaign, before the Spanish forces routed them on November 7. Hidalgo subsequently engaged in pointless violence, ordering or overseeing the execution of over four hundred Spaniards in Guadalajara and Valladolid. It was outside Guadalajara that the insurgents were finally decisively beaten on January 17, 1811. Hidalgo managed to escape, but was caught in late March, and was shot on July 30. His head, along with those of three other leaders, was placed in a metal cage and displayed on the corners of the city's granary, where they hung for the next decade.[79]

The revolution continued in the south of Mexico, where José María Morelos (1765–1815), a supporter of Hidalgo, had begun drafting troops in October 1810. He hated the Spaniards deeply (calling them "the enemies of mankind"), especially the merchants notorious for their monopolistic practices. The son of a mestizo artisan and his creole wife, this mule driver who had worked himself up to the position of parish priest was successful in fighting the Spaniards by moving away from the counterproductive violent approach that Hidalgo had advocated.

By specializing in guerrilla actions, Morelos and his men were able to establish control of the countryside in the south in 1811 and 1812 and to capture the town of Oaxaca. In 1813, Morelos organized elections that led to the formation of a congress, which eventually lost confidence in his leadership after a string of military defeats. No longer the chief executive, Morelos did remain a member of the insurgent leadership until the royalists hunted him down, tried him, and executed him in December 1815. Since popular support failed to keep the flame burning, the independence movement now died out.[80]

The dream of an autonomous New Spain did not fade away, however, and was rekindled in 1820 when an expeditionary force, ready to sail to Buenos Aires to quench the revolution, revolted. The spark of rebellion spread across the Spanish military, forcing Ferdinand to reestablish the Constitution of 1812.[81] Afraid of too large a role for the people in the political process, Mexico's national elite found native son Agustín de Iturbide (1783–1824), a colonel who had battled with the royalist army against both Hidalgo and Morelos, willing to become the leader of an autonomous movement. The plan that they worked out was issued in the village of Iguala on February 24, 1821. It established equality of Mexicans and Spaniards in a new order strongly reminiscent of the old one, thus reassuring the propertied classes. With civil and military leaders divided over the new government and in the face of opposition of the church hierarchy, Iturbide was able to win the town of Puebla over to his side and enter the city in triumph in August 1821.[82] A few days before, captain general Juan O'Donoju had arrived from Spain. Realizing that there would be no return to the old regime, O'Donoju concluded an agreement with Iturbide, recognizing New Spain's independence as a constitutional monarchy, which was confirmed by the ruling junta on September 28. When the Spanish government declined the request for King Ferdinand or a Spanish prince to become the new Mexican sovereign, the Mexican elite pushed Iturbide forward as a candidate. He ruled for two years as emperor before his mistaken belief that the provinces intended to oust him made him decide to abdicate. Iturbide then tried to return from exile, but was captured and shot in 1824.[83]

The Guatemalan elite responded to the Plan of Iguala by declaring independence from Spain (September 15, 1821), but could not persuade the other provinces in the kingdom—Chiapas, Costa Rica, El Salvador,

Honduras, and Nicaragua—to follow her lead. Animosity toward the conservative aristocracy in Guatemala City stood in the way. Most Central American municipalities favored annexation to the Mexican Empire, although liberals were ready to back an independent republican federation. After Iturbide's fall from grace, a congress declared Central America independent on July 1, 1823, under the name United Provinces of the Center of America. Chiapas was the odd province out, remaining within the Mexican nation.[84]

Peru's position during the long period of independence struggles looked most like that of Mexico. As in Mexico City, the creole elite in the viceregal capital of Lima was bent on maintaining the imperial structure intact. If some creole leaders disagreed with Spanish policies, Peru's privileged status in the empire made them demur at the idea of setting up a junta in 1808 and 1810, never mind declaring autonomy. Moreover, Túpac Amaru's rebellion was still too fresh in their memory to consider changes in the status quo. For his part, Viceroy José Fernando de Abascal y Sousa (1743–1827) defended royalist interests in an exemplary way. He did not hesitate to wage war on the junta proclaimed in La Paz, although that city was formally located (since 1776) in the viceroyalty of the Río de la Plata. He did the same in Quito, since 1740 part of the viceroyalty of New Granada. Both juntas disintegrated when the Peruvian soldiers approached. In La Paz, the ringleaders were put to death, while in Quito prison sentences were meted out. A failed attempt to free the prisoners in Quito led to a bloodbath in which many citizens died.[85]

The steep mountains of the Andes guaranteed, however, that Chileans setting up a council in Santiago in September 1810 were initially left alone. For two and a half years the Chileans ruled themselves by means of a congress created by national elections. Then, in March 1813, Abascal dispatched an army to the south of Chile, which was nevertheless unable to defeat the enemy. Another expedition, under the command of Abascal's son-in-law Mariano Osorio, fared better, occupying city after city and finally triumphing in a battle on October 1, 1814. The men whom he defeated fled with their leader, Bernardo O'Higgins (1778–1842).[86]

In the meantime, Peru itself had become the stage of rebellion. In 1814–1815, a coalition in Cuzco of Indians and creoles, led by the cacique Mateo García Pumacahua who aspired to a better treatment of Indians, presented a dangerous challenge to colonial rule, all the more since the lower clergy lent its support. But the movement fell apart when Lima did not join and Abascal refused to negotiate the implementation of the constitution of Cádiz.[87] Conditions improved for those striving for independence after Abascal was succeeded in 1816 by Joaquín de Pezuela. The new viceroy made the mistake of underestimating his adversary, the insurgent commander José de San Martín. Pezuela awoke to reality only when news arrived that the rebel army, four thousand men strong, had crossed the Andes from Mendoza and had started the conquest of Chile. In December, Pezuela sent a force of thirty-six hundred men under Osorio by sea to reconquer Chile, and they were to be joined by two thousand local royalist troops. In spite of Lima's almost infinite trust in Osorio's capacities, San Martín's army triumphed in glorious fashion in the Battle of Maipú (April 5, 1818). Fifteen hundred royalists perished in an encounter that laid the foundation for Chile's independence. The rebels' momentum was sustained when the Chileans captured some of the ships transporting reinforcements from Cádiz, while another ship mutinied. Worse was still to come. The revolt that led to the reinstatement of the Constitution of 1812 in Spain was the work of soldiers who were about to embark for Buenos Aires. They could have been of great use to Pezuela.

Pezuela had quickly made himself hated in Lima. With the viceroyalty cut off from all supplies, he had ignored local protests and authorized free trade, enabling British merchants to flood the market. More serious still, in the view of his officers, was his refusal to abandon Lima to save the viceroyalty, whereas the highlands had the advantage of offering sufficient resources to maintain the war. These were not available in the capital. When San Martín arrived on the Peruvian coast from Chile in September 1820, the patience of Pezuela's men began to run out. In January, they forced him to abdicate, and his troops evacuated the capital city soon afterward. Lima thus fell into the hands of San Martín's army, reinforced by scores of brigands turned guerrillas. This paved the way for an open town council meeting on July 15, 1821, that proclaimed Peru independent. But there were no enthusiastic crowds to greet the proclamation. Only a small group of ambitious lawyers, priests, and professionals had genuinely aspired to self-rule. The rest of the civilian population could not but accept the act of independence.[88]

San Martín took it upon himself to rule the new republic, focusing more on government matters than military tactics. But as an administrator he was not very successful, largely due to factors beyond his control, such as the lack of income that compelled him to dip into local resources, alienating creoles and Spaniards alike. On the military front, San Martín remained very passive, perhaps because of his addiction to opium—prescribed for him to counter the effects of tuberculosis—or perhaps because he expected the independence movement to spread automatically to the rest of Peru. San Martín seems to have realized that he had reached a dead end, for in July 1822, after a meeting with Bolívar in Guayaquil, he decided to leave America.[89] He sailed to Europe, where he would go to his grave in 1850.

It was now up to Bolívar to complete the conquest of Peru. His tactics were the complete opposite of those of San Martín, concentrating as he did on securing the highlands before he would move on to Lima. He realized as well that the Peruvian people were not devoted to either side and would yield only to the most powerful. He decided, moreover, that they would at last pay for the war effort. Bolívar created a new army, recruited and organized by fellow Venezuelan Antonio José de Sucre (1795–1830), sizeable but nowhere near as large as the numbers that Pumacahua had mobilized in 1814–1815. The two men led a force of six thousand Colombians and three thousand Peruvians against royalist troops on the plateau of Junín (August 6, 1824), where the rebels' cavalry made the difference. Three months later, on December 9, an army under Sucre's command defeated the royalists at Ayacucho in a decisive battle. The Spanish general signed an unconditional surrender. After Ayacucho, Sucre captured Upper Peru, declaring it an independent state in February 1825. An assembly met, made up of propertied creoles who had first been royalists, had then pursued autonomy, and now finally embraced independence.[90]

The wars of independence were thus completed in the interior of South America, having begun on opposite ends of the continent.[91] They bypassed the Caribbean colonies of Puerto Rico, Santo Domingo, and Cuba, the latter remaining as the pearl in Spain's crown. One reason, as we have seen, for Cuba's continued allegiance to the Crown was the fear of an uprising like the one in nearby Saint-Domingue. But perhaps of equal importance was that the island's Bourbon reformers had never ignored local interests and sensibilities. Unlike Mexico, for example, Cuba did not have to finance its own defense. Mexicans actually paid for most of the fortifications erected under Charles III, enabling the rapid expansion of Cuba's sugar industry. Nor was the traditional process of accommodation undermined in subsequent years. Although a number of conspiracies revealed dissatisfactions among some groups, Cuba's elite had no reason to abandon its place in the Spanish Empire.[92]

The Dawn of Republicanism

Once the struggle for independence was under way, its ideologues ostracized the Spaniards and their regime. Two of the men who set up the autonomous junta in Bogotá in 1810 explained in a document that the Bourbon reforms had failed. Spanish America, they maintained, was "an immense land where government does not permit the sciences, nor arts, nor agriculture, nor commerce, where schools, factories, industry, and work are lacking, and where people are reduced to a servile state."[93] In Buenos Aires, the president of the Assembly of the United Provinces noted in a speech in 1813 that the despotic regime had humiliated all social classes. Such critics broke with precedent. The charge of despotism had in the past been leveled against unjust alcaldes and corregidores. Now it referred to Spanish governors or authorities in the provincial capitals as well, and by extension to all Spanish government.[94] Finally, a British traveler who resided in Caracas in 1811, the year that Venezuela declared its independence, noticed: "Within these few years [of revolution in Spanish America], a new spirit has arisen in America, which is spreading with the rapidity of a religious fanaticism. I mean an affectation of total independence, as Americans, in every respect, not merely politically, but even to a fastidiousness of acknowledging any obligations to Europe. . . . In numerous and increasing instances, this spirit rises to a species of fanatical hatred against Europeans, who are termed ferocious, cruel, and perfidious, whilst the Americans are magnanimous, mild, and just."[95]

When the insurgencies had succeeded, anti-Spanish policies were enacted into law. Unmarried Spaniards—supposedly lacking ties with the new nations—were expelled from Lima and Mexico City, giving rise to large-scale capital flight. In Lima, which had been home to ten thousand Spaniards only a few years before, only six hundred were left in 1822. Many Spanish natives had been arrested in their beds and deported. In

Caracas, thousands of Spaniards fled after the restoration of the republic in 1813. Those who stayed found themselves in an atmosphere made oppressive by Bolívar's decree of the war to the death. Men were sent to prison, while their wives were forced to prostitute themselves to republican officers or were humiliated by creole women. Nor was such the exclusive fate of *peninsulares* living in the larger cities. In smaller towns such as Santa Marta (New Granada), Spanish-born merchants and landowners were also arrested and their possessions confiscated.[96]

Increasing alienation from Spanish rule led to a marked revision of the past. By 1810, the Black Legend, which imputed to the Spanish an inborn tendency to engage in cruelty and murder, spread with great speed. An Argentine newspaper even extended the Black Legend to Spain itself, which purportedly had once been among Europe's most fertile provinces, but had been turned into a wasteland by the barbaric Spaniards.[97] The more Spain was maligned, the more Indians, subjected, maltreated, and killed by conquering Spaniards in the sixteenth century, were revered. The rhetorical celebration of the Indian past was virtually boundless in the first years of independence. Chile's creoles spoke of "our fathers, the Araucanians," who had successfully resisted Spanish colonialism, and whose government was superior to that of the colonial oppressors. "Araucanian" became a poetic way of saying "Chilean." The leaders of the independent polities in New Granada flirted with Indian symbols, coining money with images of Indian women dressed up with feather crowns, and using native names to replace the old Spanish designations, such as the republic Cundinamarca for the province of Santa Fe. But admiration for the Indian past did not translate into benevolent policies toward contemporary natives. The creoles viewed natives as lazy, filthy, backward, and ignorant, and presented the project to civilize them as an argument for their own self-government. At times, they conveniently referred to three centuries of Spanish oppression to explain the native plight. However, the creoles got caught up in their own propaganda, displaying pride of their conquistador ancestors but singling out the same conquerors for critique when the fate of the Indians was brought up.[98]

In other ways, the creoles broke with tradition. The revolutionaries in Venezuela were the first to embrace the principles of the French Revolution, introducing the title of citizen for all free residents, and eliminating all hereditary titles, even though no decree was passed to that effect. Two years later (1813), the General Assembly of the United Provinces of the Río de la Plata officially ordered the extinction of all titles of counts, marquises, and barons in its territories. In Chile, Central America, and Mexico, where independence was achieved at a later stage, all noble titles were abolished in 1818, 1823, and 1826, respectively. And in Argentina as well as the territories that had once formed New Spain, all public displays of coats of arms had to be removed.[99]

At one point, the spirit of egalitarianism in Buenos Aires even made it obligatory for citizens to incorporate the Phrygian Cap of Liberty into their daily attire.[100] A more lasting example of egalitarianism was the abolition of official ethnic categorization in most of Spanish America. In places like Santa Marta, two separate marriage registers had been kept in colonial days, one for the "whites descending from Spaniards" and the other for "pardos, mestizos, blacks." With the arrival of independence, all weddings in the same parish were recorded in the same book, and the only members marked with a separate designation were the slaves.[101] But radicalism had its limits. At no time did the revolutionaries question the position of women. It is rare to find references to women at all in the newspaper press. One exception was a journalist of the radical Argentine weekly *El Grito del Sud*, who cited a young lady with a complaint about the lack of interest in women's rights. Did not women, she asked, have inalienable rights? Americans, she went on, have promoted the extinction of the African slave trade, but women, who are condemned to live in obscurity and ignorance, are still not seen as worthy individuals.[102]

Popular Participation in the Revolutions

Women were not alone in being excluded from the political process. All over Spanish America, steps were taken to prevent the active participation of the majority of citizens. In most places, property qualifications were high enough to ensure that the vote was reserved for landowners, professionals, civil servants, merchants, and entrepreneurs. There were exceptions. In Paraguay in 1813, all married men and all single men over the age of twenty-three were enfranchised. In Argentina, government minister Bernardino Rivadavia introduced universal suffrage for men in 1821. This law, which remained in the books until 1854, had no census restrictions and effectively lowered the voting age from twenty-five to twenty.[103] Even where such laws were not introduced, the plebeian classes possessed means to exert their influence. Like in the old regime, the mob would continue to intervene in political life.[104] But from a modern perspective, the democratic caliber of the new polities was low, even if formal elections did take place on a regular basis with a large popular participation. A serious obstacle was that the new institutions often did not function properly. And since the old ones had lost their legitimacy, strong men stepped in, attempting to seize power. They were often the product of the wars of independence. In Buenos Aires, for example, the military's stature had grown ever since the militias' patriotic resistance to the British invaders. In the years between 1812 and 1815, the army put its stamp on domestic politics. Although tax hikes led to occasional grumbling, there was no outright hostility toward the army, which was, after all, the country's largest employer with eight thousand jobs for soldiers. Besides, it was the wealthy who paid for the military by means of export duties and extraordinary contributions.[105]

Militarization in rural settings often took the form of *caudillismo*, as it did in Venezuela. "The caudillo," writes historian John Lynch, "was a regional chieftain, deriving his power from control of local resources, especially of haciendas, which gave him access to men and supplies."[106] Simón Bolívar sought to incorporate these warlords into his army as generals or regional commanders. Once independence had been attained, he tried to co-opt the caudillos José Antonio Páez, José Francisco Bermúdez, and Santiago Mariño by assigning them their own area in the country, which was to be at their disposal. Benefiting from the distribution of confiscated lands, these men outlasted Bolívar.[107] Mexico provided a counterpoint to the southern nations. Although the army became the central institution of the new nation, to the point that it was inconceivable that the president would *not* be a general, men who had been propelled into high military rank during the independence wars were few and far between, constituting only 12 out of 118 high-ranking officers by 1840.[108]

The many thousands of men who settled the fate of Spanish America on the battlefields did not benefit from the prominent position of the army in the independent regimes. In the end, the creole elites (or rather certain factions of these elites) were victorious in the independence wars, albeit only due to the recruitment of plebeian soldiers, in particular nonwhites. By themselves, the creole rebels would never have been able to defeat the Spaniards. If, as one author has argued, the six thousand European volunteers enlisting in Bolívar's armies (usually veterans of the Napoleonic Wars) are an appreciable number, given that military engagements rarely saw more than three thousand men on either side, it should be underscored that nonwhites decided the independence wars in the favor of the creoles.[109]

Historian Brian Hamnett has usefully summed up the plebeians who participated in the independence wars. They ranged "from local proprietors, ranchers and peasant farmers, muleteers, hacienda-overseers, artisans, Indian *caciques* and community peasants, blacks (free or enslaved), mulattoes or 'pardos,' to various professional categories (lay, clerical, or military) at the local level." In several parts of Spanish America, autonomous bands fighting under their own leaders complicated the picture of war fought between revolutionary and royalist armies. Uninterested in both the royalist and rebel war objectives, plebeians in Chile had struck out on their own, combining a tradition of banditry with the pursuit of their own goals. Partly in response to harsh attempts by the creoles to keep them in check, they began to actively fight the independence movement. Elsewhere, either side managed to temporarily co-opt potentially autonomous guerrillas or bandits.[110]

The plebeians usually had specific reasons to fight for—or oppose—independence. For example, José Artigas was able to raise an army in the Banda Oriental after a viceregal decree of 1810 had alienated many rural dwellers from the Spanish Crown. Landed property was largely controlled by a small elite residing in Montevideo and Buenos Aires, many of them Spaniards, who had started to evict (creole) squatters in the closing years of the eighteenth century. The decree of 1810 added insult to injury, as it introduced a tax for all landholders who could not produce proof of their property.[111]

Fighting under the banner of independence was no obvious choice for the nonwhite groups. The Indians of Pasto (New Granada) were devoted to the royalists throughout the independence wars, not because of a principled preference for Spanish rule, but because they felt that the colonial regime guaranteed their autonomy and were assured by the reduction of their tribute. The natives of Charcas in Upper Peru pursued alliances with both warring factions in their attempt to preserve their lands and keep their autonomy. Most Spanish American nonwhites were probably indifferent to the outcome of the wars of independence, although the republicans did not ingratiate themselves with native groups, in New Granada and elsewhere, by destroying their lands in the course of the wars. Secessionist army commanders may have tried to lure the natives with promises, the actual conduct of insurgent armies often persuaded natives to remain passive, as in Upper Peru, where the Argentine army in retreat had pillaged Indian lands.[112]

Still, Spanish officers were able to fill their ranks with Indians and other nonwhites, who had to replace the countless troops from Spain who had fallen victim to malaria and yellow fever. By late 1818, the royal troops in Venezuela were made up of three thousand Europeans and ten thousand "Americans," the latter almost exclusively Indians, mulattoes, blacks, and zambos (persons of mixed Indian and black descent). Natives also formed a major part of the Spanish armies in New Granada. Most of the eight hundred men who died on the side of the royalists at the battle of San Juan de Ciénaga (November 10, 1820) were Indians who lived in the town by the same name.[113] In Mexico, however, Indians, who made up 60 percent of the population, usually chose the "patriot" side, accounting for 55 percent of the insurgent soldiers in the years 1810 to 1816. Economic reasons underlay the participation of Indians in the insurgency. Great changes had occurred since small holdings had begun to make way for larger estates and Indian villages for haciendas in the eighteenth century. Agricultural productivity declined while hunger and scarcity increasingly tormented the native Mexicans. On top of that, a manifold crisis erupted from 1808 to 1811, reminiscent of that in France at the end of the 1780s. Hunger and unemployment thus accounted for the participation in the revolution of many rural dwellers, who happened to be Indians. Subsequently new forms of economic dislocation, spawned by the war itself, led to fresh enlistments as the 1810s unfolded. But unlike some other groups participating in the revolutionary armies in Spanish America, Mexican Indians did so close to home, intent on safeguarding the integrity of their home communities.[114]

Also fighting on the side of Spanish America's rebels were free blacks and "mulattoes" (often more a social than ethnic designation), many of them with a military background. Free blacks from Caracas, thwarted by the *mantuanos* in all their efforts to claim equality with whites, were eager to fight in the royalist armies. One of the three battalions founded by Spanish army leader Pablo Morillo in 1815 was called *Pardos de Caracas*. It was destroyed in the Battle of Boyacá and only 266 men survived. Many soldiers serving in another battalion, formed at the same occasion and also composed of free blacks, died as well at Boyacá.[115]

In areas where people of African descent predominated, they tended to form a majority in the militia companies, as they did in Arequipa, Lima, and Guayaquil. In the Banda Oriental, Artigas's program, which promised a plot of land to every free black, zambo, Indian, and poor creole, drew many members of these groups to his side.[116] In Mexico, as many as five provincial companies of *pardo* (free mulatto) and *moreno* (free black) militias joined Morelos in Acapulco, enabling the former priest to take control of the Pacific lowlands. The free blacks and mulattoes in his ranks, who worked as sharecroppers, peasants, and small-scale cotton farmers, resented the extent to which *peninsulares* controlled the cotton trade. They had probably also suffered from the increasing fiscal demands in recent years. Many blacks and mulattoes next joined the mule-train driver Vicente Guerrero (1782–1831), who was, like Morelos, of African and Indian ancestry and who maintained the revolutionary momentum after Morelos's death. The goal that he fought for was equal rights for nonwhites and nothing less. In the southeastern area that coincides with the state that now bears his name, Guerrero's guerrilla war enabled him to establish civilian rule in 1818 and elevate nonwhites to office. Significantly, the largest population group in the areas that Morelos and Guerrero controlled along the Atlantic and Pacific coasts and in Oaxaca was Afro-Mexicans. It was Guerrero who managed to persuade Iturbide to include a clause in the Iguala Plan to end the caste system.[117]

It would be wrong to assume on the basis of the foregoing that free people of color entered the independence movement only after being swayed by creoles. The story of Pedro Romero reveals that they sometimes took the initiative to act against Spanish rule. Born in Matanzas, Cuba, Romero settled as an artisan in Getsemaní, the largest neighborhood of Cartagena de Indias, home to many black and mulatto artisans, most of whom were members of the pardo militias.[118] In 1810, he requested that the Crown grant his eldest son dispensation in order to take up university studies despite his being a mulatto. Before he could even have received a response, creole rebels ousted Cartagena's newly arrived Spanish governor and set up a junta. On November 11, 1811, Romero led the mulattoes and blacks from Getsemaní to storm an arms depot, before they invaded the junta meeting with lances, guns, and daggers, and forced the council to declare Cartagena's independence. Their demand to have black officers command black militias, however, fell short of a majority in the creole junta.[119]

The fugitive slaves and their descendants who formed the bulk of the *llaneros* of Venezuela initially chose the royalist side. Their decision was only natural in light of the feud that had developed between them and the *mantuano* elite in Caracas, who wanted to assert their control over the vast cattle zone of the *llanos*, which the *llaneros* considered their patrimony. In 1813, Boves won them over to the royalist cause, utilizing their capacities as horsemen. With the *llaneros* as lancers, Boves built his army around the cavalry. The *llaneros* were attracted not simply by the war against Caracas, but also by Boves's promise to redistribute the aristocracy's land among them. His pursuit of black equality they saw confirmed in the elevation of pardos to officer posts. After Boves's death in battle in December 1814, Simón Bolívar managed to get the *llaneros* on his side, mainly because they did not want to abandon their pillaging lifestyle after Morillo had refused to incorporate them into his army.[120]

If the British invasions of 1806 and 1807 had seen free blacks and slaves in Buenos Aires take up arms alongside creole militiamen, the same men went on to fight in the independence wars. Free blacks and mulattoes made up an infantry regiment and a battalion that clashed with the royalists in a number of battles, but they were exterminated in 1815 at Sipe-Sipe in the pampas of Upper Peru. Slaves from the viceregal capital formed another infantry battalion, which the government created by decreeing that masters sell a certain proportion of their able-bodied enslaved blacks. These men were automatically granted their freedom upon entering the army, although they could not enjoy their freedom until the end of their service. Still, few slaves protested against this draft. In the province of Cuyo, San Martín added another three thousand slaves to his army that helped him in his conquest of Chile, many of them natives of Kongo and Guinea.[121]

Most of these soldiers were no longer alive when San Martín entered Lima in triumph in July 1821, having died in battle or deserted.[122] Their posts were filled by slaves from Peru's coastal haciendas, none of whom would ever enjoy real freedom despite the promises of San Martín and his recruiters. Even those who left slavery behind were at best forced to remain with their masters in conditions resembling slavery. Others were reenslaved after the war came to an end.[123]

In Venezuela, meanwhile, the revolutionaries resorted to arming slaves only once the First Republic was in jeopardy. In May 1812, Miranda proclaimed the general enlistment of slaves, who would receive their freedom after ten years of service, a term soon shortened to four years. The decree did much to turn part of the elite against the regime, but even more importantly it had an adverse effect on the enslaved population. Perhaps because Archbishop Coll y Prat instructed the parish priests to ignore the decree and instead have the slaves fight for king and religion, blacks in the eastern valleys and coastal areas rose in rebellion and resorted to vandalism and murder. Their actions helped bring down the republican order.[124]

By the time the Venezuelan rebels began using slave soldiers again, four years later, the decision was partly prompted by Bolívar's desire to fulfill his promise to Haitian president Alexandre Pétion to emancipate Venezuela's slaves. But there was also a very practical motivation: there were too few creole volunteers to do the job. Besides, he feared that maintaining slavery would eventually lead to rebellion or even extermination as in Saint-Domingue. In June 1816, Bolívar decreed freedom for all male slaves bearing arms in patriot ranks. One month later, he failed in his attack on the capital city, but did attract new numbers of blacks by proclaiming total and unconditional freedom.[125] Like in Peru, the royalists vied with the rebels over slave recruitments. As one historian explains: "The slaves drafted by the Royalists and Republicans entered the armies in a variety of ways. Sometimes they would join after a commander had promulgated a decree. Other times runaway slaves joined an army to escape capture and punishment. Patriot bands often picked up slaves from plantations as they passed by."[126] After the Spanish defeat in Venezuela in 1822, blacks who had fought on the royalist side voluntarily enlisted in the victorious army. Their new battalion took part in the subsequent conquest of Peru.[127]

Slaves on both sides enlisted in the first place, hoping to attain personal freedom. However dangerous, active service was perhaps the most realistic way to strive for freedom. But once the wars were over, many slave soldiers and other nonwhites found that they had achieved very little. In Cartagena, where blacks and mulattoes had led the effort for independence and where they controlled key positions by 1815, Governor Pedro Gual disarmed them—even before warfare with Morillo's troops had ended—after reaching an agreement with the creole commander of the army and Venezuelan and French officers. More than eighty popular leaders and activists, including no small number of blacks, were imprisoned and then exiled from the city. Pedro Romero would die of hunger in Haiti, while most men and women of African descent did not fare much better. Along with the other residents, they perished in the siege laid by Pablo Morillo, which led to a plague that caused the deaths of seven thousand people.[128]

Free blacks and mulattoes who demanded the equality to which they were formally entitled under the new regime were kept at arm's length in independent Gran Colombia. The government chose to blame pardo activists for spreading discord and jeopardizing the nation's unity. The rise of pardos to positions of authority was thus nipped in the bud, as the authorities defused imputations of racial discrimination by accusing the pardos of racial enmity and by spreading rumors about impending racial warfare. How real the fear of *pardocracia* (black rule) was is suggested by the belief among congressmen and spokesmen that the government of Haiti was trying to pit blacks against whites in Venezuela, where it was said to have sent three hundred secret agents.[129]

In keeping with their fear of black power, the republican regimes moved very cautiously toward abolition of slavery. The issue first came up in the Cortes of Cádiz in March 1811, when Miguel Guridi y Alcocer, a deputy from Tlaxcala, Mexico, proposed that they forbid the slave trade, grant children born of slaves their freedom, and pay the remaining slaves for their services (albeit not as much as free people). This proposal caused so much controversy that the subject would not be raised again in the Cortes.[130] A few months later, Chile adopted a law along the lines of Guridi's proposal, but it remained a dead issue until the so-called Law of the Free Womb was reestablished in 1818. Similar legislation, providing for the freedom of all children born of slave mothers, was introduced in Argentina, Venezuela, and Paraguay.[131] Everywhere, at least on paper, the slave regime was tempered. In Peru, for example, a new slave code established that a slave would never receive more than twelve lashes, with complete exemption for women over the age of fourteen and men over fifty or with children over fourteen.[132] Chile led the way in the complete abolition (in 1823) of the "peculiar institution," followed by Central America (1825), Mexico (1829), Uruguay (1846), Colombia (1850), Argentina (1853), Peru (1854), Venezuela (1854), and finally Paraguay (1870). Abolition came later in the colonies that remained in Spanish hands: in Puerto Rico it arrived in 1873 and in Cuba in 1886.

The new regimes were not hesitant about extending freedom and equality to Indians, after the Cortes of Cádiz had set a good example. But Indians themselves were, as in Mexico, "famously unimpressed with their newfound equality, an irrelevant abstraction at best."[133] The elimination of their communities by the Cortes had made Indians protest the unilateral termination of an age-old social pact and lose faith in the old regime. Nor were they satisfied with the new regimes, in which senior political and military posts remained out of their reach. Besides, tribute was often reintroduced, as in Gran Colombia (1828), where Bolívar used the euphemism "personal contribution." In practice, the main consequence of Indian "equality" was the distribution of Indian community lands, which the natives fought tooth and nail, and the loss of the legal protection that they had enjoyed.[134] Their struggle for independence continued.

The Bourbon reforms have often been presented as the root cause of the independence movements in Spanish America. The reforms, seen as arbitrary innovations at the cost of creole officeholders and taxpayers, are supposed to have made rebels of the creole elites. That position is untenable. The colonies hardest hit by the reforms, at least financially, were Mexico and Peru, which remained largely faithful to the Spanish Crown throughout the revolutionary period. By contrast, areas that had benefited from the Bourbon reforms, in particular Venezuela and Buenos Aires, led the movement for independence. By stimulating the production of cash crops rather than precious metals, Bourbon policymakers unwittingly encouraged the emergence of new creole elites, which were as impatient as their crops were perishable. The vulnerability of Spain during the Napoleonic Wars and under French occupation made them question the wisdom of remaining within the empire. At the same time, the disappearance of the monarch—who had traditionally provided the glue in an empire made up of numerous heterogeneous zones—set in motion unanticipated chains of events that often ended in independence.

The course of the wars and the timing of independence depended as much on developments in the colonies themselves as on those in the mother country. The debates in Cádiz and the resulting constitution, Ferdinand's uncompromising policies upon his return to the throne, and the reintroduction of the Cádiz constitution in 1820 all helped shape the American revolutions, conditioning both their course and success.

Instead of pitting large Spanish armies against American-born soldiers, the wars were largely civil wars, fought by a variety of local plebeians hired by both sides and often taking up arms for their own reasons. Most of them were disappointed by what the new regimes had in store for them. The new leadership, it turned out, was bent more on consolidating its own position than on sharing power with the rank and file. And although most states were undoubtedly more democratic than their imperial forebears, new institutions often functioned poorly while those from the colonial era had lost legitimacy. The vacuum was filled by caudillos and the military, who made short shrift of the large confederations that had been the product of independence in Gran Colombia, Central America, and the Río de la Plata.

6

The Revolutions Compared

Causes, Patterns, Legacies

Seismic waves traveled through the Atlantic world in the half century after 1775, linking uprisings on either side of the Atlantic. Divergent as they were, each was a revolution in its own right. This chapter compares the revolutions by establishing the main similarities and differences. Their chief common features can be summarized as follows.

1. *The revolutions must be understood, first of all, in the context of international politics.* The costs of the Seven Years' War led to a dramatic increase of taxation in British North America, and, combined with the War of American Independence, induced the French king to call for a meeting of the Estates General. Both the Thirteen Colonies and France were thus brought to the brink of revolution. What paved the way for the Spanish American revolutions was not a war, but Napoleon's imprisonment of the Spanish king. International politics not only created the conditions, but also helped the insurgents succeed or made the eventual victory a hard-fought one. French aid to the North American rebels was as much motivated by power politics as Britain's decision to stay out of the Spanish American wars and the expedition of soldiers by Britain and Spain to revolutionary Saint-Domingue. The presence of these soldiers in the French colony was an important factor in bringing about the local abolition of slavery. It also acted as a catalyst for the ultimate drive to Haitian independence.

2. *The revolts were not foreordained. They could have been prevented, derailed, or postponed.* What is missing from the standard accounts of revolutionary upheaval is the element of contingency. Overthrow of the old regime was not even necessarily the *initial* goal of the aggrieved. As Hannah Arendt has reminded us, it "was only in the course of the eighteenth-century revolutions that men began to be aware that a new beginning could be a political phenomenon, that it could be the

result of what men had done and what they could consciously set out to do."[1]

The revolutions did not get a chance unless imperial stability was lost. Political scientists have argued for three key conditions for state stability: (a) rulers who are widely perceived as both effective and just; (b) elites who are unified and loyal to the regime; and (c) a population that is guaranteed a customary living standard. When these conditions of stability are simultaneously lost, a revolutionary situation is in the making.[2]

The first of these conditions, the perception of a just and effective ruler, was shared by North Americans through the Seven Years' War. The Thirteen Colonies kept their trust in King George III until it became clear that he supported the sweeping fiscal measures Parliament adopted in the wake of the war. When the king had lost his aura as a just ruler, it was only a matter of time before he was depicted as the "Royal Brute of Britain," as Thomas Paine called him. The problem of French King Louis XVI was not so much that he was seen as unjust. His predicament was his lack of effectiveness and the erosion of his legitimacy. Having been the traditional center of politics, Louis was no longer the sole political force to be reckoned with in the 1780s, when both the *parlements* and an almost unrestricted public opinion asserted themselves. The summoning of the Estates General in 1788 only served to confirm that France faced a power vacuum.[3] Spanish America was confronted with a power vacuum when Napoleon imprisoned King Ferdinand VII, thus removing the ultimate imperial arbiter of conflicts and, since the Americans believed that not Spain but the king ruled their provinces, eliminating the cement that held together the Spanish monarchy. Ferdinand's return to the throne in 1814 shattered the illusions of those who had kept their faith in him. The monarch revealed himself as an intransigent man, averse to any political reforms.

Apart from the king's perceived loss of legitimacy or effectiveness or his outright disappearance from the scene, the breakdown of the old regimes was also brought about by elites turning partly or entirely against the state. In France, the representatives of the First and Second Estates joined with the Third Estate and formed a new national assembly, thus symbolically and effectively ending a regime based on privilege. Besides, local elites all over France, who had collided with the king on numerous past occasions, showed allegiance to the new order. In Spanish America, urban elites everywhere assumed self-rule while maintaining loyalty to the jailed king (or preserving its myth).

However inspired they were to put an end to existing polities, rebel leaders could not win the struggle by themselves. And how they were able to form cross-class alliances is explained in the first place by the failure of the state to maintain traditional living standards. France offers the most convincing example here. Not only did the disposable incomes decline in the two years before the revolution, fiscal policies, natural catastrophes, industrial recession, and the rising price of grain created a large army of poor and hungry subjects. Likewise, many Indians joining the first stage of the revolution in Mexico were reduced to hunger and employment, while others enlisted in the years ahead, as the war kept producing new forms of deprivation.

The forging of new loyalties occurred as groups with a revolutionary agenda attracted broad popular support. Four reasons can be listed for this successful mobilization:[4]

(a) *State sponsorship or protection of unpopular economic and social arrangements, leading to the politicization of grievances.* The unpopular arrangement upheld by the state in Saint-Domingue was obviously chattel slavery, a fate shared by eight out of every nine residents. Other examples are the repeated attempts by the British government to raise revenue by introducing new taxes in North America and similar endeavors by French ministers. Colonial elites objected to the official prohibition of most forms of international trade, condemned by the authorities as "smuggling."

(b) *Exclusion of mobilized groups from state power or resources.* If such systematic debarment had not existed and the oppressed groups had been able to establish a form of power-sharing (or had believed that possible), they would not have tried to overthrow the state. While Saint-Domingue's slaves had everything to fight for, the French Third Estate and Spanish Americans resented their unequal representation in the Estates General and the Cortes of Cádiz just as much as British Americans were upset about taxation without representation.

(c) *Weak policing capacities.* Areas where a large number of troops were stationed generally saw little rebelliousness. Where armies or militias were smaller, revolts were more likely to occur. A high correlation has been observed, for example, between reduced garrison strength and slave revolt in the Caribbean between 1789 and 1815. In France, towns all over the border areas of Alsace, Lorraine, Flanders, and Picardie had garrisons that ensured that the revolution would face no serious opposition in these war zones. The Vendée, by contrast, had few troops. The difference in deterrence also helps explain why independence revolts in Mexico were concentrated in the countryside, since every major city and town had permanent garrisons of soldiers and militia as well as widespread police surveillance.[5] Although the first Stamp Act riots broke out in places where no British troops were stationed, this line of reasoning fails to account for the outbreak of the American Revolution in New England, precisely the area where a vast number of redcoats were posted. The troops who arrived in 1768 may have initially formed one-fifth of Boston's population; by 1775 they formed the majority of the population.[6]

(d) *Random state violence against mobilized groups, reinforcing the plausibility and diffusion of a revolutionary ideology.* While the Boston Massacre convinced many New Englanders of the old regime's moral bankruptcy, patriots also presented the burning of Norfolk, Virginia, in the first days of 1776 as a shocking example of what the British were capable of doing, even though Virginia soldiers, not their British foes, had done most damage to the town.[7] It actually seems that the use of indiscriminate violence did more to recruit supporters for the revolutionary cause once warfare was under way. The violence used by British soldiers against American individuals and towns convinced many a Philadelphian to enlist with the "Patriots," just like the ruthless actions of the Spanish army in Venezuela persuaded many local fence-sitters to join the insurgents.[8]

The crisis of national or imperial legitimacy therefore did not in itself lead to insurgencies. That happened only when the regime's leadership exacerbated the situation. French king Louis XVI made a fatal error when he fired his reformist ministers and replaced them with a hard-line cabinet on July 11, 1789. The British ministry overreacted to the Boston Tea Party by closing Boston Harbor, altering the Massachusetts charter, and occupying the town with British troops. Similarly, in South America, as one historian has put it, "[a]nticolonial identities emerged in response to the ways in which loyalists handled the crisis of imperial sovereignty . . . new identities did not precede and motivate political change."[9] It was under these conditions that men and women began to join the revolutionary cause, persuaded by the passionate messages conveyed by the likes of Thomas Paine and abbé Sieyès, authors who exposed the corrupt foundations of the monarchies they attacked. And yet, even at this stage, many were not convinced of the need for a regime change, especially in British North America. Loyalism was far more significant a movement than the counterrevolution would ever be in revolutionary France, even during the heyday of Jacobin Terror. Historian R. R. Palmer established that emigration from revolutionary America was much higher than it was for revolutionary France: twenty-four émigrés per thousand in America, five per thousand in France.[10]

Support of and resentment about metropolitan policies incorporated long-standing issues that were often of a purely local nature. Preexisting disputes frequently accounted for the decision to oppose or remain faithful to the old regime.[11] The Banda Oriental and the interior provinces of the Río de la Plata, Paraguay, and Upper Peru, all desirous of more autonomy, opposed Buenos Aires when the viceregal capital embarked on its revolution. Similarly, the Venezuelan towns of Coro and Maracaibo refused to side with rebellious Caracas.[12] In the Spanish American republics and in France, small towns adopted an egalitarian rhetoric in hopes of gaining power and status at a time when new administrative capitals were created. In these secondary towns, resentment had been building, often for generations, about the neglect shown by the capital cities, the lack of consultation, and the refusal of the Crown to grant them their own privileges and governing bodies.[13]

Preference for the Patriot or Loyalist cause in the Thirteen Colonies could be also determined by enduring controversies independent of the revolution. In western Queens County (New York), many Anglicans joined the Loyalist cause to protect the privileged position of their church. In response, many Presbyterians became Whigs. In Virginia's Eastern Shore, the Presbyterians first declared their allegiance and the Anglicans responded, but the outcomes were the same as in Queens County.[14] When the revolution came to New York and New Jersey, a schism in the Dutch Reformed Church already divided the population of some towns into two camps. When one side declared itself for the Patriots, the other inevitably joined the Loyalists. In the Albany (New York) area, hostility toward New England created devotion to Loyalism, and in the South Carolina backcountry, the dedication of Cherokees and banditti to Britain convinced their traditional foes to join the patriots.[15]

3. *Warfare often meant civil war, pitting countrymen against each other. The main actors in these revolutionary dramas were previously voiceless subaltern classes fighting for their own reasons, which often did not square with those of the elites. In France the sans-culottes carried the revolution forward, and in the Americas, where race and class usually coincided, nonwhites (Indians, mestizos, blacks, mulattoes) helped shape the revolutions—and the counterrevolutions.* The revolutions often turned into bloody civil wars that descended into a dialectic of violence and counterviolence, as both revolutionaries and their opponents took vengeance for acts committed by the other side or out of fear for the imminence of such acts.[16] During France's Terror, the "military Vendée" alone mourned the killing of perhaps a quarter million people. In the Americas, there was a distinct ethnic component to the scores that were settled, especially in Haiti, which lost a quarter of its people, most of whom were killed. Venezuela also lost an astounding number of its inhabitants. A royalist wrote in 1814 that towns populated by thousands of inhabitants had been reduced to a few hundred or even a few dozen. Roads and fields were littered with unburied corpses, and agriculture had been entirely abandoned.[17] The amount of violence in the American Revolutionary War may have been relatively small, but it was still disproportionate in the Indian backcountry, where settlers used revolutionary slogans to fight a bloody war against natives.

Ordinary people carried the revolutions forward in cross-class alliances that, as we have seen, were key to the dismantling of the old regimes. If the sans-culottes were a crucial factor in the French Revolution, their New World counterparts were commonly Indians, mestizos, blacks, and mulattoes. These plebeians pursued their agendas, as did the free people of color who used the revolutions to press for equal rights. In Saint-Domingue they protested their exclusion from the assemblies that named deputies to the National Assembly in Paris, and in Peru they demanded the right to vote and to be eligible for election to the Cortes of Cádiz.[18] In New England, where free blacks were too small in number to constitute an interest group of their own, they argued on behalf of their slave brothers and sisters, stressing the incompatibility of slavery with the rights of man.

One lesson revolutionary leaders in the Spanish colonies could learn from the protest movements against the Bourbon reforms in the 1780s was that coalitions with popular classes were effective. The leaders of Venezuela's first two republics paid heavily for their refusal to enlist slaves during four years of intensive warfare with the Spanish troops, in spite of the large numbers of slaves. Argentine general San Martín was more pragmatic as he prepared for his Chilean campaign. Two out of every three recruits were blacks, enslaved or free. Without their contribution, there simply would have been no rebel army.[19]

Incorporating men of African descent into their armies was not a logical choice for the revolting American elites. Concern about a possible slave uprising actually motivated numerous slaveholders, especially in regions that were home to slave societies rather than societies with slaves, to join the revolution in the first place. In South Carolina, where planters had been content under the old regime, it happened only when social disorder threatened. These men stood in such fear of a revolt from below that even during the menacing advance of the British army in 1779, the state's House of Representatives refused to assign slave soldiers to the defense. Arming slaves might come back to haunt them, they thought.[20]

Saint-Domingue's white elite turned against the French metropolitan state when it felt that black subordination was in jeopardy. After the French Revolution had reinforced the planters' craving for autonomy, the Assembly in Paris met virtually all their wishes, but the decree of May 15, 1791, which granted civil rights to some mulatto taxpayers, alienated the colonial elite from the metropolis. Slaveholders saw mulatto subordination as integral to the preservation of a society based on slave labor. Any concession to descendants of slaves could spark a slave revolt.

Slaves did not merely join one of the warring factions, but often started their own rebellion aimed at self-liberation. When did slaves rebel? The catalyst for the revolutionary uprising of Saint-Domingue's slaves was a persistent and widespread rumor.[21] They believed that the king or the Assembly in Paris had decreed their freedom but that colonial authorities withheld it.[22] The start of the revolution may have been related to the French decree that enfranchised some mulattoes. Rumors about an imagined emancipation decree had also surfaced in the early stages of the rift between Britain and the Thirteen Colonies, probably the effect of Governor Dunmore's threat to ally with slaves. One black slave in South Carolina alleged in July 1775 that he had heard a white prisoner say that the young king, George III, "was about to alter the world and set the Negroes free."[23] Anti-slavery proposals in France, Spain, Britain, and the United States also rallied slaves into action. In the most common version of the rumor, the king had abolished slavery, but local planters or governors blocked the measure. In some versions, slaves were not to be freed completely, but granted three or more freed days per week. In 1790, frustration about what slaves saw as obstructed emancipation decrees led to minor revolts in Venezuela, Cuba, and the small Caribbean island of Tortola. The rumors appeared elsewhere in subsequent years.[24] In 1795, the largest revolt in its history rocked the Dutch Caribbean island of Curaçao. Slaves assumed that after the successful invasion of a French army of the Dutch Republic, earlier that year, the emancipation issued for slaves in French colonies would extend to their island.[25] In the Spanish colonies, a decree issued by King Charles IV in 1789 had far-reaching implications, as it regulated the treatment slaves were to receive from their masters, stipulating that owners should allow slaves to interrupt their work to spend two hours each day on their own provision grounds. In Venezuela, this code resuscitated the conviction, which had been dormant for decades, that the king had issued a decree that implied immediate freedom for all slaves. Blacks took the news about the code as a confirmation of their belief. Slaveholders from various colonies succeeded in repealing the code in 1794, no doubt dreading a Haiti-like uprising.[26]

In the early nineteenth century, the debates in the Spanish Cortes and the constitution of Cádiz they spawned reinforced such rumors. Despite the fact that the king had been ousted four years before, it was he who was credited once again with granting the slaves their freedom. In some instances, though, a foreign king was mentioned as the author of the emancipation decree. Slaves of the Kongo nation in Cuba referred to the king of Kongo, who had allegedly sent letters to the island ordering the slaves' freedom.[27] Haiti was also frequently reported to be the wellspring of the decree. As late as the 1820s and 1830s, rumors were floating around about conspiracies planned from Haiti that aimed to end slavery in New World colonies.[28]

4. *Whether they took place in slave societies, in societies with slaves, or in those without, none of the revolutions aimed at creating a democratic society. The chief objective of revolutionary leaders was sovereignty, and the nature of postrevolutionary rule was usually authoritarian.* French philosophe Jean d'Alembert's distinction between "the truly enlightened public" and "the blind and noisy multitude" was echoed by revolutionary leaders. The first U.S. president never considered the revolution that he had led as one that destroyed privilege and deference. It was a political revolt first and foremost.[29] For their part, Spanish American critics of the French Revolution denounced the democracy and excessive freedom associated with Jacobin rule. Liberty, "that salutary and aromatic balsam," had the tendency to inebriate, allowing democracy to degenerate into "anarchy," the exact opposite of time-honored hierarchy.[30]

Nevertheless, democratic practices were introduced during the revolutionary years, although they often did not last. In the United States, already democratized to an extraordinary degree in colonial days, the vote was further extended after the revolution. The French constitution of 1791 gave about two-thirds of all males over twenty-five years of age the vote in the primary electoral assemblies, and another constitution, adopted two years later, was the first anywhere in the world to abolish all tax and wealth requirements for male voters, but it never went into effect.[31] The democratic character of both constitutions was, however, moderated by the eligibility of only 12 percent of the electorate to public office. In Spanish America, the overwhelming majority of male residents could cast their vote not in the wake of independence, but during the imperial crisis that had started with the king's imprisonment. In the years 1813 and 1814, they elected delegates to the imperial legislature in Cádiz. But once independence was achieved, the lower classes were again denied suffrage.[32]

Women were not included among the newly enfranchised, despite their often heroic contributions to the revolutions. Olympe de Gouges cried out in one of her plays: "O my poor sex! O women who have gained nothing from the Revolution!" If most enlightened thinkers prior to the age of revolutions had viewed education as the logical consequence of the extension of equality to all males, revolutionaries were at most willing to concede that female education should be introduced or expanded. Women's political rights did not come up for discussion. They certainly did not in Haiti, whose leaders had an aversion to *any* form of democracy. Authoritarianism was the rule there. But if Haiti's case is extreme, most other revolutions also failed to produce a democracy marked by regular elections. As one historian has observed: "Insurrection, civil war, and *coups d'état* proved more important than elections in determining the course of revolutionary politics."[33]

The threat of tyranny also reared its head everywhere. Some North American revolutionaries discerned the specter of dictatorship, accusing Washington of attempting to prolong the war in order to maintain his position as the new uncrowned head of government. His preference for a standing army over militias also seemed to point in the direction of a monarchical future. Various officers openly declared themselves for Washington assuming royal powers, arguing that the republican experiment was bound to fail.[34] Washington declined, preferring the role of lawgiver to that of dictator. The monarchical element was not missing, however, from the U.S. Constitution. Although the Founding Fathers eschewed kingly rule, the wide powers that the Constitution granted to the president derived from the example of the British monarchs.[35]

Rousseau had imagined the dictator as a supreme lawgiver. He identified as a serious problem that people had to be virtuous if they were to accept the proper laws, while in actual fact they lacked morality. To become virtuous citizens, they had to live under the very laws that they now rejected. This called for a gifted lawgiver to break the circle.[36] Like Machiavelli, Rousseau believed that there was no limit to what this lawgiver could do. He had to be entrusted with building a new state while instilling the new virtues in his population. Both could cite famous examples from Classical Antiquity: Lycurgus in Sparta, Draco and later Solon in Athens. James Madison (1751–1836), the principal author of the U.S. Constitution, found it surprising that the ancient Greeks had entrusted so much power to a single man. The only explanation he saw was that "the fears of discord and disunion among a number of counsellors exceeded the apprehension of treachery or incapacity in a single individual."[37] John Adams, on the other hand, compared the situation in which the Founding Fathers found themselves with that of Lycurgus, Solon, and a thousand other legislators in history. They were starting a political experiment that, unfortunately, "cannot be made in a laboratory, nor determined in a few hours. The operation once begun, runs over whole quarters of the globe, and is not finished in many thousands of years." Hence the need to adopt the right, balanced, constitution.[38]

By contrast with the United States, the revolution in France *did* evolve from monarchy to the rule of a dictator when Napoleon made himself the undisputed leader of France. While it seems an incongruous trajectory, there was some logic to it, as revealed in the letters of bookseller Nicolas Ruault. The editor of Beaumarchais and Voltaire and correspondent of Benjamin Franklin, Ruault was a typical representative of the Enlightenment. In a letter to his brother, he joyously reported the storming of the Bastille. He joined a Jacobin club, but refrained from radicalism, opposing republicanism from the outset. After the invasion of the royal palace in 1792, he lamented that "nothing is more baneful for a people than regime changes." Are not we as Frenchmen, he wondered, too much accustomed to the monarchy, are we capable of being republicans, are we not too flawed to subject ourselves to a completely democratic republic? Ruault's enthusiasm for the revolution reached a low before his interest in politics returned, but he made no secret of his dissatisfaction with the Directory, writing in 1795 about the 700 legislators: "The great art of founding a republic in the center of our old Europe consists in making rich and poor walk together, freely, by common consent. But this art is not found in 700 heads of those who compose the laws; it is found in one only. Seven hundred assembled poets will not make a good epic poem, just as little as seven hundred painters can make a beautiful and grand painting. A great masterpiece, of whatever kind, cannot be the work of several men, since it would lack uniformity and unity. . . . We have to find a Lycurgus or a Solon, a Franklin, and trust him with making us this political masterpiece."[39]

Always the student of Rousseau, Simón Bolívar maintained that history showed that men submitted to the rule of a capable lawgiver and tried to effect change by means of constitutions.[40] He believed that individuals obeyed only their own interests and wondered how to fill the moral void left by a church that had been forced to retreat from its prominent position in society.[41] In 1819, therefore, he proposed a Moral Power alongside the executive, legislative, and judicial powers. The two chambers constituting this power, one of Morality and one of Education, were to keep a watch on public behavior, reward virtue, castigate vice, and propagate simple rules for the upbringing of young children.

Laurel wreaths would crown moral "champions" at annual popular festivals. Similarly, the Chilean constitution of 1823 provided for the preparation of a moral code that would "detail the duties of the citizen in all the periods of his life and in all the states of society, creating his habits, activities, duties, public instructions, rituals, and pleasures, all of which transform laws into customs and customs into civic and moral virtues."[42] Such attempts at social engineering, entirely in line with Rousseau's pleas for the glorification of patriotic virtues through honors and public rewards, were not very different from the systematic molding of citizens that Saint-Just advocated for the virtuous republic that the Jacobin leader pursued. Through the active promotion of friendship and education, the state would succeed in gradually forming moral and civic habits. And if they persisted in vice (by not having friends or otherwise), citizens could expect "terror" in the form of banishment and execution.[43]

Bolívar's moral education was to compensate for the utter inexperience of Spanish Americans in governing themselves. No representative bodies like the ones that prepared the North Americans well for independence existed in the Hispanic world. Faced with serious economic problems and centrifugal political tendencies, the creole elites saw their countries descend into authoritarian regimes and break up into smaller entities. The dissolution of the confederations of Gran Colombia (which had consisted of Colombia, Venezuela, Ecuador, and Panama), Central America, and the Río de la Plata occurred within a decade of their formation. Although the United States would not disintegrate until 1861, the new union was in danger of fracturing into two or more confederacies by the 1780s, or so James Madison thought. It strengthened his resolve at the Constitutional Convention to hem in factionalism and instability by means of a federal veto on local legislation.[44]

If Rousseau inspired the likes of Robespierre and Bolívar, educated men and women inspired by Enlightenment ideas were certainly not automatically driven to start revolutions, many championing conservative or piecemeal solutions. Peru's intellectuals, afraid of Indian rebellion, were no revolutionaries, preferring reforms within the imperial system. Colonialism was seen as rational, as long as it worked, which it did. Few therefore accepted independence until it had arrived.[45] Enlightenment ideas could be used by reformers and revolutionaries, aristocrats and sans-culottes for their own purposes. Many members of the French elites abhorred revolution but shared certain Enlightenment ideals. The *cahiers de doléances* show that provincial noblemen supported individual liberty, religious toleration, and a constitution, although they declined to give up privileges and political power. The confiscated libraries of émigrés also reveal that the revolution's harshest critics were steeped in the same philosophies as those of their adversaries.[46] Conversely, the French peasants who decisively influenced the events in the capital in the summer of 1789 did not read political literature, but typically consumed works of piety, almanacs, and books of sorcery. Literacy did not make a difference. The mobilization of peasants did not depend on their ability to read or write. The Great Fear, in fact, was prominent in areas with relatively low levels of literacy. Political works were only beginning to be read under the influence of the revolution.[47]

A French historian has suggested that the revolutionaries in France actually "invented" the Enlightenment by bringing together the works of authors such as Voltaire, Rousseau, and Raynal as they sought to legitimize the rift with the old regime. For example, in their attempt to defend the sentencing of Louis XVI—and many others after him—without due process, the Jacobins leaned on Rousseau, whose logic dictated that the perpetrator of any criminal offense could lose his civilian and natural rights. Rousseau himself had, of course, passed away long before the revolution, but Raynal, passages from whose *Histoire des Deux Indes* were used as revolutionary slogans, was still around and disagreed with the course of the revolution. Addressing the National Assembly in a pamphlet in 1791, he called for the full restoration of the powers of the king, the abolition of political clubs, and an end to popular violence. When Raynal thus showed his true colors, Robespierre remarked that the philosopher had become senile. The Jacobins of Marseille ceremonially deposited his bust at a local lunatic asylum.[48]

Insurgents outside France also selected texts or slogans that could serve the revolution, as did Saint-Domingue's blacks when they based their desire for freedom on the rights of man.[49] In Spanish America, Enlightenment works legitimized the decision to declare independence, even if not all revolutionary leaders were avid readers of such texts. Hidalgo, for example, had read hardly any, but the Inquisition still suspected him for his unorthodox views—he claimed, among other things, that plagues were not sent by God, who, he said, does not punish us with temporal chastisement.

Enlightenment concepts helped bury privilege as the organizing principle of the societies that underwent revolutionary change. Natural law philosophy had broken with the tradition that based rights on the notion of privilege. Being human was the only prerequisite for natural rights. The architects of the postrevolutionary states accordingly set about dismantling the numerous manifestations of privilege, replacing them with a vast array of individual rights. But theirs was a long and checkered struggle that did not end in a decisive victory for the advocates of equality. Slavery, after all, survived everywhere outside Haiti, at least in the short run.

Aftermaths

When the sound of the last aftershocks had faded, no revolution faced as many challenges as that of Haiti. The entire French administrative cadre had left and all Frenchmen with expertise in plantation agriculture had been killed or chased out. The almost universal illiteracy of the Haitians also spelled a dark future. Haiti's emperor Jean-Jacques Dessalines and his minister of finance were both illiterate, while Henri Christophe, one of his successors, could write only his first name and did not read. Nor did the situation improve. In the 1820s, only five members of the senate (out of twenty-four) and twenty-six members of the chamber of commons (out of eighty-two) could write their names.[50] Conditions hardly changed in the years ahead. French abolitionist Victor Schoelcher found in 1841 that only a thousand children were attending school in the entire country.[51]

Both Haitian states that emerged in the territory of Saint-Domingue suffered from the destruction wrought by the wars.[52] The population had declined by some 150,000, capital stock needed for the sugar industry had been largely destroyed, and a domestic capital market was lacking. Besides, as a free black nation afloat in a sea of slavery, Haiti had no friends, only enemies.[53] It was defenseless when a French fleet arrived in 1825 demanding war reparations at a cost of 150 million francs, an absurd amount of money. The young mainland republic to the north, by contrast, expanded economically in the decades after the peace with

Great Britain. The Revolutionary War had been comparatively short, and what destruction it had caused was minor compared to all other revolutions, not only in economic but also in demographic terms. The war dead in the United States accounted for less than 1 percent of the population, although emigration was not insignificant at 2.4 percent.[54]

The economic heritage that the Spanish Americans were unable to shed was that of silver, which came to haunt them as much as the plantation system plagued the Haitians. Silver had always played a key part in the colonial economies both as the leading export product and as a local means of exchange. Hindered by greatly increased operating costs and mismanagement, most Mexican mines ceased producing.[55] Conditions in Peru were worse. The independence wars destroyed the mines and scattered the workers and draft animals. An Englishman residing in Potosí noted: "[F]ifteen years of civil war have devastated the country, and the fortunes of the wealthiest inhabitants have been reduced to comparative insignificance: but nowhere has destruction been more mischievously active, more complete, and more manifest, than in the property of the *azogueros* [mine proprietors] of Peru."[56] Each of the former Spanish colonies lost commercial links that had existed prior to the creation of new boundaries, while setting up costly new fiscal and monetary systems, and bearing the costs of defense and law enforcement. The empire's fragmentation came at a price everywhere.[57]

Economic woes contributed to the political instability that was a hallmark of postrevolutionary societies. If insurrection, civil war, and coups d'état had determined the political course during the revolutions, they continued to wreak havoc in the following decades, not only in Haiti and Spanish America, but also in the United States, which eventually descended into a bloody war between North and South. And in France, the nineteenth century was the most volatile in the country's political history. Since the solutions that revolutions offered to structural problems were often as short-lived as the uprisings themselves, some issues refused to go away. From the perspective of natives, settlers, and empires, the American Revolution was therefore merely one phase of a struggle that lasted from the Seven Years' War through the War of 1812.[58]

Hemispheric Impact of the Revolutions

Arguably, the impact of each revolution was most pronounced in its respective hemisphere, at least in the five decades that occupy us in this book. While the institutional model was paramount in the case of the United States, the French and Haitian revolutions left legacies of both hope and fear. It has been argued that Spanish America would not have gained independence, at least in the way it did, without the example of the northern revolution. A Spanish translation of Thomas Paine's *Common Sense* by a Venezuelan, published in Philadelphia in 1811, circulated widely in Spanish America. Paine was especially well-read in the Río de la Plata, Chile, and Venezuela, where his appeal lay in his simplicity, his rhetorical style, and his emphasis on the natural rights of man.[59] But this edition was more than a translation. Apart from Paine's comments on government, the English constitution, monarchy, and finance, it contained translations of the American Declaration of Independence, the Articles of Confederation, the U.S. Constitution, and those of Massachusetts, Connecticut, New Jersey, Pennsylvania, and Virginia.[60]

The clearest example of North American inspiration is the text of a Chilean law from 1811, which translates as: "All men have certain inalienable rights which the Creator has given them in order to ensure their happiness, prosperity, and well-being." The Venezuelan declaration of independence from the same year also borrowed entire passages from its illustrious example from 1776.[61] The example of the United States went beyond mere rhetoric. A number of countries arranged the division of powers along the same lines, creating a presidential executive with veto right, a parliament consisting of a Senate and a House of Representatives, and a High Court of Justice whose members were jointly appointed by the other powers. Examples include Cundinamarca (1811, 1812), Cartagena (1812), Argentina (1819), Gran Colombia (1821), and Mexico (1824).[62] Federalism was also deemed worthy of imitation. In both Colombia and Venezuela, provincial constitutions were proclaimed after a federal constitution had been promulgated. Likewise, the provinces of Argentina wrote their own constitutions in 1819 to secure a certain degree of autonomy, while Uruguay's leader José Artigas aspired to the establishment of a federal state in the Río de la Plata according to the North American model. Finally, in imitation of the neighbors to the north, the Mexican constitution of 1824 determined that all nineteen states were to elect their own governors and legislatures.[63]

U.S. constitutionalism was not copied unquestioningly, but adapted to local political and social conditions. Some leaders opined that the moral qualities of the South Americans compared poorly to those in the North, so that it would be ill-advised to adopt U.S. institutions in Spanish America.[64] Bolívar had a high regard for the North American polity, a revolutionary society without Jacobins and without a Napoleon, but he blamed the chaos into which the first Venezuelan republic (1811–1812) descended on the fact that its constitution had been a virtual replica of that of the United States.[65]

The impact of the French Revolution was largest in the countries bordering France, where people rioted and engaged in acts of civil disobedience, buoyed by the presence or proximity of French armies. After the abolition of "feudalism" in France, the number of residents of the Rhineland who refused to pay tithes increased sharply, some men questioning clerical exemption from taxation.[66] Many Swiss also protested tax payments while referring to the revolution next door. Protest turned to celebration in several towns on the second anniversary of the storming of the Bastille, to the dismay of the government in Bern. But only in Geneva, site of much earlier turbulence, did an actual revolution take place, toppling the incumbent government in December 1792. It would take another six years before revolutionaries proclaimed republics all over Switzerland, in the hope or knowledge that nearby French troops would come to their aid, if necessary. In most places, the French were therefore received as the guardians of recent self-liberation.[67] The sister states imported the main principles of the French Revolution, the Helvetian Republic extending legal equality to all its citizens, abolishing serfdom and torture, and introducing freedom of religion, opinion, and the press.[68] Such reforms were not always simple ideological imports. Although local leaders were always eager to legislate a new order, they sometimes had little choice. For example, the French peace treaty with Venice in late 1797 determined that Venice's Great Council order "the abdication of the hereditary aristocracy."[69]

The revolutionaries in Venezuela were the first Spanish Americans to embrace the French principles. They introduced the title of citizen for all free residents and eliminated all hereditary titles, even though no decree was passed to that effect. Similar decrees followed in the United Provinces of the Río de la Plata (1813), Chile (1818), Central America (1823), and Mexico (1826).[70] The chief legal model of egalitarianism everywhere was the French Declaration of the Rights of Man and Citizen, copies of which were in great demand in the Spanish colonies from the late eighteenth century onward, despite its appearance on a list of forbidden books that King Charles IV had compiled in 1790.[71] Constitutions in Spanish America also shared the preference of the French constitution for a "parliamentary" system in which the executive branch emanated from the legislature, and in which the head of state was not directly elected.[72]

The Haitian Revolution had a lasting impact in the Atlantic world by contributing to the abolition of the slave trade in Great Britain and the United States. In Great Britain, the loss of fifty thousand sailors and soldiers in the Caribbean during the Haitian Revolution, coinciding with campaigns to abolish slavery, ended up creating negative associations with the West Indies in the metropolis. The legislators of South Carolina abolished the slave trade to their state in 1792 because they were persuaded by the connection Thomas Clarkson had made in a tract between the Haitian uprising and the large numbers of Africans who had been imported, whom the whites had been unable to control. The Haitian Revolution, coupled with slave revolts in Virginia in 1800 and 1802, helped federal advocates of abolition of the slave trade carry the day in the United States in 1807.[73] The institution of slavery, however, survived the era of revolutions largely intact, even if Bolívar proclaimed black freedom in 1816 not only to fulfill his promise made to Haitian president Pétion or to increase the size of his army, but also to prevent revolt or race war similar to that in Saint-Domingue.

Saint-Domingue obviously offered the clearest example of what slaves were capable of, her leaders emboldening blacks throughout the Americas. In Cuba, authorities found self-made drawings of Jean-François, Christophe, and Dessalines in the possession of José Antonio Aponte, the arrested organizer of an aborted slave rebellion in 1812. Free blacks and slaves, gathered in the Brazilian port of Recife in 1824, sang the praises of the "immortal Haitian" Christophe.[74] But there is no concrete proof that the Haitian Revolution inspired individual revolts, although the amount of rebelliousness did increase in the decade and a half after

1791. Still, both abolitionists and those aiming to maintain the status quo would invoke the example of "Santo Domingo" in the following decades. The first used the uprising of enslaved Haitians as a warning that similar events could transpire if no abolition occurred, while the latter sought to establish a link between abolitionist ideas and black insurgency.[75] The memory of the Haitian Revolution in the Atlantic world began to fade only once slavery was outlawed everywhere.

NOTES

CHAPTER 1. INTRODUCTION

1 Nicolas Ruault, *Gazette d'un Parisien sous la Révolution: Lettres à son frère 1783–1796*, ed. Christiane Rimbaud and Anne Vassal (Paris: Librairie Académique Perrin, 1976), 251–252.

2 To my knowledge, no monograph has attempted to link the four revolutions treated in this book, although there is no lack of works that compare two or three of these uprisings. Examples include Peggy K. Liss, *Atlantic Empires: The Network of Trade and Revolution, 1713–1826* (Baltimore: Johns Hopkins University Press, 1983); Lester D. Langley, *The Americas in the Age of Revolution, 1750–1850* (New Haven, Conn.: Yale University Press, 1996); Susan Dunn, *Sister Revolutions: French Lightning, American Light* (New York: Faber and Faber, 1999); and Joshua Simon, *The Ideology of Creole Revolution: Imperialism and Independence in American and Latin American Political Thought* (Cambridge: Cambridge University Press, 2017). To avoid the pitfall of restricting its meaning to something grand, total, and monumental, I define a revolution simply as violent regime change. Cf. Perez Zagorin, "Prolegomena to the Comparative History of Revolution in Early Modern Europe," *Comparative Studies in Society and History* 18:2 (1976), 151–174: 165. For a broader framework than the one used in this book, see David Armitage and Sanja Subrahmanyam, eds., *The Age of Revolutions in Global Context, c. 1760–1840* (New York: Palgrave Macmillan, 2010).

3 Simon Schama, *Citizens: A Chronicle of the French Revolution* (New York: Knopf, 1989), 561.

4 César Chesneau du Marsais, "Philosopher," in *The Encyclopedia of Diderot & d'Alembert Collaborative Translation Project*, trans. Dena Goodman (Ann Arbor: Michigan Publishing, University of Michigan Library, 2002), www.hdl.handle.net (accessed November 8, 2016). Originally published as "Philosophe," in *Encyclopédie ou Dictionnaire raisonné des sciences, des arts et des métiers*, vol. 12 (Paris, 1765), 509–511.

5 Volker Depkat, "Angewandte Aufklärung?," in Wolfgang Hardtwig, ed., *Die Aufklärung und ihre Weltwirkung* (Göttingen: Vandenhoeck & Ruprecht, 2010), 205–251: 207. Keith Michael Baker, "Enlightenment Idioms, Old Regime Discourses, and Revolutionary Improvisation," in Thomas E. Kaiser and Dale K. Van Kley, eds., *From Deficit to Deluge: The Origins of the French Revolution* (Stanford:

Stanford University Press, 2011), 165–197: 170–172. To define the Enlightenment in terms of sociability or public space would be to rob it of its essence. See John M. Dixon, "Henry F. May and the Revival of the American Enlightenment: Problems and Possibilities for Intellectual and Social History," *William and Mary Quarterly*, 3rd series 71:2 (2014), 255–280: 276–280.

6 Jonathan I. Israel, *Democratic Enlightenment: Philosophy, Revolution, and Human Rights, 1750–1790* (Oxford: Oxford University Press, 2012), 790. Carla Hesse, "Towards a New Topography of Enlightenment," *European Review of History—Revue européenne d'Histoire* 13:3 (2006), 499–508. For the most recent discussions of the Enlightenment, see Anthony Gottlieb, *The Dream of Enlightenment: The Rise of Modern Philosophy* (New York: Norton, 2016); and Caroline Winterer, *American Enlightenments: Pursuing Happiness in the Age of Reason* (New Haven, Conn.: Yale University Press, 2016).

7 Dorinda Outram, *The Enlightenment* (Cambridge: Cambridge University Press, 1995), 3. Jonathan Israel, *Enlightenment Contested: Philosophy, Modernity, and the Emancipation of Man 1670–1752* (Oxford: Oxford University Press, 2006), 553, 561, 568. David Brion Davis, *The Problem of Slavery in Western Culture* (New York: Oxford University Press, 1966), 393.

8 Darrin M. McMahon, *Enemies of the Enlightenment: The French Counter-Enlightenment and the Making of Modernity* (Oxford: Oxford University Press, 2001), 14, 32–33, 36, 71.

9 Jakob Salat, *Auch ein paar Worte über die Frage: Führt die Aufklärung zur Revolution? Mit besonderer Rücksicht auf den Plan der Verfinsterung* (Munich: Joseph Lindauer, 1802), 13. The translation is mine, as are the translations throughout this book.

10 Anna Plassart, *The Scottish Enlightenment and the French Revolution* (Cambridge: Cambridge University Press, 2015), 3.

11 Louis-Sébastien Mercier, *De J.J. Rousseau, considéré comme l'un des premiers auteurs de la Révolution*, 2 vols. (Paris: Buisson, 1791), 1:60.

12 See, for a similar approach, Jeremy Adelman, "An Age of Imperial Revolutions," *American Historical Review* 113:2 (2008), 319–340.

13 R. R. Palmer, *The Age of the Democratic Revolution: A Political History of Europe and America, 1760–1800*, 2 vols. (Princeton, N.J.: Princeton University Press, 1959–1964).

14 George Huppert, *After the Black Death: A Social History of Early Modern Europe*, 2nd ed. (Bloomington: Indiana University Press, 1998), 60. Olwen Hufton, *Europe: Privilege and Protest, 1730–1789* (Ithaca, N.Y.: Cornell University Press, 1980), 19. Robert S. Duplessis, *Transitions to Capitalism in Early Modern Europe* (Cambridge: Cambridge University Press, 1997), 53, 159, 168–179.

15 François-Xavier Guerra, "The Spanish-American Tradition of Representation and Its European Roots," *Journal of Latin American Studies* 26:1 (1994), 1–35: 24–25. D. A. Brading, "Bourbon Spain and Its American Empire," in Leslie Bethell, ed., *Colonial Spanish America* (Cambridge: Cambridge University Press, 1987), 112–162:

122. William H. Sewell, Jr., "Ideologies and Social Revolutions: Reflections on the French Case," *Journal of Modern History* 57:1 (1985), 57–85: 62.

16 Liana Vardi, "Land Tenure," in Peter Stearns, ed., *Encyclopedia of European Social History from 1350 to 2000*, 6 vols. (Detroit: Charles Scribner's Sons, 2001), 2:357–367: 358–359. Hufton, *Europe*, 47–49, 51, 58.

17 Hufton, *Europe*, 23, 25, 27–28, 34, 42–43. Duplessis, *Transitions to Capitalism*, 146.

18 James Lockhart, "Social Organization and Social Change in Colonial Spanish America," in Leslie Bethell, ed., *Cambridge History of Latin America* (Cambridge: Cambridge University Press, 1984), 2:285–319: 285–286.

19 Nicholas Henshall, *The Myth of Absolutism: Change and Continuity in Early Modern European Monarchy* (London: Longman, 1992), 135, 152, 178, 180. James D. Tracy, "Taxation and State Debt," in Thomas A. Brady, Jr., Heiko A. Oberman, and James D. Tracy, eds., *Handbook of European History, 1400–1600: Late Middle Ages, Renaissance, and Reformation* (Leiden: E. J. Brill, 1994), 563–588: 566. Roger Mettam, *Power and Faction in Louis XIV's France* (New York: Basil Blackwell, 1988), 16.

20 Christine Daniels and Michael Kennedy, eds., *Negotiated Empires: Centers and Peripheries in the New World, 1500–1820* (London: Routledge, 2002).

21 James B. Collins, *The State in Early Modern France* (Cambridge: Cambridge University Press, 1995), 184. Linda Kirk, "The Matter of Enlightenment," *Historical Journal* 43:4 (December 2000), 1129–1143: 1135–1136.

22 Jonathan R. Dull, *The French Navy and the Seven Years' War* (Lincoln: University of Nebraska Press, 2005), 2. Bailey Stone, *The Genesis of the French Revolution: A Global-Historical Interpretation* (Cambridge: Cambridge University Press, 1994), 25, 37. John Brewer, *The Sinews of Power: War, Money and the English State, 1688–1783* (Cambridge, Mass.: Harvard University Press, 1988), 171, 173.

23 Franz A. J. Szabo, *The Seven Years' War in Europe, 1756–1763* (Harlow, U.K.: Pearson Longman, 2008), 7. Brewer, *Sinews of Power*, 174. Dull, *French Navy*, 13–14.

24 Dull, *French Navy*, 6–15.

25 Frank W. Brecher, *Losing a Continent: France's North American Policy, 1753–1763* (Westport, Conn. and London: Greenwood Press, 1998), 10. Dull, *French Navy*, 16–17, 20–25. T. R. Clayton, "The Duke of Newcastle, the Earl of Halifax, and the American Origins of the Seven Years' War," *Historical Journal* 24:3 (1981), 571–603.

26 Brecher, *Losing a Continent*, 2.

27 Szabo, *Seven Years' War in Europe*, 424, 425, 430. Brewer, *Sinews of Power*, 174.

28 What miraculously saved Frederick the Great, as he himself acknowledged, was the death of Russia's czarina Elisabeth and her succession by Peter III, a great admirer of all things Prussian.

29 Dull, *French Navy*, 37. Stone, *Genesis of the French Revolution*, 40–41.

30 J. H. Parry, *Trade and Dominion: The European Oversea Empires in the Eighteenth Century* (London: Weidenfeld and Nicholson, 1971), 112. Patrick Villiers, *Marine royale, corsaires et trafic dans l'Atlantique: De Louis XIV à Louis XVI* (Lille: Société Dunkerquoise d'Histoire et d'Archéologie, 1991). Daniel Baugh, *The Global Seven*

Years War: Britain and France in a Great Power Contest, 1754–1763 (Harlow, U.K.: Pearson, 2011), 627–628. John Lynch, *Bourbon Spain 1700–1808* (Oxford: Blackwell, 1989), 317–318.

31 Stephen Brumwell, *Redcoats: The British Soldier and War in the Americas, 1755–1763* (Cambridge: Cambridge University Press, 2002), 24, 42, 74. The most comprehensive treatment of the war in North America is Fred Anderson, *Crucible of War: The Seven Years' War and the Fate of Empire in British North America, 1754–1766* (New York: Knopf, 2000).

32 Szabo, *Seven Years' War in Europe*, 411–412, 423, 432. Cf. Richard Pares, *War and Trade in the West Indies, 1739–1763* (Oxford: Clarendon Press, 1936).

33 Larry Neal, "Interpreting Power and Profit in Economic History: A Case Study of the Seven Years War," *Journal of Economic History* 37:1 (1977), 20–35: 31 (table 6), 34–35. J. F. Wright, "The Contribution of Overseas Savings to the Funded National Debt of Great Britain, 1750–1815," *Economic History Review* 50:4 (1997), 657–674: 666.

34 W. O. Henderson, "The Berlin Commercial Crisis of 1763," *Economic History Review*, New Series 15:1 (1962), 89–102: 94. Ingrid Mittenzwei, *Preussen nach dem Siebenjährigen Krieg* (Berlin: Akademie-Verlag, 1979), 10–11.

CHAPTER 2. CIVIL WAR IN THE BRITISH EMPIRE

1 Georgiana C. Nammack, *Fraud, Politics, and the Dispossession of the Indians: The Iroquois Land Frontier in the Colonial Period* (Norman: University of Oklahoma Press, 1969), 88–91. Gregory H. Nobles, "Breaking into the Backcountry: New Approaches to the American Frontier, 1750–1800," *William and Mary Quarterly*, 3rd series 46:4 (1989), 641–670: 646. For the frontier earlier in the century, see Warren R. Hofstra, "'The Extension of His Majesties Dominions': The Virginia Backcountry and Reconfiguration of Imperial Frontiers," *Journal of American History* 84:4 (1998), 1281–1312.

2 Alan Taylor, *The Divided Ground: Indians, Settlers, and the Northern Borderlands of the American Revolution* (New York: Knopf, 2006), 37.

3 Colin G. Calloway, *The Scratch of a Pen: 1763 and the Transformation of North America* (Oxford: Oxford University Press, 2006), 4.

4 Ian K. Steele, *Warpaths: Invasions of America* (Oxford: Oxford University Press, 1994), 175, 179. Michael N. McConnell, *A Country Between: The Upper Ohio Valley and Its Peoples, 1724–1774* (Lincoln: University of Nebraska Press, 1992), 19, 21, 30, 47.

5 McConnell, *A Country Between*, 41–42, 63–70.

6 Steele, *Warpaths*, 182, 198. Matthew C. Ward, *Breaking the Backcountry: The Seven Years' War in Virginia and Pennsylvania, 1754–1765* (Pittsburgh: University of Pittsburgh Press, 2003), 13–14, 21.

7 Mlada Bukovansky, *Legitimacy and Power Politics: The American and French Revolutions in International Political Culture* (Princeton, N.J.: Princeton University Press, 2002), 116, drawing on Gordon S. Wood, *The Radicalism of the American Revolution* (New York: Vintage Books, 1993), chaps. 7–8.

8 Jack P. Greene, *Pursuits of Happiness: The Social Development of Early Modern British Colonies and the Formation of American Culture* (Chapel Hill: University of North Carolina Press, 1988), 186–189. Michael J. Rozbicki, "The Curse of Provincialism: Negative Perceptions of Colonial American Plantation Gentry," *Journal of Southern History* 63:4 (1997), 727–752: 727, 750–751.

9 *The Revolutionary Journal of Baron Ludwig von Closen, 1780–1783*, trans. and ed. Evelyn M. Acomb (Chapel Hill: University of North Carolina Press, 1958), 187.

10 Bernard Bailyn, "Political Experience and Enlightenment Ideas in Eighteenth-Century America," *American Historical Review* 67:2 (1962), 339–351: 346. J. H. Elliott, *Empires of the Atlantic World: Britain and Spain in America 1492–1830* (New Haven, Conn.: Yale University Press, 2006), 134–135, 332–333.

11 Richard R. Beeman, *The Varieties of Political Experience in Eighteenth-Century America* (Philadelphia: University of Pennsylvania Press, 2004), 75, 103, 106, 208, 250. Property qualifications in the Caribbean colonies were no more restrictive than those in the North American South, but the proportion of voters was lower, because slaves and free blacks (as well as Jews) were excluded from the vote. Andrew Jackson O'Shaughnessy, *An Empire Divided: The American Revolution and the British Caribbean* (Philadelphia: University of Pennsylvania Press, 2000), 133.

12 Alan Tully, "The Political Development of the Colonies after the Glorious Revolution," in Jack P. Greene and J. R. Pole, eds., *The Blackwell Encyclopedia of the American Revolution* (Cambridge, Mass.: Blackwell, 1991), 28–38: 28–29. Beeman, *Varieties of Political Experience*, 14. Jack P. Greene, *Negotiated Authorities: Essays in Colonial Political and Constitutional History* (Charlottesville: University of Virginia Press, 1994), 89. Charles M. Andrews, *The Colonial Period of American History* (New Haven, Conn.: Yale University Press, 1938), 4:215. James Lang, *Conquest and Commerce: Spain and England in the Americas* (New York: Academic Press, 1975), 229.

13 Thomas C. Barrow, *Trade and Empire: The British Customs Service in Colonial America 1660–1775* (Cambridge, Mass.: Harvard University Press, 1967), 87.

14 Jack P. Greene, *Imperatives, Behaviors, and Identities: Essays in Early American Cultural History* (Charlottesville: University of Virginia Press, 1992), 197–198.

15 Andrew Burnaby, *Travels through the Middle Settlements in North-America. In the Years 1759 and 1760: With Observations upon the State of the Colonies* (Dublin: Printed for R. Marchbank, 1775), 42–43.

16 Greene, *Imperatives, Behaviors, and Identities*, 188–189.

17 John J. McCusker and Russell R. Menard, *The Economy of British America 1607–1789: With Supplementary Bibliography* (Chapel Hill: University of North Carolina Press, 1991 [1985]), 268.

18 Ibid., 108, 130, 160.

19 Kenneth Morgan, *Bristol and the Atlantic Trade in the Eighteenth Century* (Cambridge: Cambridge University Press, 1993), 89. McCusker and Menard, *Economy of British America*, 286.

20 English foodstuffs to the British Islands accounted for 8.6 percent (1699–1701), 17.9 percent (1722–1724), 27.0 percent (1752–1754), and 46.7 percent (1772–1774) of all English foodstuffs exports. Computed on the basis of Ralph Davis, "English Foreign Trade, 1700–1774," *Economic History Review*, 2nd series, 15:2 (1962), 285–303: 302–303.

21 Hermann Wellenreuther, "Exploring Misunderstandings: Atlantic Political Culture in the Early Modern World," in Horst Pietschmann, ed., *Atlantic History: History of the Atlantic System 1580–1830* (Göttingen: Vandenhoeck & Ruprecht, 2002), 140–167: 165–166.

22 Michael A. McDonnell, *The Politics of War: Race, Class, and Conflict in Revolutionary Virginia* (Chapel Hill: University of North Carolina Press, 2007), 25. Robert V. Wells, *The Population of the British Colonies in America before 1776: A Survey of Census Data* (Princeton, N.J.: Princeton University Press, 1975), 112.

23 For the Caribbean, Newfoundland, Nova Scotia, and New England, I have relied on Wells, *Population of the British Colonies*, 47, 61, 70, 79, 89, 97, 173, 183, 196, 208, 238, 253. For the Middle Colonies and the South, I used McCusker and Menard, *Economy of British America*, 136, 172, 203.

24 Eric Hinderaker and Peter C. Mancall, *At the Edge of Empire: The Backcountry in British North America* (Baltimore: Johns Hopkins University Press, 2003), 107, 109, 116–119, 125. Anderson, *Crucible of War*, 330–339. Ward, *Breaking the Backcountry*, 7, 55–58. Calloway, *Scratch of a Pen*, 47–48.

25 Anderson, *Crucible of War*, 538–542. Francis Jennings, *Empire of Fortune: Crowns, Colonies, and Tribes in the Seven Years War in America* (New York: Norton, 1988), 442–447.

26 Calloway, *Scratch of a Pen*, 73, 76, 81–82, 90.

27 Jon William Parmenter, "Pontiac's War: Forging New Links in the Anglo-Iroquois Covenant Chain, 1758–1766," *Ethnohistory* 44:4 (1997), 617–654: 620, 621, 624, 626, 638, 639. Nammack, *Fraud, Politics*, 93, 105. Gregory T. Knouff, *The Soldiers' Revolution: Pennsylvanians in Arms and the Forging of Early American Identity* (University Park: Pennsylvania State University Press, 2004), 25. Colin G. Calloway, *The American Revolution in Indian Country: Crisis and Diversity in Native American Communities* (Cambridge: Cambridge University Press, 1995), 23. Woody Holton, *Forced Founders: Indians, Debtors, Slaves, and the Making of the American Revolution in Virginia* (Chapel Hill: University of North Carolina Press for the Omohundro Institute of Early American History and Culture, 1999), 7–13. Calloway, *Scratch of a Pen*, 109–110.

28 Ward, *Breaking the Backcountry*, 3–4.

29 For the consequences in other parts of Europe, see Franco Venturi, "Church and Reform in Enlightenment Italy: The Sixties of the Eighteenth Century," *Journal of Modern History* 48:2 (1976), 215–232: 216.

30 From the text of the Declaratory Act of 1766, quoted in James H. Kettner, *The Development of American Citizenship, 1608–1870* (Chapel Hill: University of North Carolina Press for the Institute of Early American History and Culture, 1978), 132.

31 Andrew Eliot, *A Sermon Preached before His Excellency Francis Bernard, Esq; Governor, the Honorable His Majesty's Council, and the Honorable House of Representatives, of the Province of the Massachusetts-Bay in New England, May 29th 1765: Being the Anniversary for the Election of His Majesty's Council for the Province* (Boston: Green and Russell, 1765), 43.

32 Frank Wesley Pitman, *The Development of the British West Indies 1700–1763* (New Haven, Conn.: Yale University Press, 1917), 281–282. Pares, *War and Trade*, 396–397. Barrow, *Trade and Empire*, 142.

33 Robert Middlekauff, *The Glorious Cause: The American Revolution, 1763–1789* (New York: Oxford University Press, 1982), 60–61. Margaret Ellen Newell, *From Dependency to Independence: Economic Revolution in Colonial New England* (Ithaca, N.Y.: Cornell University Press, 1988), 267–269.

34 Henry Hulton, "Account of Travels" (ms.), John Carter Brown Library, Providence, R.I., 111, 113. Cf. Benjamin H. Irvin, "Tar, Feathers, and the Enemies of American Liberties, 1768–1776," *New England Quarterly* 76:2 (2003), 197–238: 210–211. R. S. Longley, "Mob Activities in Revolutionary Massachusetts," *New England Quarterly* 6:1 (1933), 98–130: 126–127.

35 Gordon S. Wood, *The Creation of the American Republic, 1776–1787* (New York: Norton, 1972), 319–321. Pauline Maier, "Popular Uprisings and Civil Authority in Eighteenth-Century America," *William and Mary Quarterly*, 3rd series 27:1 (1970), 3–35: 8–9, 12. Richard Maxwell Brown, "Violence and the American Revolution," in Stephen G. Kurtz and James H. Hutson, eds., *Essays on the American Revolution* (Chapel Hill: University of North Carolina Press, 1973), 81–120: 97. Paul A. Gilje, *The Road to Mobocracy: Popular Disorder in New York City, 1763–1834* (Chapel Hill: University of North Carolina Press for the Institute of Early American History and Culture, 1987), 10, 12.

36 Peter Linebaugh and Marcus Rediker, *The Many-Headed Hydra: Sailors, Slaves, Commoners, and the Hidden History of the Revolutionary Atlantic* (Boston: Beacon, 2000), 227–236. Brown, "Violence and the American Revolution," 98–103.

37 Douglass Adair and John A. Schutz, *Peter Oliver's Origin and Progress of the American Rebellion* (Stanford: Stanford University Press, 1961), 58–60. Philip Ranlet, *The New York Loyalists* (Knoxville: University of Tennessee Press, 1986), 12.

38 Eliga H. Gould, *The Persistence of Empire: British Political Culture in the Age of the American Revolution* (Chapel Hill: University of North Carolina Press for the Omohundro Institute of Early American History and Culture, 2000), 110–119. Edward Countryman, *The American Revolution*, rev. ed. (New York: Hill & Wang, 2003), 40–42. Newell, *From Dependency to Independence*, 281–282. The classic work on the Stamp Act is Edmund S. Morgan and Helen M. Morgan, *The Stamp Act Crisis: Prologue to Revolution* (Chapel Hill: University of North Carolina Press for the Institute of Early American History and Culture, 1953). See also P. D. G. Thomas, *British Politics and the Stamp Act Crisis: The First Phase of the American Revolution, 1763–1767* (Oxford: Clarendon Press, 1975).

39 Middlekauff, *Glorious Cause*, 107–117.

40 O'Shaughnessy, *Empire Divided*, 82–104. Robert J. Chaffin, "The Townshend Acts Crisis, 1767–1770," in Greene and Pole, *Blackwell Encyclopedia*, 126–145: 126–136.

41 Newell, *From Dependency to Independence*, 239, 296. Laurel Thatcher Ulrich, "'Daughters of Liberty': Religious Women in Revolutionary New England," in Ronald Hoffman and Peter J. Albert, eds., *Women in the Age of the American Revolution* (Charlottesville: University of Virginia Press, 1989), 211–243: 215, 225.

42 Ronald Hoffman, *A Spirit of Dissension: Economics, Politics, and the Revolution in Maryland* (Baltimore: Johns Hopkins University Press, 1973), 37. Middlekauff, *Glorious Cause*, 179–185. Ranlet, *New York Loyalists*, 29. Robert A. Gross, *The Minutemen and Their World* (New York: Hill & Wang, 1976), 39. Holton, *Forced Founders*, 90–91. O'Shaughnessy, *Empire Divided*, 105–107.

43 Barbara Clark Smith, "Food Rioters and the American Revolution," *William and Mary Quarterly*, 3rd series 51:1 (1994), 3–38: 29. Gilje, *Road to Mobocracy*, 40. Marc Egnal and Joseph A. Ernst, "An Economic Interpretation of the American Revolution," *William and Mary Quarterly*, 3rd series 29:1 (1972), 3–32: 21.

44 Hoffman, *Spirit of Dissension*, 124. Richard B. Sheridan, "The British Credit Crisis of 1772 and the American Colonies," *Journal of Economic History* 20:2 (1960), 161–186: 171. Thomas M. Doerflinger, "Philadelphia Merchants and the Logic of Moderation, 1760–1775," *William and Mary Quarterly*, 3rd series 40:2 (1983), 197–226: 197–198.

45 T. H. Breen, *Tobacco Culture: The Mentality of the Great Tidewater Planters on the Eve of Revolution* (Princeton, N.J.: Princeton University Press, 1985), 31–32. Sheridan, "British Credit Crisis," 184. Holton, *Forced Founders*, 60–65. Some historians have argued for a connection between the revolution and the debt burden of tobacco planters: Charles A. Beard, *Economic Origins of Jeffersonian Democracy* (New York: Macmillan, 1915). Isaac S. Harrell, *Loyalism in Virginia: Chapters in the Economic History of the Revolution* (Durham, N.C.: Duke University Press, 1926). But see Emory G. Evans, "Planter Indebtedness and the Coming of the Revolution in Virginia," *William and Mary Quarterly*, 3rd series 19:4 (1962), 511–533, and Evans, "Private Indebtedness and the Revolution in Virginia, 1776 to 1796," *William and Mary Quarterly*, 3rd series 28:3 (1971), 349–374. Staughton Lynd and David Waldstreicher present the revolution as a movement to free North Americans from Britain's economic restrictions in "Free Trade, Sovereignty, and Slavery: Toward an Economic Interpretation of American Independence," *William and Mary Quarterly*, 3rd series 68:4 (2011), 597–630.

46 Benjamin Woods Labaree, *The Boston Tea Party* (New York: Oxford University Press, 1964), 59–61, 70, 73.

47 John Shy, *Toward Lexington: The Role of the British Army in the Coming of the American Revolution* (Princeton, N.J.: Princeton University Press, 1965), 62, 67, 69, 81–83, 192, 195, 269.

48 Ibid., 143, 295–296, 303, 305–306.

49 Labaree, *Boston Tea Party*, 126–145. Middlekauff, *Glorious Cause*, 230. Tea parties were also held in other ports, including New York City and Chestertown, Virginia: Gilje, *Road to Mobocracy*, 59; Keith Mason, "Localism, Evangelicalism, and Loyalism: The Sources of Discontent in the Revolutionary Chesapeake," *Journal of Southern History* 56:1 (1990), 23–54: 27–28. For the fate of the Boston Tea Party in the American public memory, see Alfred F. Young, *The Shoemaker and the Tea Party: Memory and the American Revolution* (Boston: Beacon, 1999).

50 Philip S. Foner, *Labor and the American Revolution* (Westport, Conn.: Greenwood, 1976), 123–126.

51 Middlekauff, *Glorious Cause*, 233–235, 247–248.

52 Hermann Wellenreuther, *Von Chaos und Krieg zu Ordnung und Frieden: Der Amerikanische Revolution erster Teil, 1775–1783* (Berlin: LIT Verlag, 2006), 26, 29–30. Hermann Wellenreuther, "Associations, the People, Committee of Observation and Inspection and the Culture of Rights, 1774–1776," in Wellenreuther, ed., *The Revolution of the People: Thoughts and Documents on the Revolutionary Process in North America, 1774–1776* (Göttingen: Universitätsverlag Göttingen, 2006), 13–65: 18. Holton, *Forced Founders*, 102, 120, 124.

53 Wellenreuther, "Associations," 19, 26, 34. David H. Villiers, "'King Mob' and the Rule of Law: Revolutionary Justice and the Suppression of Loyalism in Connecticut, 1774–1783," in Robert M. Calhoon, Timothy Barnes, and George A. Rawlyk, eds., *Loyalists and Community in North America* (Westport, Conn.: Greenwood, 1994), 17–30: 18. William Stone, trans., *Letters of Brunswick and Hessian Officers during the American Revolution* (New York: Da Capo Press, 1970), 150–151.

54 Richard Alan Ryerson, *The Revolution Is Now Begun: The Radical Committees of Philadelphia, 1765–1776* (Philadelphia: University of Pennsylvania Press, 1978), 39, 46–47, 182, 188.

55 Wellenreuther, *Von Chaos und Krieg*, 27. Wellenreuther, "Associations," 35, 64.

56 J. T. Headley, *The Chaplains and Clergy of the Revolution* (New York: Charles Scribner, 1864), 23. Wellenreuther, *Von Chaos und Krieg*, 55. Kettner, *Development of American Citizenship*, 161–163.

57 Kettner, *Development of American Citizenship*, 170–171. Erich Angermann, "Ständische Rechtstraditionen in der amerikanischen Unabhängigkeitserklärung," *Historische Zeitschrift* 200 (1965), 61–91: 79–81. Arthur S. Marks, "The Statue of King George III in New York and the Iconology of Regicide," *American Art Journal* 13:3 (1981), 61–82: 65. *A Dialogue, between the Devil and George III. tyrant of Britain, &c. &c. &c. &c.* (Boston: Benjamin Edes and Sons, 1782), 6.

58 Bernard Bailyn, *The Ideological Origins of the American Revolution*, enlarged ed. (Cambridge, Mass.: Belknap, 1992), 76–81. Wood, *Creation of the American Republic*, 32, 35, 52, 61, 108. Drew R. McCoy, *The Elusive Republic: Political Economy in Jeffersonian America* (Chapel Hill: University of North Carolina Press, 1980), 67–68.

59 Linebaugh and Rediker, *Many-Headed Hydra*, 236–240.

60 Taylor, *Divided Ground*, 80. McConnell, *A Country Between*, 244, 252, 256, 258, 260, 262.

61 Eric Hinderaker, *Elusive Empires: Constructing Colonialism in the Ohio Valley, 1673–1800* (Cambridge: Cambridge University Press, 1997), 187, 200–201. Cal-

loway, *American Revolution in Indian Country*, 31. The reluctance stemmed from a desire to end the war rapidly: Knouff, *Soldiers' Revolution*, 40.

62 Calloway, *American Revolution in Indian Country*, 33–34, 43–44, 83.

63 Taylor, *Divided Ground*, 100–102. Knouff, *Soldiers' Revolution*, 163. Calloway, *American Revolution in Indian Country*, 47.

64 Calloway, *Scratch of a Pen*, 37. McConnell, *A Country Between*, 240.

65 Jim Piecuch, "Incompatible Allies: Loyalists, Slaves, and Indians in Revolutionary South Carolina," in John Resch and Walter Sargent, eds., *War and Society in the American Revolution: Mobilization and Home Fronts* (DeKalb: Northern Illinois University Press, 2007), 191–214, 193. Gregory Evans Dowd, *A Spirited Resistance: The North American Indian Struggle for Unity, 1745–1815* (Baltimore: Johns Hopkins University Press, 1992), 52–53. Wayne E. Lee, *Crowds and Soldiers in Revolutionary North Carolina: The Culture of Violence in Riot and War* (Gainesville: University Press of Florida, 2001), 159. Calloway, *American Revolution in Indian Country*, 49.

66 Lee, *Crowds and Soldiers*, 160.

67 Barbara Alice Mann, *George Washington's War on Native America* (Westport, Conn.: Praeger, 2005), 31, 37, 45, 47. Robert G. Parkinson, *The Common Cause: Creating Race and Nation in the American Revolution* (Chapel Hill: University of North Carolina Press for the Omohundro Institute of Early American History and Culture, 2016), 432–437. Calloway, *American Revolution in Indian Country*, 49, 51, 53. John E. Selby, *The Revolution in Virginia, 1775–1783* (Williamsburg, Va.: Colonial Williamsburg Foundation, 1988), 199. See also Max M. Mintz, *Seeds of Empire: The American Revolutionary Conquest of the Iroquois* (New York: New York University Press, 1999).

68 Peter Silver, *Our Savage Neighbors: How Indian War Transformed Early America* (New York: Norton, 2008), 42–44, 53–57. Hinderaker, *Elusive Empires*, 214. Mann, *George Washington's War*, 132, 137–141, 151. Mann lists another thirty people killed on Killbuck's Island. Dowd, *Spirited Resistance*, 65, 82–83, 85–86. William R. Nester, *The Frontier War for American Independence* (Mechanicsburg, Pa.: Stackpole Books, 2004), 322–323. The Moravian missions had been attacked by northern Indians in August 1781, when three hundred warriors plundered homes and livestock, spared the residents, but captured the missionaries: Dowd, *Spirited Resistance*, 83.

69 Calloway, *American Revolution in Indian Country*, 57, 61, 107, 174. Karim M. Tiro, "The Dilemmas of Alliance: The Oneida Indian Nation in the American Revolution," in Resch and Sargent, *War and Society*, 215–234: 229. Hinderaker, *Elusive Empires*, 204. David J. Silverman, *Red Brethren: The Brothertown and Stockbridge Indians and the Problem of Race in Early America* (Ithaca, N.Y.: Cornell University Press, 2010), 107–120.

70 Calloway, *American Revolution in Indian Country*, 282. Nester, *Frontier War*, 21.

71 McCoy, *Elusive Republic*.

72 *An Oration on the Beauties of Liberty, or the Essential Rights of the Americans, Delivered at the Second Baptist-Church in Boston, Upon the Last Annual Thanksgiving, Dec. 3d, 1772. Dedicated to the Right Honorable the Earl of Dartmouth*, 4th ed. (Boston: E. Russell, 1773), xxvii–xxviii. In actual fact, British troops tended to be better soldiers than American colonists.

73 Middlekauff, *Glorious Cause*, 260–273.

74 Ibid., 312, 320–332. David Armitage, *The Declaration of Independence: A Global History* (Cambridge, Mass.: Harvard University Press, 2007), 44–52.

75 Friederike Baer, "The Decision to Hire German Troops in the War of American Independence: Reactions in Britain and North America, 1774–1776," *Early American Studies* 13:1 (2015), 111–150: 111–112. Wellenreuther, *Von Chaos und Krieg*, 171. Rodney Atwood, *The Hessians: Mercenaries from Hessen-Kassel in the American Revolution* (Cambridge: Cambridge University Press, 1980).

76 *An Eyewitness Account of the American Revolution and New England Life: The Journal of J. F. Wasmus, German Company Surgeon, 1776–1783*, trans. Helga Doblin, ed. Mary C. Lynn (New York: Greenwood, 1990), 26.

77 James Kirby Martin, "A 'Most Undisciplined, Profligate Crew': Protest and Defiance in the Continental Ranks, 1776–1783," in Ronald Hoffman and Peter J. Albert, eds., *Arms and Independence: The Military Character of the American Revolution* (Charlottesville: University of Virginia Press, 1984), 119–140: 121–125 (quote on 124). David Noel Doyle, *Ireland, Irishmen and Revolutionary America, 1760–1820* (Dublin: Published for the Cultural Relations Committee of Ireland by the Mercier Press, 1981), 142. Don Higginbotham, "The War for Independence, to Saratoga," in Greene and Pole, *Blackwell Encyclopedia*, 296–308: 298. Wellenreuther, *Von Chaos und Krieg*, 169.

78 John Shy, "Looking Backward, Looking Forward: War and Society in Revolutionary America," in Resch and Sargent, *War and Society*, 3–19: 14. James Kirby Martin and Mark Edward Lender, *A Respectable Army: The Military Origins of the Republic, 1763–1789* (Arlington Heights, Ill.: Harlan Davidson, 1982), 69–72, 76–77, 89, 93. McDonnell, *Politics of War*, 6, 11, 278–280.

79 Wim Klooster, *Illicit Riches: Dutch Trade in the Caribbean* (Leiden: KITLV Press, 1998), 96.

80 Janice E. Thompson, *Mercenaries, Pirates, and Sovereigns: State-Building and Extraterritorial Violence in Early Modern Europe* (Princeton, N.J.: Princeton University Press, 1996), 25–26. Martin and Lender, *Respectable Army*, 143, 145.

81 William M. Fowler, Jr., *Rebels under Sail: The American Navy during the Revolution* (New York: Charles Scribner's Sons, 1976), 281. Paul A. Gilje, "Loyalty and Liberty: The Ambiguous Patriotism of Jack Tar in the American Revolution," *Pennsylvania History* 67 (Spring 2000), 165–193: 170. Francis D. Cogliano, *American Maritime Prisoners in the Revolutionary War: The Captivity of William Russell* (Annapolis: Naval Institute Press, 2001), 28–29. Young, *Shoemaker and the Tea Party*, 58.

82 John Shy, *A People Numerous and Armed: Reflections on the Military Struggle for American Independence*, rev. ed. (Ann Arbor: University of Michigan Press, 1990), 224–226. David Hackett Fisher, *Washington's Crossing* (Oxford: Oxford University Press, 2004).

83 Theodore Corbett, *No Turning Point: The Saratoga Campaign in Perspective* (Norman: University of Oklahoma Press, 2012), 136–137. Andrew Jackson O'Shaughnessy, *The Men Who Lost America: British Leadership, the American Revolution, and the Fate of Empire* (New Haven, Conn.: Yale University Press, 2013), 102–103.

84 Piers Mackesy, *The War for America, 1775–1783* (Lincoln: University of Nebraska Press, 1993 [1964]), 511, 514. Higginbotham, "War for Independence," 302–304. Martin and Lender, *Respectable Army*, 114. A. Temple Patterson, *The Other Armada: The Franco-Spanish Attempt to Invade Britain in 1779* (Manchester: Manchester University Press, 1960). For the alliance with France, see Ronald Hoffman and Peter J. Albert, eds., *Diplomacy and Revolution: The Franco-American Alliance of 1778* (Charlottesville: University of Virginia Press for the United States Capitol Historical Society, 1981).

85 Don Higginbotham, "The War for Independence, after Saratoga," in Greene and Pole, *Blackwell Encyclopedia*, 309–320: 312–314. Middlekauff, *Glorious Cause*, 562–570. Sylvia R. Frey, "Between Slavery and Freedom: Virginia Blacks in the American Revolution," *Journal of Southern History* 49:3 (1983), 375–398: 383.

86 O'Shaughnessy, *Empire Divided*, 230–231.

87 Kathleen DuVal, *Independence Lost: Lives on the Edge of the American Revolution* (New York: Random House, 2015), 158, 217, 224.

88 Ranlet, *New York Loyalists*, 169.

89 Howard H. Peckham, *The Toll of Independence: Engagements and Battle Casualties of the American Revolution* (Chicago: University of Chicago Press, 1974), 130. One author has added that perhaps ten thousand American sailors died aboard British prison ships in New York harbor: Gilje, "Loyalty and Liberty," 174.

90 Elizabeth A. Fenn, *Pox Americana: The Great Smallpox Epidemic of 1775–82* (New York: Hill & Wang, 2001); Harry M. Ward, *Between the Lines: Banditti of the American Revolution* (Westport, Conn.: Praeger, 2002), 3.

91 Lee, *Crowds and Soldiers*, 179, 190, 197, 199. Ward, *Between the Lines*, 3, 151. Martin, "A 'Most Undisciplined, Profligate Crew,'" 131–132. Edward Countryman, "Consolidating Power in Revolutionary America: The Case of New York, 1775–1783," *Journal of Interdisciplinary History* 6:4 (1976), 645–677: 653. Sung Bok Kim, "The Limits of Politicization in the American Revolution: The Experience of Westchester County, New York," *Journal of American History* 80:3 (December 1993), 868–889: 877–879. Countryman, *American Revolution*, 154.

92 John Resch, "The Revolution as a People's War: Mobilization in New Hampshire," in Resch and Sargent, *War and Society*, 70–102: 100.

93 Wells, *Population of the British Colonies*, 196, 212, 238, 253.

94 O'Shaughnessy, *Empire Divided*, 130–131, 142–143, 146–147, 151–155, 160 (quote on 152).

95 Edward Countryman, *A People in Revolution: The American Revolution and Political Society in New York, 1760–1790* (New York: Norton, 1989 [1981]), 111.

96 Adele Hast, *Loyalism in Revolutionary Virginia: The Norfolk Area and the Eastern Shore* (Ann Arbor, Mich.: UMI Research Press, 1982), 171. Bruce G. Merritt, "Loyalism and Social Conflict in Revolutionary Deerfield, Massachusetts," *Journal of American History* 57:2 (1970), 277–289: 281. Rebecca Starr, "'Little Bermuda': Loyalism on Daufuskie Island, South Carolina, 1775–1783," in Calhoon, Barnes, and Rawlyk, *Loyalists and Community*, 55–63: 57–58.

97 Knouff, *Soldiers' Revolution*, 52–53. John Shy, "The American Revolution: The Military Conflict Considered as a Revolutionary War," in Kurtz and Hutson, *Essays on the American Revolution*, 121–156: 147. Gross, *Minutemen and Their World*, 66.

98 Milton M. Klein, "Why Did the British Fail to Win the Hearts and Minds of New Yorkers?," *New York History* 64:4 (1983), 356–375: 365. Ranlet, *New York Loyalists*, 80. Joseph Tiedemann, "Communities in the Midst of the American Revolution: Queens County, New York, 1774–1775," *Journal of Social History* 18:1 (1984), 57–78: 58–62. Robert M. Calhoon, Timothy M. Barnes, and George A. Rawlyk, "Introduction," in Calhoon, Barnes, and Rawlyk, *Loyalists and Community in North America*, 4. Kim, "Limits of Politicization," 869. Ryerson, *Revolution Is Now Begun*, 145. Loyalists were not allowed to vote in New York, Rhode Island, Maryland, and the Carolinas: Robert J. Dinkin, *Voting in Revolutionary America: A Study of Elections in the Original Thirteen States, 1776–1789* (Westport, CT: Greenwood, 1982), 43.

99 Wellenreuther, *Von Chaos und Krieg*, 270, 298. David Dobson, *Scottish Emigration to Colonial America 1607–1785* (Athens: University of Georgia Press, 1994), 166. Ranlet, *New York Loyalists*, 159. Esther Clark Wright, "The Evacuation of the Loyalists from New York in 1783," *Nova Scotia Historical Review* 4 (1984), 5–25. Gordon T. Stewart and George A. Rawlyk, *A People Highly Favored of God: The Nova Scotia Yankees and the American Revolution* (Toronto: Macmillan, 1972). Gary B. Nash, *The Unknown American Revolution: The Unruly Birth of Democracy and the Struggle to Create America* (New York: Viking, 2005), 405. See, for their subsequent vicissitudes, Mary Beth Norton, *The British Americans: The Loyalist Exiles in England, 1774–1789* (Boston: Little, Brown, 1972); Simon Schama, *Rough Crossings: Britain, the Slaves and the American Revolution* (New York: HarperCollins, 2006); Maya Jasanoff, *Liberty's Exiles: American Loyalists in the Revolutionary World* (New York: Knopf, 2011).

100 Countryman, *American Revolution*, 171. Middlekauff, *Glorious Cause*, 21.

101 Wood, *Creation of the American Republic*, 136–137, 151–156. Countryman, *People in Revolution*, 75. Beeman, *Varieties of Political Experience*, 281–282.

102 Wellenreuther, *Von Chaos und Krieg*, 560, 562. Ryerson, *Revolution Is Now Begun*, 252. Dinkin, *Voting in Revolutionary America*, 6, 32, 34–36, 39, 107. Countryman, *People in Revolution*, 169.

103 Ryerson, *Revolution Is Now Begun*, 65–66, 190, 201–203, 207. Wood, *Creation of the American Republic*, 62, 71, 86, 113. Lance Banning, "The Problem of Power:

Parties, Aristocracy, and Democracy in Revolutionary Thought," in Jack P. Greene, ed., *The American Revolution: Its Character and Limits* (New York: New York University Press, 1987), 112, 114. Holton, *Forced Founders*, 192–197. Terry Bouton, *Taming Democracy: "The People," the Founders, and the Troubled Ending of the American Revolution* (New York: Oxford University Press, 2007).

104 Smith, "Food Rioters," 25, 34. Countryman, *American Revolution*, 137–138. Countryman, *People in Revolution*, 289.

105 Martin and Lender, *Respectable Army*, 196–197. McDonnell, *Politics of War*, 479, 482.

106 Twenty thousand female followers of the American army have been counted, while each British regiment included sixty women, i.e., about one woman for every eleven men in uniform. Linda K. Kerber, "'History Can Do It No Justice': Women and the Reinterpretation of the American Revolution," in Hoffman and Albert, *Women in the Age of the American Revolution*, 3–44: 12–13. Ward, *Between the Lines*, 7. See also Mary Beth Norton, *Liberty's Daughters: The Revolutionary Experience of American Women, 1750–1800* (Ithaca, N.Y.: Cornell University Press, 1996). For women's role in agriculture, see Joy Day Buel and Richard Buel, Jr., *The Way of Duty: A Woman and Her Family in Revolutionary America* (New York: Norton, 1984).

107 Dinkin, *Voting in Revolutionary America*, 42. Linda K. Kerber, *Women of the Republic: Intellect and Ideology in Revolutionary America* (Chapel Hill: University of North Carolina Press, 1980).

108 Cassandra Pybus, "Jefferson's Faulty Math: The Question of Slave Defections in the American Revolution," *William and Mary Quarterly*, 3rd series 62:2 (2005), 243–264: 248. Julius Sherrard Scott III, "The Common Wind: Currents of Afro-American Communication in the Era of the Haitian Revolution" (Ph.D. diss., Duke University, 1986), 118. Herbert Aptheker, *American Negro Slave Revolts* (New York: Columbia University Press, 1943), 201–205. Peter Wood, "'Liberty Is Sweet': African-American Freedom Struggles in the Years before White Independence," in Alfred F. Young, ed., *Beyond the American Revolution: Explorations in the History of American Radicalism* (DeKalb: Northern Illinois University Press, 1993), 149–184: 157–158.

109 Shane White, *Somewhat More Independent: The End of Slavery in New York City, 1770–1810* (Athens: University of Georgia Press, 1991), 142. Robert Olwell, "'Domestick Enemies': Slavery and Political Independence in South Carolina, May 1775–March 1776," *Journal of Southern History* 55:1 (1989), 21–48: 42. McDonnell, *Politics of War*, 22, 49. Ward, *Between the Lines*, 170, 176–177. Hast, *Loyalism in Revolutionary Virginia*, 46–47. Jacqueline Jones, "Race, Sex, and Self-Evident Truths: The Status of Slave Women during the Era of the American Revolution," in Hoffman and Albert, *Women in the Age of the American Revolution*, 293–337: 295.

110 Olwell, "'Domestick Enemies,'" 41. Schama, *Rough Crossings*, 67. Holton, *Forced Founders*, 153. McDonnell, *Politics of War*, 137, 144, 148–149. Hast, *Loyalism in Revolutionary Virginia*, 72. Philip Ranlet, "The British, Slaves, and Smallpox in Revolutionary Virginia," *Journal of Negro History* 84:3 (1999), 217–226.

111 Schama, *Rough Crossings*, 110–113. Eliga H. Gould, *Among the Powers of the Earth: The American Revolution and the Making of a New World Empire* (Cambridge, Mass.: Harvard University Press, 2012), 147–157.

112 Philip D. Morgan and Andrew Jackson O'Shaughnessy, "Arming Slaves in the American Revolution," in Christopher Leslie Brown and Philip D. Morgan, eds., *Arming Slaves from Classical Times to the Modern Age* (New Haven, Conn.: Yale University Press, 2006), 180–208: 192, 198–199. Cf. John Wood Sweet, *Bodies Politic: Negotiating Race in the American North, 1730–1830* (Baltimore: Johns Hopkins University Press, 2003), 216. The best general overviews of the black contribution to the revolution are Gary B. Nash, *The Forgotten Fifth: African Americans in the Age of Revolution* (Cambridge, Mass.: Harvard University Press, 2006); Alan Gilbert, *Black Patriots and Loyalists: Fighting for Emancipation in the War for Independence* (Chicago: University of Chicago Press, 2012); and Gerald Horne, *The Counter-Revolution of 1776: Slave Resistance and the Origins of the United States of America* (New York: New York University Press, 2014).

113 Thomas J. Davis, "Emancipation Rhetoric, Natural Rights, and Revolutionary New England: A Note on Four Black Petitions in Massachusetts, 1773–1777," *New England Quarterly* 62:2 (1989), 248–263. Daniel R. Mandell, "'A Natural and Unalienable Right': New England Revolutionary Petitions and African American Identity," in Michael A. McDonnell, Clare Corbould, Frances M. Clarke, and W. Fitzhugh Brundage, eds., *Remembering the Revolution: Memory, History, and Nation Making from Independence to the Civil War* (Amherst: University of Massachusetts Press, 2013), 41–57.

114 Gary B. Nash and Jean R. Soderlund, *Freedom by Degrees: Emancipation in Pennsylvania and Its Aftermath* (New York: Oxford University Press, 1991), 89. Mason, "Localism, Evangelicalism, and Loyalism," 42.

115 Don E. Fehrenbacher, *The Slaveholding Republic: An Account of the United States Government's Relations to Slavery*, completed and edited by Ward M. McAfee (Oxford: Oxford University Press, 2001), 28.

116 Countryman, *American Revolution*, 130.

117 Darren Staloff, *Hamilton, Adams, Jefferson. The Politics of Enlightenment and the American Founding* (New York: Hill & Wang, 2005), 62. Douglas R. Egerton, "Black Independence Struggles and the Tale of Two Revolutions: A Review Essay," *Journal of Southern History* 64:1 (1998), 95–116: 105. Ira Berlin, *Many Thousands Gone: The First Two Centuries of Slavery in North America* (Cambridge, Mass.: Belknap, 1998), 229. Joanne Pope Melish, *Disowning Slavery: Gradual Emancipation and "Race" in New England, 1780–1860* (Ithaca, N.Y.: Cornell University Press, 1998), 63–66.

118 Douglas R. Egerton, *Death or Liberty: African Americans and Revolutionary America* (Oxford: Oxford University Press, 2009), 115–116. Nash and Soderlund, *Freedom by Degrees*, 111. Berlin, *Many Thousands Gone*, 234.

119 McDonnell, *Politics of War*, 485.

120 Paul Finkelman, "Slavery and the Northwest Ordinance: A Study in Ambiguity," *Journal of the Early Republic* 6:4 (1986), 343–370: 345–346.

CHAPTER 3. THE WAR ON PRIVILEGE AND DISSENSION

1 James B. Collins, *The Ancien Régime and the French Revolution* (Toronto: Wadsworth/Thomson Learning, 2002), 56–57. Jack A. Goldstone, *Revolution and Rebellion in the Early Modern World* (Berkeley: University of California Press, 1991), 202, 207.

2 Florin Aftalion, *The French Revolution: An Economic Interpretation* (Cambridge: Cambridge University Press, 1990), 196.

3 Thomas Manley Luckett, "Hunting for Spies and Whores: A Parisian Riot on the Eve of the Revolution," *Past and Present* 156 (1977), 116–143: 123, 128–131, 138–140.

4 François R. Velde and David R. Weir, "The Financial Market and Government Debt Policy in France, 1746–1793," *Journal of Economic History* 52:1 (1992), 1–39: 5–8, 36. Eugene Nelson White, "Was There a Solution to the Ancien Regime's Financial Dilemma?," *Journal of Economic History* 49:3 (September 1989), 545–568: 558–567. But for the structural problems of France's royal finances, see Marie-Laure Legay, "Capitalisme, crises de trésorerie et donneurs d'avis: une relecture des années 1783–1789," *Revue Historique* 312:3 (2010), 577–608; Gail Bossenga, "Financial Origins of the French Revolution," in Kaiser and Van Kley, *From Deficit to Deluge*, 37–66.

5 David M. Bien, "Offices, Corps, and a System of State Credit: The Uses of Privilege under the Ancien Régime," in Keith M. Baker, ed., *The French Revolution and the Creation of Modern Political Culture* (Oxford: Pergamon, 1987), 1:89–114: 111.

6 Bailey Stone, *The Parlement of Paris, 1774–1789* (Chapel Hill: University of North Carolina Press, 1981), 181.

7 Bailey Stone, *Reinterpreting the French Revolution: A Global-Historical Perspective* (Cambridge: Cambridge University Press, 2002), 87.

8 The calling of the Estates General had first been demanded by the Paris *parlement*: John Hardman, *The Life of Louis XVI* (New Haven, Conn.: Yale University Press, 2016), 278–283.

9 Collins, *Ancien Régime*, 51, 59–60. Without authorization, women in some parts of France compiled their own *cahiers*: Christine Fauré, "Doléances, declarations et petitions, trois forms de la parole publique des femmes sous la Révolution," *Annales historiques de la Révolution française*, no. 344 (2006), 2–16: 6–7.

10 Beatrice Fry Hyslop, *A Guide to the General Cahiers of 1789: With the Texts of Unedited Cahiers* (Morningside Heights, N.Y.: Columbia University Press, 1936), 414.

11 Clergy: e.g., the *cahiers* of the sénechaussée of Beziers and the lower clergy of the diocese of Nantes: Hyslop, *Guide to the General Cahiers*, 222, 375. Nobility: John Markoff, *The Abolition of Feudalism: Peasants, Lords, and Legislators in the French Revolution* (University Park: Pennsylvania State University Press, 1996), 47. Third Estate: Collins, *Ancien Régime*, 62–63.

12 Hilton Root, *Peasants and King in Burgundy: Agrarian Foundations of French Absolutism* (Berkeley: University of California Press, 1987), 202–203.

13 Markoff, *Abolition of Feudalism*, 40, 58, 78, 109, 201. Stone, *Reinterpreting the French Revolution*, 91.

14 George V. Taylor, "Revolutionary and Nonrevolutionary Content in the Cahiers of 1789: An Interim Report," *French Historical Studies* 7:4 (1972), 479–502: 492–493.

15 Thomas Munck, *The Enlightenment: A Comparative Social History 1721–1794* (London: Arnold, 2000), 103. Keith M. Baker, "Sieyès," in François Furet and Mona Ozouf, *A Critical Dictionary of the French Revolution* (Cambridge, Mass.: Belknap, 1989), 313–323.

16 Alan Forrest, *The French Revolution* (Oxford: Blackwell, 1995), 20–22.

17 Collins, *Ancien Régime*, 78–80.

18 Schama, *Citizens*, 408–416.

19 Stone, *Reinterpreting the French Revolution*, 96–98.

20 Forrest, *French Revolution*, 32–33. Cf. Mary Ashburn Miller, *A Natural History of Revolution: Violence and Nature in the French Revolutionary Imagination, 1789–1794* (Ithaca, N.Y.: Cornell University Press, 2011). One historian has recently downplayed the amount of violence used by the Parisian population during the Revolution: Micah Alpaugh, *Non-violence and the French Revolution: Political Demonstrations in Paris, 1787–1795* (Cambridge: Cambridge University Press, 2015).

21 Alan Forrest, *The Revolution in Provincial France: Aquitaine, 1789–1799* (Oxford: Clarendon Press, 1996), 129. The term "brigands" could mean something different to different classes: Clay Ramsay, *The Ideology of the Great Fear: The Soissonnais in 1789* (Baltimore: Johns Hopkins University Press, 1992), 138–147.

22 Abel Poitrineau, *La vie rurale en Basse-Auvergne au XVIIIe siècle (1726–1789)* (Paris: P.U.F., 1965), 586, 731, 741.

23 Georges Lefebvre, *The Great Fear of 1789: Rural Panic in Revolutionary France* (New York: Pantheon Books, 1973; original French edition 1932), 50.

24 Ibid., 94–95.

25 Clarke Garrett, "The Myth of the Counterrevolution in 1789," *French Historical Studies* 18:3 (1994), 784–800: 796, 797, 799. Markoff, *Abolition of Feudalism*, 218 (table 5.1).

26 Markoff, *Abolition of Feudalism*, 222–225, 231, 248. Patrice Higonnet, *Class, Ideology, and the Rights of Nobles during the French Revolution* (Oxford: Clarendon Press, 1981), 82. Forrest, *Revolution in Provincial France*, 133–139.

27 Jean Bart, *La Révolution française en Bourgogne* (Clermont-Ferrand: La Française d'Edition et d'Imprimerie, 1996), 129.

28 Rafe Blaufarb, *The Great Demarcation: The French Revolution and the Invention of Modern Property* (New York: Oxford University Press, 2016).

29 Ibid., 1–5.

30 Furet, "Night of August 4," in Furet and Ozouf, *Critical Dictionary*, 107–114.

31 Peter McPhee, *Revolution and Environment in Southern France, 1780–1830: Peasants, Lords, and Murder in the Corbières* (Oxford: Oxford University Press, 1999), 125–127. For the connection between environmental concerns and political move-

ments during the Revolution, see Kieko Matteson, *Forests in Revolutionary France: Conservation, Community, and Conflict, 1669–1848* (Cambridge: Cambridge University Press, 2015).

32 Collins, *Ancien Régime*, 99, 103, 109–112. Timothy Tackett, *Religion, Revolution, and Regional Culture in Eighteenth-Century France: The Ecclesiastical Oath of 1791* (Princeton, N.J.: Princeton University Press, 1986), 22, 24. Rodney J. Dean, *L'Assemblée constituante et la réforme ecclesiastique, 1790* (Paris: Rodney Dean, 2014). Joseph F. Byrnes, *Priests of the French Revolution: Saints and Renegades in a New Political Era* (University Park: Pennsylvania State University Press, 2014).

33 Tackett, *Religion, Revolution, and Regional Culture*, 8–11, 69, 155, 231–232. Furet, "Civil Constitution of the Clergy," in Furet and Ozouf, *Critical Dictionary*, 449–457. Markoff, *Abolition of Feudalism*, 230.

34 Tackett, *Religion, Revolution, and Regional Culture*, 164–165, 181, 200–201, 289.

35 Donald Greer, *The Incidence of the Emigration during the French Revolution* (Cambridge, Mass.: Harvard University Press, 1951). Palmer, *Age of the Democratic Revolution*, 1:188. Massimo Boffa, "Emigrés," in Furet and Ozouf, *Critical Dictionary*, 324–336: 325–326. Higonnet, *Class, Ideology, and the Rights of Nobles*, 58–59, 84.

36 Higonnet, *Class, Ideology, and the Rights of Nobles*, 63, 67. J. Percy Keating, "John Keating and His Forebears," *Records of the American Catholic Historical Society* 29:4 (1918), 289–335: 310.

37 Taylor, "Revolutionary and Nonrevolutionary Content," 487.

38 Marcel Gauchet, "Rights of Man," in Furet and Ozouf, *Critical Dictionary*, 818–828: 819–820, 823. Annie Jourdan, "The 'Alien' Origins of the French Revolution: American, Scottish, Genevan, and Dutch Influences," *Proceedings of the Western Society for French History* 35 (2007), 185–205.

39 Marcel Gauchet, *La revolution des pouvoirs: la souveraineté, le peuple et la représentation, 1789–1799* (Paris: Gallimard, 1995), 58–59. Ladan Boroumand, *La guerre des principes: Les assemblées révolutionnaires face aux droits de l'homme et à la souveraineté de la nation mai 1789–juillet 1794* (Paris: Éditions de l'École des Hautes Études en Sciences Sociales, 1999), 70–71. Mona Ozouf, "Equality," in Furet and Ozouf, *Critical Dictionary*, 669–683: 676. Baker, "Sieyès," 319–320.

40 Forrest, *French Revolution*, 79–80. Ozouf, "Equality," 672.

41 Jean-Pierre Gross, "Progressive Taxation and Social Justice in Eighteenth-Century France," *Past and Present*, no. 140 (1993), 79–126: 104–105, 107–108.

42 David Patrick Geggus, *Haitian Revolutionary Studies* (Bloomington: Indiana University Press, 2002), 159.

43 Laura Mason and Tracey Rizzo, *The French Revolution: A Document Collection* (Boston: Houghton Mifflin, 1999), 111.

44 *Requête des dames à l'Assemblée* and *Remontrances plaintes et doléances des Dames Françoises, à l'occasion de l'Assemblée des Etats-Generaux*, both in *Les femmes dans la Revolution française*, 2 vols. (Paris: EDHIS, 1982), vol. 1. For the intersection of de Gouges's work on gender with her critique of black slavery, see Lisa

Beckstrand, *Deviant Women of the French Revolution and the Rose of Feminism* (Madison, N.J.: Fairleigh Dickinson University Press, 2009), 97–121.

45 Jon Cowans, *To Speak for the People: Public Opinion and the Problem of Legitimacy in the French Revolution* (New York: Routledge, 2001), 58. Dominique Godineau, *The Women of Paris and Their French Revolution* (Berkeley: University of California Press, 1998; original French edition 1988), 100. Suzanne Desan, "'War between Brothers and Sisters': Inheritance Law and Gender Politics in Revolutionary France," *French Historical Studies* 20:4 (1997), 597–634: 598, 601, 608, 611, 613. Desan, "Pétitions de femmes en faveur d'une réforme révolutionnaire de la famille," *Annales historiques de la Révolution française* 344 (2006), 27–46: 45. Desan, *The Family on Trial in Revolutionary France* (Berkeley: University of California Press, 2004). The (temporary) emancipation of women painters in these years is discussed in Marie-Josèphe Bonnet, *Liberté, égalité, exclusion: femmes peintres en Révolution, 1770–1804* (Paris: Vendémiaire, 2012).

46 For the background of women's engagement on this occasion, see David Garrioch, "The Everyday Lives of Parisian Women and the October Days of 1789," *Social History* 24:3 (1999), 231–249.

47 Godineau, *Women of Paris*, 98–99, 102–103. Olwen H. Hufton, *Women and the Limits of Citizenship in the French Revolution* (Toronto: University of Toronto Press, 1992). Martine Lapied, "Parole publique des femmes et conflictualité pendant la Révolution, dans le Sud-Est de la France," *Annales historiques de la Révolution française* 344 (2006), 47–62.

48 Raymonde Monnier, *Le Faubourg Saint-Antoine (1789–1815)* (Paris: Société des Etudes Robespierristes, 1981), 18, 25, 56, 72, 122, 297.

49 Ibid., 91, 93–94, 98, 116, 125.

50 Michel Vovelle, *La mentalité révolutionnaire: Société et mentalités sous la révolution française* (Paris: Messidor/Éditions sociales, 1985), 70–82. Colin Lucas, "The Crowd and Politics between 'Ancien Régime' and Revolution in France," *Journal of Modern History* 60:3 (1988), 421–457: 422.

51 Mona Ozouf, *La fête révolutionnaire 1789–1799* (Paris: Éditions Gallimard, 1976), 69.

52 Lynn A. Hunt, "Committees and Communes: Local Politics and National Revolution in 1789," *Comparative Studies in Society and History* 18:3 (1976), 321–346: 324–325, 332–333, 340, 343. Haim Burstin, *Révolutionnaires: Pour une anthropologie politique de la Révolution Française* (Paris: Vendémiaire, 2013). The departments were a creation of the revolution. In the summer and fall of 1789, the Assembly replaced the division in provinces by departments, which were subdivided into districts, which were themselves subdivided into cantons.

53 Isser Woloch, *The New Regime: Transformations of the French Civic Order, 1789–1820s* (New York: Norton, 1994), 63–67, 71–73, 82, 89–90.

54 Palmer, *Age of the Democratic Revolution*, 1:501. Root, *Peasants and King in Burgundy*, 66.

55 Samuel F. Scott, "The Regeneration of the Line Army during the French Revolution," *Journal of Modern History* 42:3 (1970), 307–330: 318.

56 Ling-Ling Sheu, *Voltaire et Rousseau dans le théâtre de la Révolution française (1789–1799)*, foreword by Roland Mortier (Brussels: Éditions de l'Université de Bruxelles, 2005), 10–11. Schama, *Citizens*, 133.

57 Timothy Tackett, *When the King Took Flight* (Cambridge, Mass.: Harvard University Press, 2003).

58 J. M. Roberts, *The French Revolution*, 2nd ed. (Oxford: Oxford University Press, 1997), 41.

59 David Andress, "The Denial of Social Conflict in the French Revolution: Discourses around the Champ de Mars Massacre, 17 July 1791," *French Historical Studies* 22:2 (1999), 183–209: 207–209.

60 Mona Ozouf, "Varennes," in Furet and Ozouf, *Critical Dictionary*, 155–164: 162.

61 Higonnet, *Class, Ideology, and the Rights of Nobles*, 76. Boffa, "Emigrés," 326–327. Six thousand men deserted through the end of the year: Greer, *Incidence of the Emigration*, 26; Samuel Scott, *The Response of the Royal Army to the French Revolution: The Role and Development of the Line Army 1789–93* (Oxford: Clarendon Press, 1978), 109, adds that between September 15 and December 1, 1792, 2,160 officers emigrated.

62 Owen Connelly, *The French Revolution and Napoleonic Era* (Fort Worth: Harcourt, 1991), 97.

63 François Furet, *Revolutionary France 1770–1880* (Oxford: Blackwell, 1992; original French edition 1988), 83.

64 Arthur Herzberg, *The French Enlightenment and the Jews* (New York: Columbia University Press, 1968).

65 Sue Peabody, *"There Are No Slaves in France": The Political Culture of Race and Slavery in the Ancien Régime* (Oxford: Oxford University Press, 1996), chaps. 1 and 2.

66 Stone, *Reinterpreting the French Revolution*, 159. Collins, *Ancien Régime*, 127.

67 Alison Patrick, "The Second Estate in the Constituent Assembly, 1789–1791," *Journal of Modern History* 62:2 (1990), 223–252: 243. Patrice L. R. Higonnet, *Goodness beyond Virtue: Jacobins during the French Revolution* (Cambridge, Mass.: Harvard University Press, 1998), 78, 104, 173.

68 Higonnet, *Goodness beyond Virtue*, 127, 157, 161.

69 Jennifer Harris, "The Red Cap of Liberty: A Study of Dress Worn by French Revolutionary Partisans," *Eighteenth-Century Studies* 14:3 (1981), 283–312: 283, 286.

70 Albert Soboul, *The Parisian Sans-Culottes and the French Revolution 1793–4* (Oxford: Clarendon Press, 1964), 100–105. Higonnet, *Goodness beyond Virtue*, 285.

71 Higonnet, *Goodness beyond Virtue*, 160. Collins, *Ancien Régime*, 132–134. Connelly, *French Revolution and Napoleonic Era*, 107–109.

72 Timothy Tackett, *The Coming of the Terror in the French Revolution* (Cambridge, Mass.: Belknap, 2015), 192–193.

73 Cowans, *To Speak for the People*, 78, 196. Furet, *Revolutionary France*, 111.

74 See Aftalion, *French Revolution*, 111, for a grassroots view of hoarding.

75 Higonnet, *Goodness beyond Virtue*, 83. Gross, "Progressive Taxation," 111, 113. Michael L. Kennedy, "The Best and the Worst of Times: The Jacobin Club Network

from October 1791 to June 1793," *Journal of Modern History* 56:4 (1984), 635–666: 661. Bronislaw Backo, *Ending the Terror: The French Revolution after Robespierre* (Cambridge: Cambridge University Press, 1994), 76. Soboul, *Parisian Sans-Culottes*, 107.

76 Guy Ikni, "Sur les biens communaux," *Annales Historiques de la Révolution Française* 54:247 (1982), 71–94: 78–79. Patrice Higonnet, "Sans-Culottes," in Furet and Ozouf, *Critical Dictionary*, 393–399. Cf. Diane Ladjouzi, "Les journées des 4 et 5 septembre 1793 à Paris: Un mouvement d'union entre le peuple, la Commune de Paris et la Convention pour un exécutif révolutionnaire," *Annales historiques de la Révolution française* 72:3 (2000), 27–44. Connelly, *French Revolution and Napoleonic Era*, 141–142. Monnier, *Faubourg Saint-Antoine*, 82.

77 Hufton, *Women and the Limits of Citizenship*, 57–58, 69–70, 75, 80–82.

78 Furet, *Revolutionary France*, 117–119.

79 Cited in Andrew Jainchill, "The Constitution of the Year III and the Persistence of Classical Republicanism," *French Historical Studies* 26:3 (2003), 399–435: 410.

80 Matthew Shaw, *Time and the French Revolution: The Republican Calendar, 1789–Year IV* (Woodbridge, U.K.: Boydell & Brewer, 2011). Sanja Perovic, *The Calendar in Revolutionary France: Perceptions of Time in Literature, Culture, Politics* (Cambridge: Cambridge University Press, 2012). On the failure of revolutionary festivals, see Joseph F. Byrnes, "Celebration of the Revolutionary Festivals under the Directory: A Failure of Sacrality," *Church History* 63:2 (1994), 201–220.

81 Serge Bianchi, "Les curés rouges dans la Révolution française," *Annales Historiques de la Révolution Française* 57:262 (1985), 446–479: 475–477. Richard S. Clay, *Iconoclasm in Revolutionary Paris: The Transformation of Signs* (Oxford: Voltaire Foundation, 2012).

82 Bronislaw Backo, "Vandalism," in Furet and Ozouf, *Critical Dictionary*, 860–868. Higonnet, *Goodness beyond Virtue*, 139. James Livesey, "Agrarian Ideology and Commercial Republicanism in the French Revolution," *Past and Present*, no. 157 (1997), 94–121: 100.

83 Stanley J. Idzerda, "Iconoclasm during the French Revolution," *American Historical Review* 60:1 (1954), 13–26: 15–16.

84 Edmund Burke, *Reflections on the Revolution in France* (Oxford: Oxford University Press, 1993), 61, 173, 291–292.

85 Wil Verhoeven, *Americomania and the French Revolution Debate in Britain, 1789–1802* (New York: Cambridge University Press, 2013), 32–69. Mori, *Britain in the Age of the French Revolution*, 14. George Taylor, *The French Revolution and the London Stage 1789–1805* (New York: Cambridge University Press, 2000), 42–43. Cf. R. B. McDowell, *Ireland in the Age of Imperialism and Revolution, 1760–1801* (Oxford: Clarendon Press, 1979), 351.

86 Inge Stephan, *Literarischer Jakobinismus in Deutschland (1789–1806)* (Stuttgart: J. B. Metzlersche Verlagsbuchhandlung, 1976), 33. Winfried Dotzauer, "Die Freimaurerei und die Französische Revolution in Deutschland," in Meinrad Schaab, ed., *Oberrheinische Aspekte des Zeitalters der Französischen Revolution* (Stuttgart:

W. Kohlhammer Verlag, 1990), 41–84: 60. Jörg Schweigard, "Studentische Netzwerke im Zeichen der Französischen Revolution: Politische Gruppenbildungen, Meinungstransfers und Symbole an süddeutschen Hochschulen (1791–1794)," *Aufklärung* 24 (2012), 317–344.

87 Anatole G. Mazour, "The Russian Ambassador in France 1789–1792," *Russian Review* 1:2 (1942), 86–93: 88–90.

88 Roberts, *French Revolution*, 62.

89 Higonnet, *Goodness beyond Virtue*, 92, 177–178, 227. Harris, "Red Cap of Liberty," 285.

90 Mona Ozouf, *L'École de la France: Essais sur la Révolution, l'utopie et l'enseignement* (Paris: Gallimard, 1984), 83. Patrice Gueniffey and Ran Halévi, "Clubs and Popular Societies," in Furet and Ozouf, *Critical Dictionary*, 458–473: 459. Ozouf, "Girondins," in Furet and Ozouf, *Critical Dictionary*, 351–361: 357. Boroumand, *La guerre des principes*, 312. Higonnet, *Goodness beyond Virtue*, 26, 156.

91 Ran Halévi, "The Constituent Revolution and Its Ambiguities," in Jack R. Censer, ed., *The French Revolution and Intellectual History* (Chicago: Dorsey Press, 1989), 139–151: 151.

92 Cowans, *To Speak for the People*, 117, 127, 144.

93 Stone, *Reinterpreting the French Revolution*, 72.

94 Scott, *Response of the Royal Army*, 18, 188–189. Forrest, *French Revolution*, 116–121. Stone, *Reinterpreting the French Revolution*, 165. Janet Polasky, *Revolutions without Borders: The Call to Liberty in the Atlantic World* (New Haven, Conn.: Yale University Press, 2015), 232–244.

95 Boroumand, *La guerre des principes*, 464, 481.

96 Martyn Lyons, *France under the Directory* (Cambridge: Cambridge University Press, 1975), 86–87, quoted in Stone, *Reinterpreting the French Revolution*, 188–189.

97 Frederick C. Schneid, "The French Army," in Frederick C. Schneid, ed., *European Armies of the French Revolution, 1789–1802* (Norman: University of Oklahoma Press, 2015), 13–35: 21. F. M. Anderson, ed., *The Constitutions and Other Select Documents Illustrative of the History of France, 1789–1907*, 2nd ed. (Minneapolis: H. W. Wilson, 1908), 184–185.

98 Collins, *Ancien Régime*, 212–213. Jacques Godechot, *La vie quotidienne en France sous le Directoire* (Paris: Librairie Hachette, 1977), 22–23.

99 Cowans, *To Speak for the People*, 151.

100 "Law on Suspects," in Mason and Rizzo, *French Revolution: A Document Collection*, 230–232.

101 Boroumand, *La guerre des principes*, 483.

102 Dan Edelstein, *The Terror of Natural Rights: Republicanism, the Cult of Nation, and the French Revolution* (Chicago: University of Chicago Press, 2009), 142–147, 154–163.

103 Furet, *Revolutionary France*, 135. His most recent biography is Peter McPhee, *Robespierre: A Revolutionary Life* (New Haven, Conn.: Yale University Press, 2012).

104 George Armstrong Kelly, "Conceptual Sources of the Terror," *Eighteenth-Century Studies* 14:1 (1980), 18–36: 34. Mona Ozouf, "War and Terror in French Revolutionary Discourse, 1792–1794," *Journal of Modern History* 56:4 (1984), 579–597: 584. For the view that the events of 1789 led inexorably to the Terror, see Marisa Linton, *Choosing Terror: Virtue, Friendship, and Authenticity in the French Revolution* (Oxford: Oxford University Press, 2013), 9.

105 Boroumand, *La guerre des principes*, 461, 467.

106 Higonnet, *Goodness beyond Virtue*, 52. Dagmar von Gersdorff, *Goethe's Mutter: Eine Biographie* (Frankfurt am Main: Insel Verlag, 2001), 333.

107 For the Terror outside Paris, see Richard Ballard, *The Unseen Terror: The French Revolution in the Provinces* (London: I.B. Tauris, 2011).

108 David L. Longfellow, "Silk Weavers and the Social Struggle in Lyon during the French Revolution, 1789–1794," *French Historical Studies* 12:1 (1981), 1–40: 1–22. The 1790s also saw furious journeymen protests against non-guild labor in various German towns: Karl H. Wegert, "Patrimonial Rule, Popular Self-Interest, and Jacobinism in Germany, 1763–1800," *Journal of Modern History* 53:3 (1981), 440–467: 452.

109 Forrest, *French Revolution*, 153–154. Higonnet, *Goodness beyond Virtue*, 277.

110 Collins, *Ancien Régime*, 164–165. Backo, *Ending the Terror*, 148–149.

111 Forrest, *French Revolution*, 141, 152. Furet, "Chouannerie," in Furet and Ozouf, *Critical Dictionary*, 3–10: 5.

112 The other departments were Loire-Inférieure, Maine-et-Loire, and Deux–Sèvres.

113 Hugh Gough, "Genocide and the Bicentenary: The French Revolution and the Revenge of the Vendée," *Historical Journal* 30:4 (1987), 977–988: 980–981.

114 Jean-Clément Martin, *La Vendée et la France* (Paris: Seuil, 1987), 312–317. England's support for the insurgents led the Directory to consider helping the United Irish to rise in rebellion. One director hoped Ireland would be England's Vendée: Marianne Elliott, *Partners in Revolution: The United Irishmen and France* (New Haven, Conn.: Yale University Press, 1982), 87.

115 Markoff, *Abolition of Feudalism*, 293–294, 366–367, 389. Forrest, *French Revolution*, 147, 149, 151. T. J. A. Le Goff and D. M. G. Sutherland, "The Social Origins of Counter-Revolution in Western France," *Past and Present* 99 (1983), 65–87: 76–78. David Andress, *The Terror: The Merciless War for Freedom in Revolutionary France* (New York: Farrar, Straus and Giroux, 2006), 161.

116 McPhee, *Robespierre*, 217–220. Backo, *Ending the Terror*, 16–17. The Parisian population supported his downfall: Colin Jones, "The Overthrow of Maximilien Robespierre and the 'Indifference' of the People," *American Historical Review* 119:3 (2014), 689–713: 709.

117 Denis Woronoff, *The Thermidorean Regime and the Directory, 1794–1799* (Cambridge: Cambridge University Press, 1984), 23–24. Collins, *Ancien Régime*, 195–196.

118 Patrice Gueniffey, "La Révolution ambigüe de l'an III: la Convention, l'élection directe et le problème des candidatures," in Roger Dupuy and Marcel Morabito,

eds., *1795: Pour une République sans Révolution* (Rennes: Presses Universitaires de Rennes, 1996), 49–78: 50–54.

119 Furet, *Revolutionary France*, 154, 193. Collins, *Ancien Régime*, 196. Woronoff, *Thermidorean Regime*, 119.

120 Holger Böning, *Revolution in der Schweiz: das Ende der Alten Eidgenossenschaft; die Helvetische Republik 1798–1803* (Frankfurt am Main: Peter Lang, 1985), 117. Raymond Grew, "Finding Social Capital: The French Revolution in Italy," *Journal of Interdisciplinary History* 29:3 (1999), 407–433: 420–421. E. H. Kossmann, *De Lage Landen 1780–1840: Anderhalve eeuw Nederland en België*, 4th ed. (Amsterdam: Elsevier, 1984), 42–44. Edward de Maesschalck, *Overleven in revolutietijd: Een ooggetuige over het Franse bewind (1792–1815)* (Leuven: Davidsfonds, 2003), 97–98. T. C. W. Blanning, *The French Revolution in Germany: Occupation and Resistance in the Rhineland,1792–1802* (Oxford: Oxford University Press, 1983), 125, 215, 221, 225, 286. Hansgeorg Molitor, *Vom Untertan zum administré: Studien zur französischen Herrschaft und zum Verhalten der Bevölkerung im Rhein-Mosel-Raum von den Revolutionskriegen bis zum Ende der Napoleonische Zeit* (Wiesbaden: Franz Steiner Verlag, 1980), 172.

121 Sheu, *Voltaire et Rousseau dans le théâtre*, 11–12, 75. A new emphasis on individuality emerged, as reflected in contemporary utopian novels: Anne-Rozenn Morel, "Le principe de fraternité dans les fictions utopiques de la Révolution française," *Dix-Huitième Siècle* 41:1 (2009), 120–136: 135.

122 Woloch, *New Regime*, 181–183, 190, 192–193.

123 Ruault, *Gazette d'un Parisien*, 376. Aftalion, *French Revolution*, 167–171. Collins, *Ancien Régime*, 209.

124 Godechot, *La vie quotidienne*, 110–111.

125 Robert Legrand, *Babeuf et ses compagnons de route* (Paris: Société des Études Robespierristes, 1981), 177.

126 Woronoff, *Thermidorean Regime*, 46–47. Legrand, *Babeuf et ses compagnons de route*, 246–247. David Thompson, *The Babeuf Plot: The Making of a Republican Legend* (London: Trench, Trubner, 1947), 48.

127 Furet, *Revolutionary France*, 173–174. Woronoff, *Thermidorean Regime*, 60–61.

CHAPTER 4. FROM PRIZE COLONY TO BLACK INDEPENDENCE

1 Moreau de Saint-Méry, *Description topographique, physique, civile, politique et historique de la partie française de l'isle Saint-Domingue*, ed. Blanche Maurel and Étienne Taillemite (Paris: Société de l'Histoire des Colonies Françaises, Librairie Larose, 1958), 119–120, 723, 1165.

2 Olivier Pétré-Grenouilleau, *Nantes au temps de la traite des Noirs* (Paris: Hachettes Littératures, 1998), 34, 38.

3 Calculated on the basis of Patrick Villiers, *Le commerce colonial atlantique et la guerre d'indépendance des Etats-Unis d'Amérique* (New York: Arno Press, 1977), 443. Saint-Domingue accounted for 77.0 percent and 85.6 percent, respectively, of the value of the exports from Bordeaux and Nantes.

4 Jacques Cauna, *Au temps des isles à sucre: Histoire d'une plantation de Saint-Domingue au XVIIIe siècle* (Paris: A.C.C.T., Éditions Karthala, 1987), 19.

5 Robert Chagny, "Barnave et le débat colonial à l'Assemblée Constituante," in Michel Hector, ed., *La Révolution française et Haïti: filiations, ruptures, nouvel-les dimensions: Colloque organisé par la Société Haïtienne d'Histoire et de Géogra-phie et le Comité haïtien du Bicentenaire de la Révolution française (5–8 décembre 1989)* (Port-au-Prince: Editions Henri Deschamps, Société Haïtienne d'Histoire et de Géographie, 1995), 400–418: 401–402.

6 Susan M. Socolow, "Economic Roles of the Free Women of Color of Cap Fran-çais," in David Barry Gaspar and Darlene Clark Hine, eds., *More Than Chattel: Black Women and Slavery in the Americas* (Bloomington: Indiana University Press, 1996), 279–297: 280. Charles Frostin, *Histoire de l'autonomisme colon de la partie de St. Domingue aux XVIIe et XVIIIe siècles. Contribution à l'étude du senti-ment américain d'indépendance* (Lille: Université de Lille III, 1973), 834. Moreau de Saint-Méry, *Description*, 316.

7 Robert Louis Stein, *The French Sugar Business in the Eighteenth Century* (Baton Rouge: Louisiana State University Press, 1988), 37–38, 80–82. Françoise Thésée, *Négociants bordelais et colons de Saint-Domingue: La maison Henry Romberg, Bapst et Cie 1783–1793* (Paris: Société Française d'Histoire d'Outre-Mer, 1972), 209–210.

8 G. Debien, "L'esprit d'indépendance chez les colons de Saint-Domingue au XVIIIe siècle et l'appel aux Anglais en 1793," *Revue d'Histoire et de Géographie d'Haïti* 17 (1946), 1–46: 8–9.

9 Frostin, *Histoire de l'autonomisme colon*, 616–617, 619.

10 Villiers, *Marine royale*, 430, 434–435. Pitman, *Development of the British West Indies*, 234. Liliane Crété, *La traite des nègres sous l'ancien régime: Le nègre, le sucre et la toile* (Paris: Librarie Académique Perrin, 1989), 233. Michel-René Hilliard d'Auberteuil, *Considérations sur l'état présent de la colonie française de Saint-Domingue: Ouvrage politique et législatif; présenté au ministre de la marine*, 2 vols. (Paris: Grangé, 1776–1777), 1:58. Moreau de Saint-Méry, *Description*, 1166. Frostin, *Histoire de l'autonomisme colon*, 626. For a comparison between Saint-Domingue and Jamaica, see Trevor Burnard and John Garrigus, *The Plantation Machine: Atlantic Capitalism in French Saint-Domingue and British Jamaica* (Philadelphia: University of Pennsylvania Press, 2016).

11 Debien, "L'esprit d'indépendance," 14.

12 Frostin, *Histoire de l'autonomisme colon*, 641, 727, 729–730. Debien, "L'esprit d'indépendance," 15.

13 Frostin, *Histoire de l'autonomisme colon*, 648, 722–724.

14 Moreau de Saint-Méry, *Description*, 33–34. Frostin, *Histoire de l'autonomisme colon*, 834. Hilliard d'Auberteuil, *Considérations*, 2:45.

15 John D. Garrigus, *Before Haiti: Race and Citizenship in French Saint-Domingue* (New York: Palgrave Macmillan, 2006), 118. Cauna, *Au temps des isles à sucre*, 87–90. Frostin, *Histoire de l'autonomisme colon*, 692, 703–705.

16   Garrigus, *Before Haiti*, 118. Stewart R. King, *Blue Coat or Powdered Wig: Free People of Color in Pre-revolutionary Saint Domingue* (Athens: University of Georgia Press, 2001), 124.

17   Frostin, *Histoire de l'autonomisme colon*, 688–689, 692. Moreau de Saint-Méry, *Description*, 34.

18   Frostin, *Histoire de l'autonomisme colon*, 693–699. Garrigus, *Before Haiti*, 142.

19   Frostin, *Histoire de l'autonomisme colon*, 661. Garrigus, *Before Haiti*, 169.

20   Socolow, "Economic Roles," 281–284. King, *Blue Coat or Powdered Wig*, 50, 187. Garrigus, *Before Haiti*, 71–72, 74. Frostin, *Histoire de l'autonomisme colon*, 662.

21   Gérard Barthélémy, "Spécificité, idéologie et rôle des Noirs libres pendant la période de l'indépendance d'Haïti (Premier aperçu pour une étude du groupe des noirs libres)," in Michel Hector, ed., *La Révolution française et Haïti: filiations, ruptures, nouvelles dimensions: Colloque organisé par la Société Haïtienne d'Histoire et de Géographie et le Comité haïtien du Bicentenaire de la Révolution française (5–8 décembre 1989)*, 2 vols. (Port-au-Prince: Editions Henri Deschamps, Société Haïtienne d'Histoire et de Géographie, 1995), 1:169–184. King, *Blue Coat or Powdered Wig*, 64.

22   King, *Blue Coat or Powdered Wig*, 54, 65. Garrigus, *Before Haiti*, 103, 207.

23   Cf. Stuart B. Schwartz, "The Formation of a Colonial Identity in Brazil," in Nicholas Canny and Anthony Pagden, eds., *Colonial Identity in the Atlantic World, 1500–1800* (Princeton, N.J.: Princeton University Press, 1987), 15–50: 16.

24   Garrigus, *Before Haiti*, 95. Gabriel Debien, *Études antillaises (XVIIIe Siècle)* (Paris: Librairie Armand Colin, 1956), 75. Yvan Debbasch, *Couleur et liberté: Le jeu de critère ethnique dans un ordre juridique esclavagiste* (Paris: Librarie Dalloz, 1967), 38–39, 53–54, 74–75. Julien Raymond, *Réclamations adressées à l'Assemblé Nationale, par les personnes de Couleur, Propriétaires & Cultivateurs de la Colonie Françoise de Saint-Domingue* (Paris: s.n., 1790). Julien Raymond, *Observations sur l'origine et les progrés du préjugé des colons blancs contre les hommes de couleur; Sur les inconvéniens de le perpétuer; la nécessité, la facilité de le détruire; sur le projet du Comité colonial, etc.* (Paris: Belin, Desenne, Bailly, Bureau du Patriote François, 1791), 8. King, *Blue Coat or Powdered Wig*, 168.

25   Peabody, *"There Are No Slaves in France,"* 74. le jeune Weuves, *Réflexions historiques et politiques sur le commerce de France avec ses colonies de l'Amérique* (Geneva: L. Cellot, 1780), 280–281. For the pre-revolutionary position of blacks and "mulattoes" in France, see Pierre H. Boulle, *Race et l'esclavage dans la France de l'Ancien Régime* (Paris: Perrin, 2007).

26   Sankar Muthu, *Enlightenment against Empire* (Princeton, N.J.: Princeton University Press, 2003), 3–5, 101–102, 120–121. Srinivas Aravamudan, "Progress through Violence or Progress from Violence? Interpreting the Ambivalences of the *Histoire des Deux Indes*," in Valérie Cossy and Deidre Dawson, eds., *Progrès et violence au XVIIIe siècle* (Paris: Honoré Champion, 2001), 259–280, 268, 272.

27   Léo Elisabeth, *La société martiniquaise aux XVIIe et XVIIIe siècles, 1664–1789* (Paris: Éditions Karthala, Fort-de-France: SHM, 2003), 411, 438. Guillaume

Thomas Raynal, *Essai sur l'administration de St. Domingue* (s.l.: s.n., 1785), 38–39, 199.

28 Debbasch, *Couleur et liberté*, 54. Hilliard d'Auberteuil, *Considérations*, 2:88.

29 Garrigus, *Before Haiti*, 143, 156.

30 John Garrigus, "Blue and Brown: Contraband Indigo and the Rise of a Free Colored Planter Class in French Saint-Domingue," *Americas* 50:2 (October 1993), 233–263: 235 (table 1).

31 David P. Geggus, "Sugar and Coffee Cultivation in Saint Domingue and the Shaping of the Slave Labor Force," in Ira Berlin and Philip D. Morgan, eds., *Cultivation and Culture: Labor and the Shaping of Slave Life in the Americas* (Charlottesville: University of Virginia Press, 1993), 73–98: 79–82. Cf. for a slightly different picture in one part of the south: Arlette Gautier, "Les origines ethniques des esclaves déportés à Nippes, Saint-Domingue, de 1721 à 1770 d'après les archives notariales," *Revue Canadienne des Études Africaines* 23:1 (1989), 28–39.

32 Stein, *French Sugar Business*, 45.

33 Cauna, *Au temps des isles à sucre*, 116–117. Hilliard d'Auberteuil, *Considérations*, 1:136. Justin Girod-Chantrans, *Voyage d'un suisse dans différentes colonies d'Amérique pendant la derniere guerre, avec une table d'observations météorologiques faites à Saint-Domingue* (Neuchatel: De l'Imprimerie de la Société Typographique, 1785), 137, 161.

34 Cf. Debien, *Études antillaises*, 173.

35 "Le début de la révolte de Saint Domingue dans la Plaine du Cap, vécu par Louis de Calbiac," *Généalogie et Histoire de la Caraïbe Bulletin* 48 (1993), 774–784: 780–781.

36 David P. Geggus, "Slave and Free Colored Women in Saint Domingue," in Gaspar and Hine, *More Than Chattel*, 259–278: 260.

37 *Manuscrit d'un voyage de France à Saint Domingue, à la Havanne et aux Unis Etats Damérique* (ms.), John Carter Brown Library, Providence, R.I., 169–171. Moreau de Saint-Méry, *Description*, 55.

38 Hilliard d'Auberteuil, *Considérations*, 1:137–138.

39 Hein Vanhee, "Central African Popular Christianity and the Making of Haitian Vodou Religion," in Linda Heywood, ed., *Central Africans and Cultural Transformations in the American Diaspora* (Cambridge: Cambridge University Press, 2002), 243–264: 248–250.

40 Carolyn E. Fick, *The Making of Haiti: The Saint Domingue Revolution from Below* (Knoxville: University of Tennessee Press, 1990), 49–57. Moreau de Saint-Méry, *Description*, 1131–1135. Bernard Moitt, "Slave Women and Resistance in the French Caribbean," in Gaspar and Hine, *More Than Chattel*, 239–258: 246–247. For a book-length study of the maroons, see Jean Fouchard, *The Haitian Maroons: Liberty or Death*, trans. A. Faulkner Watts, preface by C. L. R. James (New York: E. W. Blyden Press, 1981).

41 Laurent Dubois, *Avengers of the New World: The Story of the Haitian Revolution* (Cambridge, Mass.: Harvard University Press, 2004), 54.

42 Blanche Maurel, *Cahiers de doléances de la colonie de Saint-Domingue pour les États Généraux de 1789* (Paris: Librairie Ernest Leroux, 1933), 36, 205.

43 Nicolas-Robert, marquis de Cocherel, *Apperçu sur la Constitution de Saint-Domingue, par M. de Cocherel, l'un de ses Députés* (s.l: s.n. [1789 or 1790]), 1–2. P. J. Laborie, *Réflexions sommaires addressées à la France et à la colonie de S. Domingue* (Paris: De l'Imprimerie de Chardon [1789?]), 40.

44 Maurel, *Cahiers de doléances*, 63, 89, 95, 100.

45 Ibid., 70, 73. *Du commerce des colonies* (Versailles: Ph.-D. Pierres, 1789), 15–16, 26, 34.

46 *Motion de M. de Cocherel, député de S. Domingue, à la Séance du Samedi 29 Août 1789, soir* (Versailles: Baudouin, 1789), 1–2. Jean-François, comte de Reynaud de Villeverd, *Motion de M. le Comte de Reynaud, député de Saint-Domingue, à la Séance du 31 Août* (Versailles: Baudouin, 1789), 4. *Réponse succincte des Députés de S. Domingue, au mémoire des commerçans des ports de mer, distribué dans les Bureaux de l'Assemblée Nationale, le 9 Octobre 1789* (Versailles: Baudouin, 1789), 6. *Réponse des Députés des Manufactures et du Commerce de France, au Motions de MM. De Cocherel & de Raynaud, Députés de l'Isle de St. Domingue à l'Assemblée Nationale* (Versailles: Ph.-D. Pierres, 1789), 32–33.

47 Bernard Journu-Auber, *Rapport et projet de décret sur les effets de la Révolution dans les Colonies françaises au-delà du Cap de Bonne-Espérance, présentés à l'Assemblée Nationale le 7 Janvier 1792, l'an 4 de la Liberté, au nom du Comité des Colonies* (Paris: L'Imprimerie Nationale, 1792), 12–13.

48 Thésée, *Négociants bordelais*, 127. Peabody, *"There Are No Slaves in France,"* 119.

49 Dubois, *Avengers of the New World*, 77. Laborie, *Réflexions sommaires*, 4–5n. *Observations de M. de Cocherel, Député de Saint-Domingue, à l'Assemblée Nationale, sur la demande des Mulâtres* (Paris: l'Imprimerie de Clousier, 1789), 11–12.

50 Garrigus, *Before Haiti*, 236–237. *Extrait du procès-verbal de l'Assemblée des Citoyens—Libres de Couleur, & Propriétaires des Isles & Colonies Françoises, constituée sous le titre de Colons Américains* (s.l.: s.n., 1789). *Adresse à l'Assemblée-Nationale, pour les Citoyens-Libres de Couleur, des Isles & Colonies Françoises, 18 Octobre 1789* (s.l.: s.n., 1789), 1–2. *Réclamations adres-sées à l'Assemblé Nationale, par les personnes de Couleur, Propriétaires & Cultivateurs de la Colonie Françoise de Saint-Domingue* (s.l.: s.n., 1789), 6. J. M. C., *Précis des gémissemens des sang-mêlés dans les colonies françoises* (Paris: Baudouin, 1789), 7, 13.

51 Robin Blackburn, *The Overthrow of Colonial Slavery 1776–1848* (London: Verso, 1988), 171–172.

52 Garrigus, *Before Haiti*, 240. M. Grégoire, *Lettre aux Philantropes, sur les malheurs, les droits et les réclamations des Gens de couleur de Saint-Domingue, et des autres îles françoises de l'Amérique* (Paris: Belin, Desenne, Bailly, Bureau du Patriote François, 1790), 7, 18. For Grégoire, see Rita Hermon-Belot, *L'abbé Grégoire: La politique de la vérité* (Paris: Seuil, 2000); Alyssa Goldstein Sepinwall, *The Abbé Grégoire and the French Revolution: The Making of Modern Universalism* (Chapel Hill: University of North Carolina Press, 2005).

53 Laborie, *Réflexions sommaires*, 33. Louis Charton, *Observation de M. Charton à la motion de M. Moreau de Saint-Méry* (s.l.: s.n., 1789), 2. J. Marie de Bordes, *Défense des colons de Saint-Domingue; ou Examen rapide de la nouvelle déclaration des droits de l'homme, en ce qu'elle a particulièrement de relatif aux colonies* (Philadelphia: Moreau de Saint-Méry, 1796), 36. *Coup d'oeil sur la question de la traite et de l'esclavage des Noirs, considéré dans son rapport avec le Droit naturel* (Paris: Momoro, 1790), 10–11. *De l'état des nègres rélativement à la prosperité des colonies françaises et de leur métropole; discours aux réprésentans de la nation* (Paris: s.n., 1789), 12–13. Cf. *Du commerce des colonies*, 36–37.

54 David Duval-Sanadon, *Réclamations et observations des colons, sur l'idée de l'Abolition de la Traite et de l'affranchissement des Nègres*, 2nd ed. (Paris: s.n., 1789), 32–33. Jean-Baptiste, baron Mosneron de Launay, *Discours sur les Colonies et la Traite des Noirs, Prononcé le 26 Février 1790, par M. Mosneron de l'Aunay, Député du Commerce de Nantes près l'Assemblée Nationale, à la Société des amis de la Constitution* (Paris: s.n., 1790), 11. *De l'état des nègres*, 17.

55 Jean-Daniel Piquet, *L'émancipation des Noirs dans la Révolution française (1789–1795)* (Paris: Éditions Karthala, 2002), 199–204.

56 Société des Amis des Noirs, *Réflexions sur le Code Noir, et Dénonciation d'un crime affreux, commis à Saint-Domingue; Adressées à l'Assemblé Nationale* (Paris: L'Imprimerie du Patriote François, 1790), 8–9. Piquet, *L'émancipation des Noirs*, 201–202.

57 Maurel, *Cahiers de doléances*, 112. Raymond, *Observations sur l'origine et les progrés*, 13. Jean Siffrein Maury, *Opinion de M. l'Abbé Maury, député de Picardie, sur le droit d'initiative que réclament les assemblées coloniales pour toutes les loix relatives à l'état des personnes dans les colonies; sur l'admissibilité des hommes de couleur aux droits de citoyen actif, ou aux emplois publics; Prononcée dans l'Assemblée Nationale, le vendredi 13 mai 1791* (Paris: L'Imprimerie Nationale, 1791), 9. Garrigus, *Before Haiti*, 243, 258–259. Garrigus estimates that around a thousand men would have benefited from the May 15 decree. A contemporary estimate was four to five hundred: *Débats entre les accusateurs et les accusés, dans l'affaire des colonies, imprimés en exécution de la Loi du 4 Pluviôse* (Paris: L'Imprimerie Nationale, 1795), 1:261.

58 Malick W. Ghachem, *The Old Regime and the Haitian Revolution* (New York: Cambridge University Press, 2012), 244–246.

59 *Journal général politique, de littérature, et de commerce*, June 16, 1791. *Délibération des quatre Comités réunis de Constitution, de Marine, d'Agriculture & Commerce & des colonies. Du 12 Septembre 1791* (Paris: L'Imprimerie Nationale, 1791), 3, 11. Cf. Pierre-Victor, baron Malouet, *Opinion de M. Malouet, sur la Législation des Colonies, relativement à l'état des personnes et au régime intérieur* (s.l.: s.n., n.d.), 14.

60 J.-P. Brissot de Warville, *Discours sur la nécessité de maintenir le décret rendu le 15 mai 1791, en faveur des hommes de couleur libres, prononcé le 12 septembre 1791, à la séance de la Société des Amis de la Constitution, séante aux Jacobins* (Paris: s.n., 1791).

61 Frostin, *Histoire de l'autonomisme colon*, 713. Geggus, *Haitian Revolutionary Studies*, 10. Garrigus, *Before Haiti*, 244. Conditions in Guadeloupe also amounted to a veritable civil war: Anne Pérotin-Dumon, *Être patriotique sous les tropiques: La Guadeloupe, la colonisation et la Révolution (1789-1794)* (Basse-Terre: Société d'Histoire de la Guadeloupe, 1985), 138-139.

62 Thésée, *Négociants bordelais*, 130. Dubois, *Avengers of the New World*, 86.

63 John D. Garrigus, "Vincent Ogé 'jeune' (1757-91): Social Class and Free Colored Mobilization on the Eve of the Haitian Revolution," *Americas* 68:1 (2011), 33-62. Geggus, *Haitian Revolutionary Studies*, 11. Dubois, *Avengers of the New World*, 87-88.

64 Elisabeth, *La société martiniquaise*, 447, 450-453. Debien, *Études antillaises*, 119.

65 Blackburn, *Overthrow of Colonial Slavery*, 172. Dubois, *Avengers of the New World*, 79-80.

66 Frédéric Régent, *Esclavage, métissage, liberté: La Révolution française en Guadeloupe, 1789-1802* (Paris: Bernard Grasset, 2004), 219-221.

67 Fick, *Making of Haiti*, 91, Dubois, *Avengers of the New World*, 106-107.

68 "Le début de la révolte de Saint Domingue," 774-776. The role of vodou in the rebellion's organization has been exaggerated in the past: Geggus, *Haitian Revolutionary Studies*, 77-78.

69 Cauna, *Au temps des isles à sucre*, 19, 212. Thésée, *Négociants bordelais*, 158-159.

70 John K. Thornton, "'I Am the Subject of the King of Congo': African Political Ideology and the Haitian Revolution," *Journal of World History* 4:2 (1993), 181-214: 201-202. Dubois, *Avengers of the New World*, 123-124. Bryan Edwards, *An Historical Survey of the French Colony in the Island of St. Domingo: Comprehending a Short Account of Its Ancient Government, Political States, Population, Productions, and Exports; a Narrative of the Calamities Which Have Desolated the Country Ever since the Year 1789, with Some Reflections on Their Causes and Probable Consequences; and a Detail of the Military Transactions of the British Army in That Island to the End of 1794* (London: John Stockdale, 1797), 105, 143.

71 Blackburn, *Overthrow of Colonial Slavery*, 195. Robert Louis Stein, *Léger Félicité Sonthonax: The Lost Sentinel of the Republic* (Rutherford, N.J.: Fairleigh Dickinson University Press, 1985), 24.

72 Stein, *Léger Félicité Sonthonax*, 20-23, 42, 44-45.

73 Ibid., 46-55.

74 David Patrick Geggus, *Slavery, War, and Revolution: The British Occupation of Saint Domingue 1793-1798* (Oxford: Clarendon Press, 1982), 64. Stein, *Léger Félicité Sonthonax*, 59-61, 65, 67-68. *Dénonciation des colons de Saint-Domingue, en état d'arrestation dans la Ville de Nantes, soussignés; contre Polverel et Sonthonax, ci-devant Commissaires Civils aux Isles sous le vent, pour y rétablir l'ordre & la tranquillité publique. A la Convention Nationale et au peuple français* (s.l.: s.n., 1793). For the daily stream of exiles, see the rubric "departures" in the *Journal Politique du Port-au-Prince et Affiches Américaines* of August 11, 1793. For Jamaica, see Philip Wright and G. Debien, "Les colons de Saint-Domingue passés à la

Jamaïque (1792–1835)," *Bulletin de la Société d'Histoire de la Guadeloupe* 26 (1975), 1–217: 44.

75 Stein, *Léger Félicité Sonthonax*, 69–70. Dubois, *Avengers of the New World*, 155–157. Fick, *Making of Haiti*, 158–159. *Extrait d'une lettre, sur les malheurs de Saint-Domingue en général, et principalement sur l'incendie de la ville du Cap Français* (Paris: l'Imprimerie de Pain, 1793), 19.

76 Stein, *Léger Félicité Sonthonax*, 75. Fick, *Making of Haiti*, 159.

77 Stein, *Léger Félicité Sonthonax*, 79, 88–89. *Journal des Révolutions de la partie française de St.-Domingue* [Philadelphia], October 7, 1793. Dubois, *Avengers of the New World*, 162–165. Garrigus, *Before Haiti*, 271–272. Victor Hugues introduced a modified version of this system as the administrator of Guadeloupe: Laurent Dubois, *A Colony of Citizens: Revolution and Slave Emancipation in the French Caribbean, 1787–1804* (Chapel Hill: University of North Carolina Press, 2004), 206–209.

78 Piquet, *L'Émancipation des Noirs*, 484. Jean-Charles Benzaken, "Louis-Pierre Dufay, député abolitionniste et homme d'affaires avisé. Esquisse biographique," *Annales historiques de la Révolution française* 368 (2012), 61–85.

79 Louis Pierre Dufay, *Compte rendu sur la situation actuelle de SaintDomingue* (Paris: L'Imprimerie Nationale, 1794), 8–9.

80 Yves Bénot, "Comment la Convention a-t-elle voté l'abolition de l'esclavage en l'an II?" *Annales Historiques de la Révolution Française*, nos. 293–294 (1993), 349–361: 353–355.

81 Pierre Pluchon, *Toussaint Louverture: Une révolutionnaire noir d'Ancien Régime* (Paris: Fayard, 1989), 85. Piquet, *L'Émancipation des Noirs*, 348. Blackburn, *Overthrow of Colonial Slavery*, 223. For a careful reconstruction of the demise of slavery in Saint-Domingue, see Jeremy D. Popkin, *You Are All Free: The Haitian Revolution and the Abolition of Slavery* (New York: Cambridge University Press, 2010).

82 Alain Yacou, "La stratégie espagnole d'éradication de Saint-Domingue Français 1790–1804," in Paul Butel and Bernard Lavallé, eds., *L'espace caraïbe, enjeu et théâtre des luttes impériales, XVIe–XIXe siècle* (Talence: Maison des Pays Ibériques, 1996), 277–293: 280–283. Ada Ferrer, "Cuba en la sombra de Haití: noticias, sociedad y esclavitud," in María Dolores González-Ripoll, Consuelo Naranjo, Ada Ferrer, Gloria García, and Josef Opatrný, *El rumor de Haití en Cuba: temor, raza y rebeldía, 1789–1844* (Madrid: Consejo Superior de Investigaciones Científicas, 2004), 179–231: 190–191. The Spanish troops stood by idly as Jean-François's men massacred seven hundred white Frenchmen in July 1794: ibid., 193.

83 Pluchon, *Toussaint Louverture*, 134.

84 His most recent biography, which I was unable to consult for this edition, is Philippe Girard, *Toussaint Louverture: A Revolutionary Life* (New York: Basic Books, 2016).

85 Geggus, *Haitian Revolutionary Studies*, 16.

86 Fick, *Making of Haiti*, 159–160. Pluchon, *Toussaint Louverture*, 93, 96.

87 Fick, *Making of Haiti*, 163–164, 168–169, 172, 173. Geggus, *Slavery, War, and Revolution*, 64, 101, 313. Mr. Gros, *Recit historique sur les evenemens qui se sont succédés dans les camps de la Grande-Rivière, du Dondon, de Sainte-Suzanne & autres, depuis le 26 octobre 1791 jusqu'au 24 decembre de la même année* (Paris: L. Potier de Lille, 1793), 5.

88 Pluchon, *Toussaint Louverture*, 97. Geggus, *Slavery, War, and Revolution*, 103. Michael Duffy, *Soldiers, Sugar, and Seapower: The British Expeditions to the West Indies and the War against Revolutionary France* (Oxford: Clarendon Press, 1987), 62.

89 Garrigus, *Before Haiti*, 245–246. Geggus, *Slavery, War, and Revolution*, 69–70, 77–78, 114.

90 Duffy, *Soldiers, Sugar, and Seapower*, 257, 369. Geggus, *Slavery, War, and Revolution*, 275. See Duffy, *Soldiers, Sugar, and Seapower*, 44, 54, 196, for the numbers of British troops sent.

91 Duffy, *Soldiers, Sugar, and Seapower*, 111–113. Geggus, *Slavery, War, and Revolution*, 127–129, 328.

92 Duffy, *Soldiers, Sugar, and Seapower*, 148. This number would grow to six thousand by 1798: Dubois, *Avengers of the New World*, 216.

93 Hubert Cole, *Christophe, King of Haiti* (New York: Viking, 1967), 30–31. Deborah Jenson, "Jean-Jacques Dessalines and the African Character of the Haitian Revolution," *William and Mary Quarterly*, 3rd series 69:3 (2012), 615–638.

94 Pluchon, *Toussaint Louverture*, 101, 102, 107–109. Fick, *Making of Haiti*, 184, 186. Geggus, *Slavery, War, and Revolution*, 116. Geggus, *Haitian Revolutionary Studies*, 17–18, 125.

95 Pluchon, *Toussaint Louverture*, 111, 117–118, 122–126, 144. Geggus, *Haitian Revolutionary Studies*, 19.

96 Pluchon, *Toussaint Louverture*, 162, 200, 202–203. Geggus, *Slavery, War, and Revolution*, 201, 247, 258–260. Fick, *Making of Haiti*, 186, 188, 194196.

97 Marcus Rainsford, *A Memoir of Transactions That Took Place in St. Domingo, in the Spring of 1799; Affording an Idea of the Present State of That Country, the Real Character of Its Black Governor, Toussaint L'ouverture, and the Safety of Our West-India Islands from Attack or Revolt; Including the Rescue of a British officer under Sentence of Death* (London: R. B. Scott, 1802), 11–12.

98 Geggus, *Haitian Revolutionary Studies*, 19–20.

99 Geggus, *Slavery, War, and Revolution*, 203, 305. Pluchon, *Toussaint Louverture*, 135–136. Dubois, *Avengers of the New World*, 188–189.

100 Pluchon, *Toussaint Louverture*, 189–191, 202–203. C. L. R. James, *The Black Jacobins: Toussaint L'Ouverture and the San Domingo Revolution* (2nd ed., New York: Vintage Books, 1989), 217–220, 257. Fick, *Making of Haiti*, 198–199.

101 James, *Black Jacobins*, 236. Garrigus, *Before Haiti*, 303.

102 Dubois, *Avengers of the New World*, 223. Pluchon, *Toussaint Louverture*, 200. For the tumultuous two decades after 1789 in the entire island of Hispaniola, see Graham T. Nessler, *Islandwide Struggle for Freedom: Revolution, Emancipation,*

and Reenslavement in Hispaniola, 1789–1809 (Chapel Hill: The University of North Carolina Press, 2016).

103 Geggus, *Haitian Revolutionary Studies*, 25–26. Dubois, *Avengers of the New World*, 234, 251. Joseph Saint-Rémy, *Pétion et Haïti: Étude monographique et historique*, 2nd ed., 5 vols. in one (Paris: Librairie Berger-Levrault et Cie, 1956, ed. François Dalencour), 1:11–12. Lespinasse, "Autour d'un centenaire," in *Gens d'autrefois . . . Vieux Souvenirs . . .* , 63–78: 67–68.

104 Marcus Rainsford, *An Historical Account of the Black Empire of Hayti: Comprehending a View of the Principal Transactions in the Revolution of Santo Domingo; with its Antient and Modern State* (London: James Cundee, 1805), 220.

105 Geggus, *Haitian Revolutionary Studies*, 25–26. Dubois, *Avengers of the New World*, 264–265, 267.

106 Dubois, *Avengers of the New World*, 274–278. Hénock Trouillot, "La Guerre de l'Indépendance d'Haïti: Les grands prêtres du vodou contre l'armée française," *Revista de Historia de América* 72 (1971), 259–327: 264.

107 Rainsford, *Historical Account*, 327. Boisrond Tonnerre, *Mémoires pour servir à l'histoire d'Haïti* (Port-au-Prince: Editions Fardin, 1981), 75. Bernard Gainot and Mayeul Macé, "Fin de campagne à Saint-Domingue, novembre 1802–novembre 1803," *Outre-mers* 90 (2003), 15–40. Joseph Élisée Peyre-Ferry, *Journal des opérations militaires de l'armée française à Saint-Domingue 1802–1803 sous les ordres des capitaines-généraux Leclerc et Rochambeau* (Paris: Les Éditions de Paris, 2006), 171, 188.

108 Philippe R. Girard, "Caribbean Genocide: Racial War in Haiti, 1802–4," *Patterns of Prejudice* 39:2 (1995), 138–161. Rainsford, *Memoir of Transactions*, 22. Peyre-Ferry, *Journal des opérations militaires*, 53. Dubois, *Avengers of the New World*, 289.

109 Garrigus, *Before Haiti*, 303–307. Trouillot, "La Guerre de l'Indépendance," 273, 288.

110 A French source estimated that 50,270 of the 58,545 men died in the first four months after disembarking, predominantly of yellow fever: Trouillot, "La Guerre de l'Indépendance," 295. See also J. R. McNeill, *Mosquito Empires: Ecology and War in the Greater Caribbean, 1620–1914* (New York: Cambridge University Press, 2010), 260–265.

111 David Geggus, "British Opinion and the Emergence of Haiti, 1791–1805," in James Walvin, ed., *Slavery and British Society, 1776–1846* (Baton Rouge: Louisiana State University Press, 1982), 123–149: 137.

112 Michel-Rolph Trouillot, *Silencing the Past: Power and the Production of History* (Boston: Beacon, 1995), 94–95.

113 Geggus, *Haitian Revolutionary Studies*, 177.

114 B. Ardouin, *Études sur l'histoire d'Haïti suivies de la vie du Général J.-M. Borgella*, 11 vols., 2nd ed. (Port-au-Prince: chez l'éditeur, 1958), 6:8.

115 Cole, *Christophe*, 141–144. Girard, "Caribbean Genocide," 139–140, 143. Leslie J.-R. Péan, *Haïti, économie politique de la corruption: De Saint-Domingue à Haïti 1791–1870* (Paris: Maisonneuve & Larose, 2003), 87–90. Ardouin, *Études sur l'histoire*

d'Haïti, 6:14–15. Dessalines's wife tried in vain to intervene on behalf of one white family: Mademoiselle de P., *Histoire de mesdemoiselles de Saint-Javier: Les deux seules blanches conservées a Saint-Domingue*, 2nd ed. (Paris: J.-J. Blaise, 1812), 45–51.

116 Cole, *Christophe*, 144. Ardouin, *Études sur l'histoire d'Haïti*, 6:28.

117 Cole, *Christophe*, 145, 147, 151. Saint-Rémy, *Pétion et Haïti*, 4:40. Péan, *Haïti, économie politique de la corruption*, 135. Mats Lundahl, "Defense and Distribution: Agricultural Policy in Haiti during the Reign of Jean-Jacques Dessalines, 1804–1806," *Scandinavian Economic History Review* 22:2 (1984), 77–103: 82.

118 Saint-Rémy, *Pétion et Haïti*, 4:57. Cole, *Christophe*, 153. Lundahl, "Defense and Distribution," 92, 95–96.

119 Ardouin, *Études sur l'histoire d'Haïti*, 6:12. James Franklin, *The Present State of Hayti (Saint Domingo), with Remarks on Its Agriculture, Commerce, Laws, Religion, Finances, and Population, etc. etc.* (London: John Murray, 1828), 187–188. W. W. Harvey, *Sketches of Hayti; from the Expulsion of the French, to the Death of Christophe* (London: L. B. Seeley and Son, 1827), 238–239. Cole, *Christophe*, 161. In 1816, the Haitian authorities freed all 145 Africans on board a North American slave ship that anchored in Cap-Henry en route to Cuba: Ardouin, *Études sur l'histoire d'Haïti*, 8:66.

120 Ardouin, *Études sur l'histoire d'Haïti*, 6:34. Pamphile de Lacroix, *Mémoires pour servir à l'histoire de la révolution de Saint-Domingue*, 2 vols. (Paris: Pillet Aîné, 1819), 2:303–304, 323. Harvey, *Sketches of Hayti*, 341.

121 Robert K. Lacerte, "Xenophobia and Economic Decline: The Haitian Case, 1820–1843," *Americas* 37:4 (1981), 499–515: 503. Cole, *Christophe*, 239. Mats Lundahl, *Peasants and Poverty: A Study of Haiti* (New York: St. Martin's Press, 1979), 485, quoting O. Ernest Moore, *Haiti: Its Stagnant Society and Shackled Economy: A Survey* (New York: Exposition Press, 1972), 114.

122 Lacerte, "Xenophobia," 500. *Procès verbal des séances du Conseil général de la Nation* (Cap-Henry: P. Roux [1814]), 14–16. See also Chevalier de Prézeau, *Réfutation de la lettre du général français Dauxion Lavaysse* (Cap-Henry: P. Roux, 1814).

123 Cole, *Christophe*, 219–220.

124 Lacerte, "Xenophobia," 502, 505. John Edward Baur, "Mulatto Machiavelli, Jean Pierre Boyer, and the Haiti of His Day," *Journal of Negro History* 32:3 (1947), 307–353: 328n59. For international recognition of Haitian independence, see Julia Gaffield, *Haitian Connections in the Atlantic World: Recognition after Independence* (Chapel Hill: University of North Carolina Press, 2015).

125 Cf. David Nicholls, "A Work of Combat: Mulatto Historians and the Haitian Past, 1847–1867," *Journal of Interamerican Studies and World Affairs* 16:1 (1974), 15–38.

126 Péan, *Haïti, économie politique de la corruption*, 247, 257. Ardouin, *Études sur l'histoire d'Haïti*, 7:15. Cole, *Christophe*, 178, 190.

127 Saint-Rémy, *Pétion et Haïti*, 5:124.

128 Pierre-Eugène de Lespinasse, *Gens d'autrefois . . . Vieux Souvenirs* (Paris: Jean d'Halluin, 1961), 84–97.

129 Harvey, *Sketches of Hayti*, 144–145.

130 Saint-Rémy, *Pétion et Haïti*, 5:51–55.

131 Lundahl, "Defense and Distribution," 87. Lundahl, *Peasants and Poverty*, 263, 269. Péan, *Haïti, économie politique de la corruption*, 89–90, 141. Ardouin, *Études sur l'histoire d'Haïti*, 7:10, 27, 99. Leslie F. Manigat, *La politique agraire du gouvernement d'Alexandre Pétion (1807–1818)* (Port-au-Prince: Imp. La Phalange, 1962), 26–32, 47. Vertus Saint-Louis, "L'assassinat de Dessalines et les limites de la société haïtienne face au marché international," in Yves Bénot and Marcel Dorigny, eds., *Rétablissement de l'esclavage dans les colonies françaises 1802. Ruptures et continuités de la politique française (1800–1830). Aux origines d'Haïti. Actes du colloque international tenu à l'Université de Paris VIII les 20, 21 et 22 juin 2002* (Paris: Maisonneuve & Larose, 2003), 161–177: 163, 168–170.

132 Ardouin, *Études sur l'histoire d'Haïti*, 8:108.

CHAPTER 5. MULTIPLE ROUTES TO SOVEREIGNTY

1 J. H. Elliott, "Spain and Its Empire in the Sixteenth and Seventeenth Centuries," in Elliott, *Spain and Its World, 1500–1700: Selected Essays* (New Haven, Conn.: Yale University Press, 1989), 7, 15–16.

2 The figures for New Spain and Peru are found in Timothy E. Anna, *The Fall of the Royal Government in Peru* (Lincoln: University of Nebraska Press, 1979), 2. For New Granada and the Caribbean islands, I have relied on George Reid Andrews, *Afro-Latin-America, 1800–2000* (Oxford: Oxford University Press, 2004), 202, and for the Río de la Plata on Andrews as well as on John Lynch, *The Spanish American Revolutions 1808–1826*, 2nd ed. (New York: Norton, 1986), 38, 106; and Heraclio Bonilla, "Peru and Bolivia," in Leslie Bethell, ed., *Spanish America after Independence, c. 1820–c. 1870* (Cambridge: Cambridge University Press, 1987), 238–282: 264.

3 Stuart Schwartz, "The Landed Elite," in Louisa Schell Hoberman and Susan Migden Socolow, eds., *The Countryside in Colonial Latin America* (Albuquerque: University of New Mexico Press, 1996), 97–121: 113.

4 The two taxes for the nobility were the *media annata*, due at the creation of the title and when someone succeeded to it, and the *lanzas*, an annual tax that could be paid in cash in 160,000 *reales de vellón*: Paul Rizo-Patrón Boylan, *Linaje, dote y poder: La nobleza de Lima de 1700 a 1850* (Lima: Pontificia Universidad Católica del Perú, Fondo Editorial, 2001), 29–30.

5 Peter F. Guardino, *Peasants, Politics, and the Formation of Mexico's National State: Guerrero, 1800–1857* (Stanford: Stanford University Press, 1996), 25.

6 George Reid Andrews, "Spanish American Independence: A Structural Analysis," *Latin American Perspectives* 12:1 (1985), 105–132: 113.

7 Luis Felipe Pellicer, *La vivencia del honor en la provincial de Venezuela, 1774–1809: estudio de casos* (Caracas: Fundación Polar, 1996), 42, 116–117. Marianela Ponce, *El ordenamiento jurídico y el ejercicio del derecho de libertad de los esclavos en la Provincia de Venezuela 1730–1768* (Caracas: Academia Nacional de la Historia, 1994), 38–39.

8 Margarita Garrido, *Reclamos y representaciones: variaciones sobre la política en el Nuevo Reino de Granada, 1770–1815* (Santafé de Bogotá: Banco de la República, 1993), 31. Doris M. Ladd, *The Mexican Nobility at Independence 1780–1826* (Austin: University of Texas Press, 1976), 71. Inés Quintero, "Honor, riqueza y desigualdad en la provincia de Venezuela, siglo XVIII," in Bernd Schröter and Christian Büschges, eds., *Beneméritos, aristócratas y empresarios: Identidades y estructuras sociales de las capas altas urbanas en América hispánica* (Frankfurt am Main: Iberoamericana, 1999), 183–198: 189, 191, 194–195.

9 Pellicer, *Vivencia del honor*, 26, 28, 33, 35–38. For the concept of honor in Mexico, see Patricia Seed, *To Love, Honor, and Obey in Colonial Mexico: Conflicts over Marriage Choice, 1574–1821* (Stanford: Stanford University Press, 1988).

10 Lyman L. Johnson, "Francisco Baquero: Shoemaker and Organizer," in David G. Sweet and Gary B. Nash, eds., *Struggle and Survival in Colonial America* (Berkeley: University of California Press, 1981), 86–101: 90–91. Marie Laure Rieu-Millán, *Los diputados americanos en las Cortes de Cádiz (Igualdad o independencia)* (Madrid: Consejo Superior de Investigaciones Científicas, 1990), 158.

11 Lockhart, "Social Organization and Social Change," 298. Lyman L. Johnson, "Estimaciones de la población de Buenos Aires en 1744, 1778 y 1840," *Desarrollo Económico* 19:73 (1979), 107–119: 117. Sarah C. Chambers, *From Subjects to Citizens: Honor, Gender, and Politics in Arequipa, Peru, 1780–1854* (University Park: Pennsylvania State University Press, 1999), 47, 87. For the scope of race mixture in New Granada, see Germán Colmenares, *La provincia de Tunja en el Nuevo Reino de Granada: Ensayo de historia social (1539–1800)* (Bogotá: Universidad de los Andes, Facultad de Artes y Ciencias, Departamento de Historia, 1970), 203.

12 Jesús A. Cosamalón Aguilar, "Amistades peligrosas: matrimonios indígenas y espacios de convivencia interracial (Lima 1795–1820)," in Scarlett O'Phelan Godoy, ed., *El Perú en el siglo XVIII: La Era Borbónica* (Lima: Pontificia Universidad Católica del Perú, Instituto Riva-Agüero, 1999), 345–368: 351, 367.

13 Lyle N. McAlister, *Spain and Portugal in the New World 1492–1700* (Minneapolis: University of Minnesota Press, 1984), 438.

14 Peter Bakewell, "Conquest after the Conquest: The Rise of Spanish Domination in America," in Richard L. Kagan and Geoffrey Parker, *Spain, Europe and the Atlantic World: Essays in Honour of John H. Elliott* (Cambridge: Cambridge University Press, 1995), 296–315: 298.

15 H. Pietschmann, "Burocracia y corrupción en Hispanoamérica colonial: una aproximación tentativa," *Nova Americana* 5 (1982), 11–37: 23–24.

16 Mark A. Burkholder and D. S. Chandler, *From Impotence to Authority: The Spanish Crown and the American Audiencias, 1687–1808* (Columbia: University of Missouri Press, 1977), 90.

17 Zacarías Moutoukias, "Power, Corruption, and Commerce: The Making of the Local Administrative Structure in Seventeenth-Century Buenos Aires," *Hispanic American Historical Review* 68 (1988), 771–801: 776.

18 Lynch, *Bourbon Spain*, 253. Colin M. MacLachlan, *Spain's Empire in the New World: The Role of Ideas in Institutional and Social Change* (Berkeley: University of California Press, 1988), 126–127, 130. Mark D. Szuchman, "From Imperial Hinterland to Growth Pole: Revolution, Change, and Restoration in the Río de la Plata," in Mark D. Szuchman and Jonathan C. Brown, eds., *Revolution and Restoration: The Rearrangement of Power in Argentina, 1776–1860* (Lincoln: University of Nebraska Press, 1994), 1–26: 5.

19 Lynch, *Bourbon Spain*, 332.

20 Ernesto J. A. Maeder, "La Iglesia misional y la evangelización del mundo indígena," in Leandro de Sagatizábal, ed., *Nueva Historia de la Nación Argentina*, vol. 2, pt. 2 (Buenos Aires: Planeta, 1999), 433–468: 460–461. D. A. Brading, *The First America: The Spanish Monarchy, Creole Patriots, and the Liberal State, 1492–1867* (Cambridge: Cambridge University Press, 1991), 497–500. Lynch, *Bourbon Spain*, 281–283.

21 O. Carlos Stoetzer, *The Scholastic Roots of the Spanish American Revolution* (New York: Fordham University Press, 1979), 97.

22 Leon G. Campbell, *The Military and Society in Colonial Peru, 1750–1810* (Philadelphia: American Philosophical Society, 1978), 33–34.

23 Burkholder and Chandler, *From Impotence to Authority*, 88, 99.

24 MacLachlan, *Spain's Empire in the New World*, 127.

25 Geoffrey J. Walker, *Spanish Politics and Imperial Trade, 1700–1789* (Bloomington: Indiana University Press, 1979), 223.

26 Lynch, *Bourbon Spain*, 344. Miles Wortman, "Government Revenue and Economic Trends in Central America, 1787–1819," *Hispanic American Historical Review* 55:2 (1975), 251–286: 256.

27 Timothy E. Anna, "Spain and the Breakdown of the Imperial Ethos: The Problem of Equality," *Hispanic American Historical Review* 62:2 (1982), 254–272: 264.

28 Carlos Marichal, "La bancarrota del virreinato: finanzas, guerra y política en la Nueva España, 1770–1808," in Josefina Zoraida Vázquez, ed., *Interpretaciones del siglo XVIII mexicano: El impacto de las reformas borbónicas* (Mexico City: Editorial Patria, 1992), 153–186: 162–186. Brian R. Hamnett, "The Appropriation of Mexican Church Wealth by the Spanish Bourbon Government. The 'Consolidación de Vales Reales,' 1805–1809," *Journal of Latin American Studies* 1:2 (1969), 85–113: 85–87, 101. "Relacion de gobierno del virrey Francisco Gil de Taboada y Lemos, 1796," in Manuel Atanascio Fuentes and Ambrosio Cerdan de Landa Simon Pontero, eds., *Memorias de los vireyes que han gobernado el Perú durante el tiempo del coloniaje español*, 6 vols. (Lima: Librería Central de Felipe Bailly, 1859), 6:286–287. Rizo-Patrón Boylan, *Linaje, dote y poder*, 64–65n111. Anna, *Fall of the Royal Government in Peru*, 11–16.

29 Stoetzer, *Scholastic Roots*, 152–153.

30 Andrews, "Spanish American Independence," 115–116. Bernard Lavallé, "Crisis agraria y cambios en la relación esclavista: Trujillo (Perú) durante el último siglo colonial," *Jahrbuch für die Geschichte von Staat, Wirtschaft und Gesellschaft*

Lateinamerikas 35 (1998), 45–72. Carmen Vivanco Lara, "Bandolerismo colonial peruano: 1760–1810: Caracterización de una respuesta popular y causas económicas," in Carlos Aguirre and Charles Walker, eds., *Bandoleros, abigeos y montoneros: Criminalidad y violencia en el Perú, siglos XVIII–XX* (Lima: Instituto de Apoyo Agrario, 1990), 25–56: 36–37. P. Michael McKinley, *Pre-revolutionary Caracas: Politics, Economy, and Society, 1777–1811* (Cambridge: Cambridge University Press, 1985), 122–125.

31 Brading, *First America*, 467–468.

32 John Leddy Phelan, *The People and the King: The Comunero Revolt in Colombia, 1781* (Madison: University of Wisconsin Press, 1978), 111, 159–161. John Lynch, "The Origins of Spanish American Independence," in Leslie Bethell, ed., *The Cambridge History of Latin America, Volume III: From Independence to c. 1870* (Cambridge: Cambridge University Press, 1985), 3–50: 32–34. Anthony McFarlane, "Civil Disorders and Popular Protests in Late Colonial New Granada," *Hispanic American Historical Review* 64:2 (1984), 17–54, places the *comuneros* revolt in a tradition of social protest.

33 John R. Fisher, *Bourbon Peru, 1750–1824* (Liverpool: Liverpool University Press, 2003), 100. Alberto Flores Galindo, *Buscando un Inca: identidad y utopía en los Andes* (Havana: Casa de las Américas, 1986), 97.

34 See, in addition to Flores Galindo, *Buscando un Inca*, Manuel Burga, *Nacimiento de una utopia: muerte y resurrección de los incas* (Lima: Instituto de Apoyo Agrario, 1988).

35 Flores Galindo, *Buscando un Inca*, 98–99.

36 Brading, *First America*, 519.

37 For the age of revolutions in the Luso-Atlantic world, see Gabriel Paquette, *Imperial Portugal in the Age of Atlantic Revolutions: The Luso-Brazilian World, c. 1770–1850* (Cambridge: Cambridge University Press, 2013).

38 The most up-to-date analysis of the events in Bayonne and the subsequent challenges to the Spanish Empire is Barbara H. Stein and Stanley J. Stein, *Crisis in an Atlantic Empire: Spain and New Spain, 1808–1810* (Baltimore: Johns Hopkins University Press, 2014), 45–74. For the response to the French Revolution in Spain and New Spain, see Gabriel Torres Puga, *Opinión pública y censura en Nueva España: Indicios de un silencio imposible (1767–1794)* (Mexico City: El Colegio de México, 2010), chap. 5.

39 John Lynch, "British Policy and Spanish America, 1783–1808," *Journal of Latin American Studies* 1:1 (1969), 1–30.

40 William Spence Robertson, "The Juntas of 1808 and the Spanish Colonies," *English Historical Review* 31:124 (1916), 573–585: 576. D. A. G. Waddell, "International Politics and Latin American Independence," in Leslie Bethell, ed., *The Independence of Latin America* (Cambridge: Cambridge University Press, 1987), 195–232: 196–197.

41 Cf. the memorandum by Captain Sir Home Popham (who would later lead the failed expedition to Buenos Aires), dated October 14, 1804, in Carlos A. Vil-

lanueva, *Napoleón y la independencia de América* (Paris: Casa Editorial Garnier Hermanos, 1911), 339.

42 Napoleon to vice-admiral Decrès, Bayonne, May 8, 1808; Napoleon to Murat, Bayonne, May 21, 1808, in C. Parra-Pérez, *Bayona y la política de Napoleón en América* (Caracas: Tipografía Americana, 1939), 61–62, 64–65. Murat to Napoleon, Madrid, May 15, 1808: *Lettres et documents pour servir à l'histoire de Joachim Murat 1767–1815 publié par S.A. le Prince Murat*, introduction Paul Le Brethon, 8 vols. (Paris: Plon-Nourrit et Cie., 1912), 6:114.

43 John Rydjord, "Napoleon and the Independence of New Spain," in Charles W. Hackett, George P. Hammond, and J. Lloyd Mecham, eds., *New Spain and the Anglo-American West: Historical Contributions Presented to Herbert Eugene Bolton* (Los Angeles: privately printed, 1932), 1:289–312: 293. Narciso Coll y Prat, *Memoriales sobre la independencia de Venezuela*, intro. Manuel Pérez Vila (Caracas: Academia Nacional de la Historia, 1960), 148. Villanueva, *Napoleón y la independencia de América*, 238–241, lists the names of many of these agents.

44 José Félix Blanco, *Documentos para la historia de la vida pública del Libertador de Colombia, Perú y Bolivia, publicados por dispoción del general Guzmán Blanco, ilustre americano, regenerador y presidente de los Estados Unidos de Venezuela, en 1875* (Caracas: Imprenta de "La Opinión Nacional," de Fausto Teodoro de Aldrey, 1875), 2:169, 248. Jules Mancini, *Bolívar: La emancipación de las colonias españolas desde los orígenes hasta 1815* (Paris: Librería de la V.da de Ch. Bouret, 1930), 248. José Domingo Díaz, *Recuerdos sobre la rebelión de Caracas* (Caracas: Academia Nacional de la Historia, 1961), 55–56. Mario Briceño-Iragorry, *Casa León y su tiempo (Aventura de un anti-héroe)* (Caracas: Tipografía Americana, 1947), 105.

45 Murat to Napoleon, Madrid, May 15, 1808, and Murat to Gil de Lemos, minister of the Navy, Madrid, May 15, 1808, Le Brethon, *Lettres et documents*, 6:114, 116. Parra-Pérez, *Bayona y la política*, 66–67. Rydjord, "Napoleon and the Independence of New Spain," 1:291. Miguel Artola, "Los afrancesados y América," in *Miscelánea americanista, I: Homenaje a D. Antonio Ballesteros Beretta (1880–1949)* (Madrid: Consejo Superior de Investigaciones Científicas, 1951), 79–105: 91. Richmond F. Brown, "Dilemmas of a Creole Loyalist: José de Aycinena and Central America's Crisis of Independence, 1808–1824," *Colonial Latin American Historical Review* 12:3 (2003), 249–273: 257.

46 After a few years, the government of independent Cartagena de Indias tried to approach Napoleon in order to request military aid in the form of soldiers or, if that was not possible, weapons for the defense against Spain and Great Britain. The diplomatic mission eventually failed: C. Parra-Pérez, *Una misión diplomática venezolana ante Napoleón en 1813* (Caracas: s.n., 1953), 17–18, 26, 41–42, 51, 74, 87–89. See also Christophe Belaubre, Jordana Dym, and John Savage, eds., *Napoleon's Atlantic: The Impact of Napoleonic Empire in the Atlantic World* (Leiden: Brill, 2010).

47 Ladd, *Mexican Nobility*, 105.

48 Simon Collier, *Ideas and Politics of Chilean Independence, 1808–1833* (Cambridge: Cambridge University Press, 1968), 51.

49 Marco Antonio Landavazo Arias, *La máscara de Fernando VII: discurso e imaginario monárquicos en una época de crisis: Nueva Espana, 1808–1822* (Mexico City: Colegio de México, Centro de Estudios Históricos; Morelia, Michoacán [Mexico]: Universidad Michoacana de San Nicolás de Hidalgo; Zamora, Michoacán [Mexico]: Colegio de Michoacán, 2001), 86, 106. Ladd, *Mexican Nobility*, 106.

50 *Noticia de las devotas rogativas con que la ciudad de Lima imploró el auxilio divino en las actuales circunstancias de la monarquía; escrita por encargo de la ilustre hermandad de la archicofradía de N. Madre y Señora del Rosario, por el D.D. Justo Figuerola individuo del ilustre colegio de abogados de esta Rel Audiencia, y veintiquatro de dicha hermandad* (Lima: en la imprenta de los niños expósitos, 1808), 10, 15, 18–19, 37–38.

51 Guardino, *Peasants, Politics*, 31–32. Rieu-Millán, *Los diputados americanos*, 329n29. Landavazo Arias, *La máscara de Fernando VII*, 122. Fund-raising drives in Buenos Aires were unsuccessful: Tulio Halperín-Donghi, *Politics, Economics and Society in Argentina in the Revolutionary Period*, trans. Richard Southern (Cambridge: Cambridge University Press, 1975), 159–160.

52 Jeremy Adelman, *Sovereignty and Revolution in the Iberian Atlantic* (Princeton, N.J.: Princeton University Press, 2006), 198–203.

53 Lynch, *Spanish American Revolutions*, 12. Collier, *Ideas and Politics*, 54. Mario Rodríguez, *The Cádiz Experiment in Central America, 1808 to 1826* (Berkeley: University of California Press, 1978), 40–41.

54 Regency decree, February 14, 1810, quoted in Anna, "Spain and the Breakdown," 257.

55 Charles R. Berry, "The Election of the Mexican Deputies to the Spanish Cortes, 1810–1822," in Nettie Lee Benson, ed., *Mexico and the Spanish Cortes, 1810–1822: Eight Essays* (Austin: University of Texas Press, 1966), 10–42: 11, 14. Rieu-Millán, *Los diputados americanos*, 36–37. From September 1810 through May 1814, a total of 86 overseas delegates attended the sessions. In all, 63 were present during the extraordinary Cortes (September 1810–September 1813), including 27 substitutes and 36 elected by American towns; 65 attended the ordinary Cortes (October 1, 1813–May 10, 1814), including 23 elected by the provinces and 42 substitutes (18 elected in Cádiz in September 1810 and 24 chosen by the towns for the extraordinary Cortes). Ibid., 31.

56 Anna, "Spain and the Breakdown," 259. Rieu-Millán, *Los diputados americanos*, 96.

57 Rieu-Millán, *Los diputados americanos*, 327–328.

58 Ibid., 146–168, 273–294.

59 Anna, "Spain and the Breakdown," 262.

60 Rieu-Millán, *Los diputados americanos*, 226–227, 262, 310–311. María Rosario Sevilla Soler, *Las Antillas y la Independencia de la América Española, 1808–1826* (Madrid: Consejo Superior de Investigaciones Científicas, Escuela de Estudios Hispano-Americanos, 1986), 74–75. Anna, "Spain and the Breakdown," 263.

61 Anthony McFarlane, "Representaciones políticas de políticas de representación en Hispanoamérica a finales del período colonial," in *XII Congreso Internacional*

AHILA, Universidade do Porto—1999 (Porto: Centro Leonardo Coimbra da Faculdade de Letras da Universidade do Porto, 2001), 11–19: 17–18.

62 Jaime E. Rodríguez, "The Origins of Constitutionalism and Liberalism in Mexico," in Rodríguez, ed., *The Divine Charter: Constitutionalism and Liberalism in Nineteenth-Century Mexico* (Lanham, Md.: Rowan & Littlefield, 2005), 1–32: 13. Berry, "Election of the Mexican Deputies," 17, 18, 25, 28. Guerra, "Spanish-American Tradition of Representation," 8. Jaime E. Rodríguez O., "La antigua provincia de Guayaquil durante la época de la independencia, 1809–1820," in Rodríguez, ed., *Revolución, independencia y las nuevas naciones de América* (Madrid: Fundación MAPFRE TAVERA, 2005), 511–556: 538–539. Jaime E. Rodríguez O., *The Independence of Spanish America* (Cambridge: Cambridge University Press, 1998), 105. See also Roberto Breña, ed., *Cádiz a debate: actualidad, contexto y legado* (Mexico City: El Colegio de México, 2014).

63 Thomas Kinder, "Journal, Made during a Voyage to Madeira and the River Plate" (ms.), John Carter Brown Library, Providence, R.I., 164. Lyman L. Johnson, *Workshop of Revolution: Plebeian Buenos Aires and the Atlantic World, 1776–1810* (Durham, N.C.: Duke University Press, 2011), 262–274.

64 The first expedition succeeded in defeating royalist troops, but resulted in a massacre, as the political commissioner in charge of the army, Juan José Castelli, summarily executed royal officials, while his troops went on a rampage, looting and killing many citizens. En route to Upper Peru, Castelli's troops encountered resistance in the town of Córdoba, led by Liniers, the local bishop, and a number of senior officials. After Castelli's victory, he had Liniers and the intendant executed, but spared the bishop. The next year, 1811, saw the defeat of his army, which disintegrated during a battle. San Martín was successfully involved in the second expedition, but judged that Upper Peru was dispensable in the war of South American liberation. The third expedition, finally, was destroyed by royalist troops in 1815. Rodríguez, *Independence of Spanish America*, 129–132. Lynch, *Spanish American Revolutions*, 50–52, 121–123. For a detailed analysis of the revolutionary period in the area that would become Bolivia, see José Luis Roca, *Ni con Lima ni con Buenos Aires: La formación de un Estado nacional en Charcas* (La Paz: Instituto Francés de Estudios Andinos/Plural Editores, 2007).

65 David Bushnell, "The Independence of Spanish South America," in Bethell, *Independence of Latin America*, 93–154: 103. José Carlos Chiaramonte, *Ciudades, provincias, Estados: Orígenes de la Nación Argentina, 1800–1846* (Buenos Aires: Compañia Editora Espasa Calpe Argentina/Ariel, 1997), 137. Similarly, the cabildo of Santiago attempted to run all of Chile. Collier, *Ideas and Politics*, 58.

66 John Street, *Artigas and the Emancipation of Uruguay* (Cambridge: Cambridge University Press, 1959), 78–99, 118, 128. Rodríguez, *Independence of Spanish America*, 134–136. Fabrício Prado, *Edge of Empire: Atlantic Networks and Revolution in Bourbon Río de la Plata* (Oakland: University of California Press, 2015), 153–180.

67 Rodríguez, *Independence of Spanish America*, 133–134.

68 *Conjuración de 1808 en Caracas para la formación de una Junta Suprema Guberna-tiva* (Caracas: s.n., 1949), 26–27. C. Parra-Pérez, *Historia de la Primera República de Venezuela* (Caracas: Academia Nacional de Historia, 1959), 2:57, 61–62. Bush-nell, "Independence of Spanish South America," 102.

69 Karen Racine, *Francisco de Miranda: A Transatlantic Life in the Age of Revolution* (Wilmington, Del.: Scholarly Resources, 2003), 107, 115–139.

70 *General Account of Miranda's Expedition, Including the Trial and Execution of Ten of His Officers. And an Account of the Imprisonment and Sufferings of the Remain-der of His Officers and Men Who Were Taken Prisoners* (New York: McFarlane and Long, 1808), 14–20, 33–34, 67–70. Racine, *Francisco de Miranda*, 155–165. Adel-man, *Sovereignty and Revolution*, 175.

71 Lynch, *Spanish American Revolutions*, 195–199. Díaz, *Recuerdos sobre la rebelión*, 98–99. Rodríguez, *Independence of Spanish America*, 117–118.

72 Adelman, *Sovereignty and Revolution*, 193. Rodríguez, *Independence of Spanish America*, 119–122. Lynch, *Spanish American Revolutions*, 199–207. Stephen K. Stoan, *Pablo Morillo and Venezuela, 1815–1820* (Columbus: Ohio State University Press, 1974), 52–53, 66–67.

73 Lynch, *Spanish American Revolutions*, 240–243. Rodríguez, *Independence of Spanish America*, 150–159. Brian R. Hamnett, "Popular Insurrection and Royal Reaction: Colombian Regions, 1810–1823," in John R. Fisher, Allan J. Kuethe, and Anthony McFarlane, eds., *Reform and Insurrection in Bourbon New Granada and Peru* (Baton Rouge: Louisiana State University Press, 1990), 292–326: 316.

74 Adelman, *Sovereignty and Revolution*, 274–277. Paul Verna, *Pétion y Bolívar: Una etapa decisiva en la emancipación de Hispanoamérica (1790–1830)*, 3rd ed. (Caracas: Ediciones de la Presidencia de la República, 1980), 151–156, 163–178, 183–185, 248–263.

75 Lynch, *Spanish American Revolutions*, 243–249. See for the imperialist dimension of Bolívar's thought: Joshua Simon, "Simón Bolívar's Republican Imperialism: An-other Ideology of American Revolution," *History of Political Thought* 33:2 (2012), 280–304.

76 Adelman, *Sovereignty and Revolution*, 294–303, 305.

77 Timothy Anna, "The Independence of Mexico and Central America," in Bethell, *Independence of Latin America*, 49–92: 56–59. Stein and Stein, *Crisis in an Atlantic Empire*, 325–357.

78 Hugh M. Hamill, Jr., *The Hidalgo Revolt* (Gainesville: University Press of Florida, 1966), 97–99, 104–105, 107–110. Lynch, *Spanish American Revolutions*, 306–307.

79 Hamill, *Hidalgo Revolt*, 88, 118–119, 122, 135, 139–140, 195, 216.

80 Guardino, *Peasants, Politics*, 64–65. Rodríguez, *Independence of Spanish America*, 165–167.

81 Anna, *Fall of the Royal Government in Peru*, 133–138, 159–160.

82 Rodríguez, *Independence of Spanish America*, 205–208. Cristina Gómez Álvarez, *El alto clero poblano y la revolución de Independencia, 1808–1821* (Mexico City: Facultad de Filosofía y Letras, Universidad Nacional Autónoma de México; Puebla: Benemérita Universidad Autónoma de Puebla, 1997), 183–184, 187.

83 Jaime E. Rodríguez O., *"We Are Now the True Spaniards": Sovereignty, Revolution, Independence, and the Emergence of the Federal Republic of Mexico, 1808–1824* (Stanford: Stanford University Press, 2012), 301–304.

84 R. L. Woodward, "Central America," in Bethell, *Spanish America after Independence*, 171–206: 175–177. See also Jordana Dym, *From Sovereign Villages to National States: City, State and Federation in Central America, 1759–1839* (Albuquerque: University of New Mexico Press, 2006).

85 Bushnell, "Independence of Spanish South America," 98–101. Rodríguez, *Independence of Spanish America*, 145.

86 Rodríguez, *Independence of Spanish America*, 136, 138, 140, 142–144.

87 John Fisher, "Royalism, Regionalism, and Rebellion in Colonial Peru, 1808–1815," *Hispanic American Historical Review* 59:2 (1979), 232–257: 257. Campbell, *Military and Society*, 223. Scarlett O'Phelan Godoy, "El mito de la 'independencia concedida': los programas políticos del siglo XVIII y del temprano XIX en el Perú y Alto Perú," in Inge Buisson et al., *Problemas de la formación del estado en Hispanoamérica* (Cologne: Böhlau, 1984), 55–92: 77.

88 Rodríguez, *Independence of Spanish America*, 144–145, 170–171, 178.

89 Bushnell, "Independence of Spanish South America," 133–134. Anna, *Fall of the Royal Government in Peru*, 193–194.

90 Lynch, *Spanish American Revolutions*, 270–273, 280–284. Brian R. Hamnett, "Process and Pattern: A Re-examination of the Ibero-American Independence Movements, 1808–1826," *Journal of Latin American Studies* 29:2 (1997), 279–328: 314.

91 Historians have seriously neglected the maritime dimension of Spanish American independence. For exceptions, see Anne Pérotin-Dumon, "La contribution des corsarios insurgentes à l'indépendance américaine: Course et piraterie dans le Golfe du Mexique et la Mer des Antilles, 1810–1830," *Bulletin de la Société d'histoire de la Guadeloupe* 53–54 (1982), 49–71; Johanna von Grafenstein, "Corso y piratería en el Golfo-Caribe durante las guerras de independencia hispanoamericanas," in Mickaël Augeron and Mathias Tranchant, eds., *La violence et la mer dans l'espace atlantique: XIIe–XIXe siècle* (Rennes: Presses Universitaires de Rennes, 2004), 269–282; Edgardo Pérez Morales, *El gran diablo hecho barco: Corsarios, esclavos y revolución en Cartagena y el Gran Caribe, 1791–1817* (Bucaramanga: Universidad Industrial de Santander, 2012); David Head, *Privateers of the Americas: Spanish American Privateering from the United States in the Early Republic* (Athens: University of Georgia Press, 2015).

92 Allan J. Kuethe, *Cuba, 1753–1815: Crown, Military, and Society* (Knoxville: University of Tennessee Press, 1986), 114–115. Jorge I. Domínguez, *Insurrection or Loyalty: The Breakdown of the Spanish American Empire* (Cambridge, Mass.: Harvard University Press, 1980), 251. For the continued ties between Spain and its former colonies, see Matthew Brown and Gabriel Paquette, eds., *Connections after Colonialism: Europe and Latin America in the 1820s* (Tuscaloosa: University of Alabama Press, 2013).

93 Quoted in Liss, *Atlantic Empires*, 207.

94 *El Redactor de la Asamblea* [Buenos Aires], May 29, 1813. Garrido, *Reclamos y representaciones*, 321.

95 Robert Semple, *Sketch of the Present State of Caracas; Including a Journey from Caracas through La Victoria to Puerto Cabello* (London: Robert Baldwin, 1812), 146–147. Semple, the well-traveled son of a Boston Loyalist, must have attended the debates in Venezuelan Congress in early July 1811, which confirmed his thesis. See Joaquin Gabaldón Márquez, ed., *El Publicista de Venezuela* (Caracas: Academia Nacional de la Historia, 1959). Semple argued that these observations also applied to the United States.

96 Stoan, *Pablo Morillo and Venezuela*, 51. Steinar A. Sæther, *Identidades e independencia en Santa Marta y Riohacha, 1750–1850* (Bogotá: Instituto Colombiano de Antropología e Historia, 2005), 193. Anna, *Fall of the Royal Government in Peru*, 183–184, 207. In Buenos Aires, an expulsion decree was eventually repealed, but all the same, Spanish residents seeking citizen rights were often thwarted, especially if they opposed the new government: Halperín-Donghi, *Politics, Economics and Society*, 172–175.

97 Collier, *Ideas and Politics*, 74–75. The Argentine article appeared on January 14, 1812, in the prospectus of the first issue of *El Grito del Sud*, organ of the Sociedad Patriótica of the Río de la Plata.

98 Collier, *Ideas and Politics*, 212–216. Garrido, *Reclamos y representaciones*, 310. Gabriel Camargo Pérez, "Etiología y metamorfosis de la voz 'Cundinamarca,'" *Boletín de Historia y Antigüedades* 73 (1986), 665–688. Hans-Joachim König, "Símbolos nacionales y retórica política en la Independencia: el caso de la Nueva Granada," in Buisson et al., *Problemas de la formación del estado*, 389–405: 394–398. Rebecca Earle, "Patriotismo criollo y el mito del indio fiel," in *XII Congreso Internacional AHILA*, 91–102: 94. José M. Portillo Valdés, *Crisis atlántica: Autonomía e independencia en la crisis de la monarquía hispana* (Madrid: Fundación Carolina, Centro de Estudios Hispánicos e Iberoamericanos, Marcial Pons Historia, 2006), 221.

99 Semple, *Sketch of the Present State of Caracas*, 137. *El Redactor de la Asamblea* [Buenos Aires], May 29 and November 20, 1813. Bushnell, "Independence of Spanish South America," 129. Woodward, "Central America," 180. Ladd, *Mexican Nobility*, 160.

100 Halperín-Donghi, *Politics, Economics and Society*, 163.

101 Sæther, *Identidades e independencia*, 239.

102 *El Grito del Sud*, September 1, 8, 15, and 22, 1812.

103 Domínguez, *Insurrection or Loyalty*, 239. Richard Alan White, *Paraguay's Autonomous Revolution: 1810–1840* (Albuquerque: University of New Mexico Press, 1978), 56. Chiaramonte, *Ciudades, provincias, Estados*, 186–187.

104 See, for example, Halperín-Donghi, *Politics, Economics and Society*, 166.

105 Tulio Halperín-Donghi, "Revolutionary Militarization in Buenos Aires 1806–1815," *Past and Present* 40 (1968), 84–107: 86, 105–106.

106 John Lynch, "Bolívar and the Caudillos," *Hispanic American Historical Review* 63:1 (1983), 3–35: 4.

107 Ibid., 16, 22, 24, 35.

108 Jan Bazant, "Mexico," in Bethell, *Spanish America after Independence*, 123–170: 131. Lynch, *Spanish American Revolutions*, 330.

109 Adam Zamoyski, *Holy Madness: Romantics, Patriots, and Revolutionaries, 1776–1871* (New York: Viking, 2000), 211.

110 Hamnett, "Process and Pattern," 312–313. Leonardo León, "Montoneros populares durante la gestión de la República: Chile, 1810–1820," *Anuario de Estudios Americanos* 68:2 (2011), 483–510: 488, 493, 505–506. Igor Goicovic Donoso, "De la indiferencia a la resistencia: Los sectores populares y la Guerra de Independencia en el norte de Chile (1817–1823)," *Revista de Indias* 74 (2014), 129–159. For the role of muleteers, see Guardino, *Peasants, Politics*, 55.

111 Ricardo D. Salvatore, "The Breakdown of Social Discipline in the Banda Oriental and the Littoral, 1790–1820," in Szuchman and Brown, *Revolution and Restoration*, 74–102: 82–83. For plebeian participation in the revolutionary process in Buenos Aires, see Gabriel di Meglio, "Un nuevo actor para un nuevo escenario: La participación política de la plebe urbana de Buenos Aires en la década de la Revolución (1810–1820)," *Boletín del Instituto de Historia Argentina y Americana "Dr. Emilio Ravignani,"* 3rd series 24 (2001), 7–43.

112 Rebecca Earle Mond, "Indian Rebellion and Bourbon Reform in New Granada: Riots in Pasto, 1780–1800," *Hispanic American Historical Review* 73:1 (1993), 99–124: 123. Sæther, *Identidades e independencia*, 200–204. Marcela Echeverri, "Popular Royalists, Empire, and Politics in Southwestern New Granada, 1809–1819," *Hispanic American Historical Review* 91:2 (2011), 237–269: 255–265. Maria Luísa Soux, "Rebelión, guerrilla y tributo: los indios en Charcas durante el proceso de independencia," *Anuario de Estudios Americanos* 68:2 (2011), 455–482: 458.

113 McNeill, *Mosquito Empires*, 280. Díaz, *Recuerdos sobre la rebelión*, 352–353. Sæther, *Identidades e independencia*, 226.

114 Richard J. Salvucci, "Agriculture and the Colonial Heritage of Latin America: Evidence from Bourbon Mexico," in Jeremy Adelman, ed., *Colonial Legacies: The Problem of Persistence in Latin American History* (New York: Routledge, 1999), 107–133: 125, 128. Barry M. Robinson, *The Mark of Rebels: Indios Fronterizos and Mexican Independence* (Tuscaloosa: University of Alabama Press, 2016), 75–78. Eric Van Young, *The Other Rebellion: Popular Violence, Ideology, and the Mexican Struggle for Independence, 1810–1821* (Stanford: Stanford University Press, 2001), 71, 138. For Indians serving in the "patriot" and royalist armies of Peru, see John Miller, *Memoirs of General Miller, in the Service of the Republic of Peru*, 2 vols. (London: Longman, Rees, Orme, Brown and Green, 1828), 2:5–6; Gustavo Pons Muzzo, ed., *La Expedición Libertadora*, 2 vols. (Lima: Comisión Nacional del Sesquicentenario de la Independencia del Perú, 1971), 2:307, 369.

115 Lino Duarte Level, *Cuadros de la historia militar y civil de Vene-zuela desde el descubrimiento y conquista de Guayana hasta la batalla de Carabobo* (Madrid: Editorial América, 1917), 451. José Marcial Ramos Guédez, "Participación de negros, mulatos y zambos en la independencia de Venezuela, 1810–1823," in Heraclio

Bonilla, ed., *Indios, negros y mestizos en la independencia* (Bogotá: Planeta, 2010), 186–202.

116 Campbell, *Military and Society*, 226. Adelman, *Sovereignty and Revolution*, 282.

117 Ben Vinson III, "Articulating Space: The Free-Colored Military Establishment in Colonial Mexico from the Conquest to Independence," *Callaloo* 27:1 (2004), 150–171: 164–165. Theodore G. Vincent, *The Legacy of Vicente Guerrero, Mexico's First Black Indian President* (Gainesville: University Press of Florida, 2001), 17, 103. Ted Vincent, "The Blacks Who Freed Mexico," *Journal of Negro History* 79:3 (1994), 257–276: 261.

118 The viceroyalty contained an estimated 70,000 slaves and 140,000 free blacks in 1800: Hamnett, "Popular Insurrection and Royalist Reaction," 292.

119 Alfonso Múnera, *El fracaso de la nación: región, clase y raza en el Caribe colombiano, 1717–1821* (Bogotá: Banco de la República, Ancora Editores, 1998), 97, 175–176, 178–179, 187, 196–197. See also Sergio Paolo Solano D., "Pedro Romero, el artesano: trabajo, raza y diferenciación social en Cartagena de Indias a finales del dominio colonial," *Historia crítica* 61 (2016), 151–170.

120 Izard, *El miedo a la revolución*, 132. Stoan, *Pablo Morillo and Venezuela*, 52, 56.

121 George Reid Andrews, *The Afro-Argentines of Buenos Aires, 1800–1900* (Madison: University of Wisconsin Press, 1980), 43, 115–118. Núria Sales de Bohigas, "Esclavos y reclutas en Sudamérica, 1816–1826," *Revista de Historia de América* 70 (1970), 279–337: 292–293. See also Halperín-Donghi, "Revolutionary Militarization," 97–98, in Halperín-Donghi, *Politics, Economics and Society*, 193–194. Marta B. Goldberg, "Los negros de Buenos Aires," in Luz María Martínez Montiel, ed., *Presencia africana en Sudamérica* (Mexico City: Consejo Nacional para la Cultura y las Artes, 1995), 529–607: 564–571. For the black contribution to the independence process in Uruguay, see Óscar D. Montaño, "Los afro-orientales. Breve reseña del aporte africano en la formación de la población uruguaya," in Martínez Montiel, *Presencia africana en Sudamérica*, 391–448: 427–432. Their avenues to freedom are the subject of Ana Fraga, "'La Patria me hizo libre': Aproximación a la condición de los esclavos durante las guerras de Independencia en la Banda Oriental," in Silvia C. Mallo and Ignacio Telesca, eds., *"Negros de la Patria": Los afrodescendientes en las luchas por la Independencia en el antiguo virreinato del Río de la Plata* (Buenos Aires: Editorial SB, 2010), 171–186.

122 Hamnett, "Process and Pattern," 316.

123 Christine Hünefeldt, *Paying the Price of Freedom: Family and Labor among Lima's Slaves, 1800–1854* (Berkeley: University of California Press, 1994), 26–27, 87. The slave population of Peru in 1795 was 40,385, or 3.6 percent of the overall population: Anna, *Fall of the Royal Government in Peru*, 16–17.

124 Stoan, *Pablo Morillo and Venezuela*, 38. John V. Lombardi, *The Decline and Abolition of Negro Slavery in Venezuela, 1820–1854* (Westport, Conn.: Greenwood, 1971), 37–38. José de Austria, *Bosquejo de la historia militar de Venezuela*, 2 vols. (Caracas: Academia Nacional de Historia, 1960), 1:330.

125 Izard, *El miedo a la revolución*, 60–61. Simón Bolívar, *Obras completas*, ed. Vicente Lecuna, 3 vols., 2nd ed. (Habana: Editorial Lex, 1950), 1:717. Lombardi, *Decline and Abolition*, 41–42.

126 Lombardi, *Decline and Abolition*, 45.

127 Duarte Level, *Cuadros de la historia militar*, 442, 450.

128 Peter Blanchard, "The Language of Liberation: Slave Voices in the Wars of Independence," *Hispanic American Historical Review* 82:3 (2002), 499–523: 507–508. Múnera, *El fracaso de la nación*, 209–210, 214.

129 Marixa Lasso, "Race War and Nation in Caribbean Gran Colombia, Cartagena, 1810–1832," *American Historical Review* 111:2 (2006), 336–361: 347, 349–350, 353–359. David Bushnell, *The Santander Regime in Gran Colombia* (Newark: University of Delaware Press, 1954), 172. See also Aline Helg, "Simón Bolívar and the Spectre of *Pardocracia*: José de Padilla in Post-Independence Cartagena," *Journal of Latin American Studies* 35 (2003), 447–471. In 1817, Bolívar had ordered the arrest of Manuel Piar, the only *pardo* general of his rebel army, accusing him of inciting racial warfare. A court-marshal condemned Piar to death.

130 Manuel Chust Calero, "De esclavos, encomenderos y mitayos. El anticolonialismo en las Cortes de Cádiz," *Mexican Studies / Estudios Mexicanos* 11:2 (1995), 179–202: 189–190.

131 Lynch, *Spanish American Revolutions*, 156. Andrews, *Afro-Argentines*, 48. Lombardi, *Decline and Abolition*, 48.

132 *Gaceta del Gobierno de Lima*, October 16, 1825.

133 Stanley C. Green, *The Mexican Republic: The First Decade, 1823–1832* (Pittsburgh: University of Pittsburgh Press, 1987), 64.

134 Virginia Guedea, "De la fidelidad a la infidencia: Los gobernadores a la parcialidad de San Juan," in Jaime E. Rodríguez O., ed., *Patterns of Contention in Mexican History* (Wilmington, Del.: Scholarly Resources, 1992), 95–123: 101. Frank Safford, "Race, Integration, and Progress: Elite Attitudes and the Indian in Colombia, 1750–1870," *Hispanic American Historical Review* 71:1 (1999), 1–33: 11–15. Elliott, *Empires of the Atlantic World*, 385. Sergio García Ávila, *Las comunidades indígenas en Michoacán: Un largo camino hacia la privatización de la tierra, 1765–1835* (Morelia: UMSNH, Instituto de Investigaciones Históricas, 2009), 334–371.

CHAPTER 6. THE REVOLUTIONS COMPARED

1 Hannah Arendt, *On Revolution* (London: Penguin, 1990 [1963]), 46.

2 Jack A. Goldstone, "Comparative Historical Analysis and Knowledge Accumulation in the Study of Revolutions," in James Mahoney and Dietrich Rueschemeyer, eds., *Comparative Historical Analysis in the Social Sciences* (Cambridge: Cambridge University Press, 2003), 41–90: 78–79.

3 Bukovansky, *Legitimacy and Power Politics*, 171. François Furet, *Interpreting the French Revolution* (Cambridge: Cambridge University Press; Paris: Éditions de la Maison des Sciences de l'Homme, 1981), 5.

4   See Jeff Goodwin, "State-Centered Approaches to Social Revolutions: Strengths and Limitations of a Theoretical Tradition," in John Foran, ed., *Theorizing Revolutions* (London: Routledge, 1997), 11–37: 17–19.

5   Geggus, *Slavery, War, and Revolution, 7.* Schama, *Citizens,* 695. Eric Van Young, "Islands in the Storm: Quiet Cities and Violent Countrysides in the Mexican Independence Era," *Past and Present* 118 (1988), 130–155: 142.

6   Four thousand redcoats arrived in 1768 in a city whose census had counted 15,520 people three years before. By July 1775, the number of troops, with their dependents, women, and children, was 13,600, while all other residents combined numbered 6,753. Josiah H. Benton, Jr., *Early Census Making in Massachusetts, 1643–1765, with a Reproduction of the Lost Census of 1765 (Recently Found) and Documents Relating Thereto* (Boston: C. E. Goodspeed, 1905), Appendix. Richard Frothingham, *History of the Siege of Boston, and of the Battles of Lexington, Concord, and Bunker Hill,* 6th ed. (Boston: Little, Brown, 1896), 235.

7   McDonnell, *Politics of War,* 168.

8   Knouff, *Soldiers' Revolution,* 56. Needless to say, military violence and abuse could also work the other way. As seen above (chapter 5), the plunder by Argentine troops in Upper Peru made natives of the area desist from recruitment into the patriot army.

9   Adelman, *Sovereignty and Revolution,* 177.

10 Palmer, *Age of the Democratic Revolution,* 1:188.

11 Similarly, old grievances against a local bishop or abbey had induced many German individuals, princes, and towns to join the Reformation in the sixteenth century.

12 For examples in New Granada and Peru, see Mond, "Riots in Pasto," 123; Garrido, *Reclamos y representaciones,* 321; and Alberto Flores Galindo, "Soldados y montoneros," in Flores Galindo, *Buscando un Inca,* 209–223.

13 Ted W. Margadant, *Urban Rivalries in the French Revolution* (Princeton, N.J.: Princeton University Press, 1992), 155, 157, 167, 453–454. Cf. Germán Cardozo Galué and Arlena Urdaneta de Cardozo, "La élite de Maracaibo en la construcción de una identidad regional (siglos XVIII–XIX)," in Bernd Schröter and Christian Büschges, eds., *Beneméritos, aristócratas y empresarios: Identidades y estructuras sociales de las capas altas urbanas en América hispánica* (Frankfurt am Main: Vervuert, 1999), 157–182: 166–167.

14 Joseph S. Tiedemann, "Presbyterianism and the American Revolution in the Middle Colonies," *Church History* 74:2 (2005), 306–344: 340. Mason, "Localism, Evangelicalism, and Loyalism," 30–31. Anglicans did not automatically side with the Crown. In Virginia, only a small minority did: William Parks, "Religion and the Revolution in Virginia," in Richard A. Rutyna and Peter C. Stewart, eds., *Virginia in the American Revolution: A Collection of Essays* (Norfolk, Va.: Old Dominion University, 1977), 38–56: 53.

15 Adrian C. Leiby, *The Revolutionary War in the Hackensack Valley: The Jersey Dutch and the Neutral Ground, 1775–1783* (New Brunswick, N.J.: Rutgers Univer-

sity Press, 1962), 19–20. Ranlet, *New York Loyalists*, 123, 153. Richard R. Beeman, "The Political Response to Social Conflict in the Southern Backcountry: A Comparative View of Virginia and the Carolinas during the Revolution," in Ronald Hoffman, Thad W. Tate, and Peter J. Albert, eds., *An Uncivil War: The Southern Backcountry during the American Revolution* (Charlottesville: University of Virginia Press for the U.S. Capitol Historical Society, 1985), 213–239: 230–231. See also Judith L. Van Buskirk, *Generous Enemies: Patriots and Loyalists in Revolutionary New York* (Philadelphia: University of Pennsylvania Press, 2002).

16 Timothy Tackett, "Interpreting the Terror," *French Historical Studies* 24:4 (Fall 2001), 569–578: 570–572, 574–575.

17 Izard, *El miedo a la revolución*, 34.

18 Víctor Peralta Ruiz, "El impacto de las Cortes de Cádiz en el Perú. Un balance historiográfico," *Revista de Indias* 68:242 (2008), 67–96: 83. For a comparison between the Cádiz constitution and the constitutions of revolutionary France and the United States, see Mónica Quijada, "Una constitución singular: La carta gaditana en perspectiva comparada," *Revista de Indias* 68:242 (2008), 15–38.

19 Hamnett, "Popular Insurrection," 293. Sales de Bohigas, "Esclavos y reclutas," 282–283.

20 Olwell, "'Domestick Enemies,'" 47. Morgan and O'Shaughnessy, "Arming Slaves in the American Revolution," 193.

21 Rumors also induced insurgents elsewhere to take up arms, especially rumors about conspiracies, which indicated that all middle ground was lost between them and the incumbent authorities. People, as Van Young has argued, tended to project a mixture of fear and aggression in these rumors. The numerous rumors spread in New Spain in 1810 and 1811 about imminent massacres of creoles by peninsular Spaniards bear some resemblance to the Great Fear that had many French peasants in its grip in the summer of 1789: Van Young, *Other Rebellion*, 329–333, 420–421; Van Young, "Islands in the Storm," 139. For the role of rumor in Pontiac's War and beyond, see Gregory Evans Dowd, "The French King Wakes Up in Detroit: 'Pontiac's War' in Rumor and History," *Ethnohistory* 37:3 (1990), 255–278.

22 Geggus, *Slavery, War, and Revolution*, 3. Michael Craton, "Slave Culture, Resistance, and the Achievement of Emancipation in the British West Indies, 1783–1838," in Walvin, *Slavery and British Society*, 100–122.

23 Holton, *Forced Founders*, 152–154. Olwell, "'Domestick Enemies,'" 34.

24 Geggus, *Slavery, War, and Revolution*, 7–8. Scott, "Common Wind," 133. Dubois, *Colony of Citizens*, 106–107.

25 Account of Pastor Jacobus Schinck, September 7, 1795, in A. F. Paula, ed., *1795: de slavenopstand op Curacao: een bronnenuitgave van de originele overheidsdocumenten* (Curaçao, N.A.: Centraal Historisch Archief, 1974), 268. A detailed treatment of the revolt is found in Cornelis Ch. Goslinga, *The Dutch in the Caribbean and in Surinam, 1791/5–1942* (Assen, Maastricht: Van Gorcum, 1990), 8–20. New perspectives are presented in Wim Klooster and Gert Oostindie, eds., *Curaçao in*

the Age of Revolutions, 1795–1800 (Leiden: KITLV Press, 2011), available online at www.booksandjournals.brillonline.com.

26 Scott, "Common Wind," 147–157. Ildefonso Leal, "La aristocracia criolla venezolana y el código negrero de 1789," *Revista de Historia* [Caracas] 2 (1961), 61–81. Consuelo Naranjo Orovio, "La amenaza haitiana, un miedo interesado: poder y fomento de la población blanca en Cuba," in González-Ripoll et al., *El rumor de Haití en Cuba*, 83–178: 89. For the complete text of the slave code, see Miguel Acosta Saignes, *Vida de los esclavos negros en Venezuela* (Havana: Casa de las Américas, 1978), 254–258.

27 Geggus, *Slavery, War, and Revolution*, 10. Matt D. Childs, *The 1812 Aponte Rebellion in Cuba and the Struggle against Atlantic Slavery* (Chapel Hill: University of North Carolina Press, 2006), 161.

28 Ferrer, "Cuba en la sombra de Haití," 226–227. Naranjo Orovio, "La amenaza haitiana," 160. For a more elaborate treatment of this topic, see Wim Klooster, "Slave Revolts, Royal Justice, and a Ubiquitous Rumor in the Age of Revolutions," *William and Mary Quarterly*, 3rd series 71:3 (2014), 401–424.

29 Roger Chartier, *The Cultural Origins of the French Revolution*, translated by Lydia G. Cochrane (Durham, N.C.: Duke University Press, 1991), 27. Joost Kloek and Wijnand Mijnhardt, with Eveline Koolhaas-Grosfeld, *1800: Blauwdrukken voor een samenleving* (Den Haag: Sdu Uitgevers, 2001), 261. Joseph J. Ellis, *His Excellency: George Washington* (New York: Knopf, 2004), 158.

30 *Viva el Rey, Gazeta del Gobierno de Chile*, February 23, 1815. Guardino, *Peasants, Politics*, 62–63. Casimiro Olañeta to Simón Bolívar, Chuquisaca, October 19, 1825, in Daniel Florencio O'Leary, *Memorias del general O'Leary*, ed. Simón B. O'Leary, 32 vols. (Caracas: Impr. de la "Gaceta Oficial"), 11:19.

31 Palmer, *Age of the Democratic Revolution*, 1:523. John Markoff, "Where and When Was Democracy Invented?," *Comparative Studies in Society and History* 41:4 (1999), 660–690: 670–671, 677. Laura F. Edwards, "The Contradictions of Democracy in American Constitutions and Practices," in Joanna Innes and Mark Philp, eds., *Re-imagining Democracy in the Age of Revolutions: America, France, Britain, Ireland, 1750–1850* (Oxford: Oxford University Press, 2013), 40–54.

32 Melvin Edelstein, *The French Revolution and the Birth of Electoral Democracy* (Surrey, U.K.: Ashgate, 2014), 34. Bushnell, *Santander Regime*, 18–19, 268–270.

33 Rafe Blaufarb, "The French Revolution: The Birth of European Popular Democracy?," *Comparative Studies in Society and History* 37:3 (1995), 608–618: 608.

34 Ellis, *His Excellency*, 138–139.

35 Eric Nelson, *The Royalist Revolution: Monarchy and the American Founding* (Cambridge, Mass.: Belknap, 2014).

36 Furet, *Interpreting the French Revolution*, 31. George Klosko, *Jacobins and Utopians: The Political Theory of Fundamental Moral Reform* (Notre Dame, Ind.: University of Notre Dame Press, 2003), 87.

37 *The Federalist No. 38* (January 12, 1788), www.constitution.org.

38 John Adams, *A Defence of the Constitutions of Government of the United States of America* (London: C. Dilly, 1787–1788), Preface.

39 Ruault, *Gazette d'un Parisien*, 154, 189, 303, 379.

40 Simón Bolívar to Guillermo White, San Cristóbal, May 26, 1820, in Bolívar, *Obras Completas*, 1:442–443. Anthony Pagden, *Spanish Imperialism and the Political Imagination: Studies in European and Spanish American Social and Political Theory, 1513–1830* (New Haven, Conn.: Yale University Press, 1990), 151.

41 J. L. Salcedo-Bastardo, *Bolívar: A Continent and Its Destiny* (Richmond, U.K.: Richmond Publishing, 1977), 117–118. Israel, *Enlightenment Contested*, 361. For an example of similar reasoning, see *Gazeta Ministerial del Gobierno de Buenos-Ayres*, September 1, 1813.

42 O. Carlos Stoetzer, "Bolívar y el Poder Moral," *Revista de Historia de América* 95 (1983), 139–158: 156. Anna Maria Battista, "El Poder Moral: la creazione irrisolta e sconfitta di Simón Bolívar," *Il pensiero politico: Rivista di Storia delle Idee Politiche e Sociali* 20 (1987), 56–78: 57–62. Bolívar also inserted the Moral Power in his 1826 constitution for Bolivia: Bolívar, *Obras completas*, 3:764. Collier, *Ideas and Politics*, 275, 323–324.

43 Peter Gay, *The Enlightenment: An Interpretation: The Science of Freedom* (New York: Norton, 1969), 532–533. Klosko, *Jacobins and Utopians*, 111–115. Andress, *The Terror*, 374.

44 Drew R. McCoy, *The Last of the Fathers: James Madison and the Republican Legacy* (Cambridge: Cambridge University Press, 1989), 40–43. Lance Banning, *The Sacred Fire of Liberty: James Madison and the Founding of the Federal Republic* (Ithaca, N.Y.: Cornell University Press, 1995), 121–127.

45 Anna, *Fall of the Royal Government in Peru*, 32.

46 Jolanta Pekacz, "Gendered Discourse as a Political Option in Pre-revolutionary France," in Cossy and Dawson, *Progrès et violence au XVIIIe siècle*, 331–346: 332. Bukovansky, *Legitimacy and Power Politics*, 96. Chartier, *Cultural Origins*, 83, 85.

47 Chartier, *Cultural Origins*, 139–140. John Markoff, "Literacy and Revolt: Some Empirical Notes on 1789 in France," *American Journal of Sociology* 92:2 (1986), 323–349: 332, 334.

48 Chartier, *Cultural Origins*, 5. Dan Edelstein, "War and Terror: The Law of Nations from Grotius to the French Revolution," *French Historical Studies* 31:2 (2008), 229–262: 256–257. Srinivas Aravamudan, *Tropicopolitans: Colonialism and Agency, 1688–1804* (Durham, N.C.: Duke University Press, 1999), 293–294.

49 Nick Nesbitt, *Universal Emancipation: The Haitian Revolution and the Radical Enlightenment* (Charlottesville: University of Virginia Press, 2008), 43, 58.

50 Ardouin, *Études sur l'histoire d'Haïti*, 6:21. Cole, *Christophe*, 215. Franklin, *Present State of Hayti*, 400.

51 Péan, *Haïti, économie politique de la corruption*, 188–189.

52 Franklin, *Present State of Hayti*, 304.

53 Mimi Sheller, *Democracy after Slavery: Black Publics and Peasant Radicalism in Haiti and Jamaica* (Gainesville: University Press of Florida, 2000), 73–77. Lundahl, *Peasants and Poverty*, 277.

54 James A. Henretta, "The War for Independence and American Economic Development," in Ronald Hoffman et al., *The Economy of Early America: The Revolutionary Period, 1763–1790* (Charlottesville: University Press of Virginia for the United States Capitol Historical Society, 1988), 45–87, 86. Jacques Barbier and Allan J. Kuethe, eds., *The North American Role in the Spanish Imperial Economy, 1760–1819* (Manchester: Manchester University Press, 1984).

55 Anne Staples, "Mexican Mining and Independence: The Saga of Enticing Opportunities," in Christon I. Archer, *The Birth of Modern Mexico, 1780–1824* (Wilmington, Del.: Scholarly Resources, 2003), 151–164: 160–161.

56 Enrique Tandeter, *Coercion and Market: Silver Mining in Colonial Potosí* (Albuquerque: University of New Mexico Press, 1993), 221–223. Anna, *Fall of the Royal Government in Peru*, 200. Edmond Temple, *Travels in Various Parts of Peru, Including a Year's Residence in Potosi*, 2 vols. (Philadelphia: E.L. Carey & A. Hart, 1833), 1:197.

57 Leandro Prados de la Escosura, "The Economic Consequences of Independence in Latin America," in Victor Bulmer-Thomas, John H. Coatsworth, and Roberto Condés Conde, eds., *The Cambridge Economic History of Latin America*, vol. 1: *The Colonial Era and the Short Nineteenth Century* (Cambridge: Cambridge University Press, 2006), 463–504: 482–483.

58 François Furstenberg, "The Significance of the Trans-Appalachian Frontier in Atlantic History," *American Historical Review* 113:3 (2008), 647–677: 650.

59 José Luis Romero, "La independencia de Hispanoamérica y el modelo político norteamericano," *Inter-American Review of Bibliography* 26 (1976), 429–455. Collier, *Ideas and Politics*, 173. Elliott, *Empires of the Atlantic World*, 391. In 1821, the year that Peru became independent, a Peruvian Indian named Anselmo Nateiu produced an abridged translation of Paine's *Common Sense* into Spanish: *Reflecciones politicas escritas bajo el titulo de Instinto Comun por el ciudadano Tomas Paine, y traducidas abreviadamente* (Lima: En la imprenta de Rio, 1821).

60 Street, *Artigas*, 185.

61 Liss, *Atlantic Empires*, 206. Albert P. Blaustein, Jan Sigler, and Benjamin R. Beede, eds., *Independence Documents of the World* (Dobbs Ferry, N.Y.: Oceana, 1977), 736, 751.

62 Abelardo Levaggi, "Origen del poder legislativo en Hispanoamérica (1810–1814)," *Revista del Instituto de Historia del Derecho Ricardo Levene* [Buenos Aires] 19 (1968), 30–63: 61. Liss, *Atlantic Empires*, 208. Bushnell, *Santander Regime*, 18. O. Carlos Stoetzer, *El pensamiento político en la América española durante el período de la Emancipación (1789–1825)*, 2 vols. (Madrid: Instituto de Estudios Políticos, 1966), 2:68, 162. George Athan Billias, *American Constitutionalism Heard Round the World, 1776–1789: A Global Perspective* (New York: New York University Press, 2009), 105–141.

63 Javier Ocampo López, *La independencia de los Estados Unidos de América y su proyección en Hispanoamérica: El modelo norteamericano y su repercusión en la independencia de Colombia. Estudio a través de la folletería de la indepen-*

dencia de Colombia (Caracas: Instituto Panamericano de Geografía e Historia, Comisión de Historia, Comité Orígenes de la Emancipación, 1979), 25–27. José Luis Romero, "La independencia de Hispanoamérica y el modelo político norteamericano," *Inter-American Review of Bibliography* 26 (1976), 429–455: 449, 452. Joseph T. Criscenti, "Argentine Constitutional History, 1810–1852: A Re-examination," *Hispanic American Historical Review* 41 (1961), 367–412: 385–386. Bazant, "Mexico," 131.

64 Chiaramonte, *Ciudades, provincias, Estados*, 407. Ocampo López, *La independencia de los Estados Unidos*, 79.

65 Pagden, *Spanish Imperialism*, 139.

66 Blanning, *French Revolution in Germany*, 209.

67 Böning, *Revolution in der Schweiz*, 54–55, 67, 82.

68 Ibid., 108, 158.

69 Giovanni Scarabello, "Aspetti dell'avventura politica della Municipalità democratica," in Stefano Pillinini, ed., *Venezia e l'esperienza "democratica" del 1797: Atti del corso di storia veneta* (Venice: Ateneo Veneto, 1998), 25–47: 32–33.

70 Semple, *Sketch of the Present State of Caracas*, 137. *El Redactor de la Asamblea* [Buenos Aires], May 29 and November 20, 1813. Bushnell, "Independence of Spanish South America," 129. Woodward, "Central America," 180. Ladd, *Mexican Nobility*, 160.

71 Romero, "Modelo norteamericano," 437.

72 Levaggi, "Origen del poder legislativo," 62. Frank Safford, "Politics, Ideology and Society," in Bethell, *Spanish America after Independence*, 62–63.

73 Alfred N. Hunt, *Haiti's Influence on Antebellum America: Slumbering Volcano in the Caribbean* (Baton Rouge: Louisiana State University Press, 1988), 108. David Brion Davis, "Impact of the French and Haitian Revolutions," in David P. Geggus, ed., *The Impact of the Haitian Revolution in the Atlantic World* (Columbia: University of South Carolina Press, 2001), 3–9: 5–6.

74 Childs, *1812 Aponte Rebellion*, 168–169. Marcus J. M. de Carvalho, *Liberdade: Rotinas e Rupturas do Escravismo no Recife, 1822–1850* (Recife: Ed. Universitária da UFPE, 2002), 197. For the influence on Cuba of the Haitian Revolution, see more generally Ada Ferrer, *Freedom's Mirror: Cuba and Haiti in the Age of Revolution* (New York: Cambridge University Press, 2014). For Brazil, see João José Reis and Flávio dos Santos Gomes, "Repercussions of the Haitian Revolution in Brazil, 1791–1850," in David Patrick Geggus and Norman Fiering, eds., *The World of the Haitian Revolution* (Bloomington: Indiana University Press, 2009), 284–313.

75 Alejandro E. Gómez, *Le spectre de la Révolution Noire: L'impact de la Révolution Haïtienne dans le monde atlantique, 1790–1886* (Rennes: Presses Universitaires de Rennes, 2013), 242. For the impact of the Haitian Revolution on the early American republic, see Ashli White, *Encountering Revolution: Haiti and the Making of the Early Republic* (Baltimore: Johns Hopkins University Press, 2010); James Alexander Dun, *Dangerous Neighbors: Making the Haitian Revolution in Early America* (Philadelphia: University of Pennsylvania Press, 2016).

INDEX

Abascal y Sousa, José Fernando de, 154–55
Abenaki, 30
abolitionism, 47, 63, 97, 102–3. *See also*
    Society of the Friends of the Blacks
absenteeism, 93, 98
Acapulco, 163
Adams, John, 34, 85, 178
Adams, Samuel, 34, 85
Ailhaud, Jean Antoine, 109
Aix-en-Province, 84
Aix-la-Chapelle, Peace of (1748), 8, 9
Albany, 173
Alembert, Jean le Rond d', 177
Allada, 98, 113
Allegheny Mountains, 9, 30
Allende, Ignacio, 151–52
Alsace, 56, 69, 172
Alvear, Carlos María de, 144
American Board of Customs Collectors,
    23, 24
Amat y Junient, Manuel de, 133
Amherst, Jeffrey, 18
Andes, 150, 154, 155
Angers, 83
Anglo-Dutch war, fourth, 39
Aranjuez, 137
Ardouin, Beaubrun, 121
Arendt, Hannah, 169
Arequipa, 163
Argentina, 127, 134, 159, 166, 167
Articles of Confederation, 43, 184
Artigas, José, 145–46, 161, 163, 184
associations. *See* committees, revolutionary
Asunción, 146

Athens, 63, 178
Augereau, Pierre, 88
Australia, 14
Austria, 3, 8–11, 68, 69, 74, 78, 79, 147
Austrian Netherlands, 8, 78, 147
Ayacucho, battle of, 156

Babeuf, François-Noël, 87
Bailén, battle of, 138
Baltic Sea, 8
Banda Oriental, 144–46, 161, 163, 173
Bank of England, 25
Barbados, 40
Barnave, Antoine, 103
Bastille, 1–2, 55, 65, 67, 71, 76
Bayonne, 137–38
Belgium. *See* Austrian Netherlands
Bentham, Jeremy, 147
Berlin, 10, 55
Bermuda, 14, 17
Bermúdez, José Francisco, 160
Biassou, Georges, 107, 112–14
Bight of Benin, 98
Bight of Biafra, 98
Black Legend, 158
blacks in the American revolution, 39,
    45–48, 176; in France, 70; in Saint-
    Domingue/Haiti, 91–125, 181; in Span-
    ish America, 161–66, 175, 176
Bogotá, Santa Fé de, 126, 149, 157
Bolívar, Simón Antonio José, 147–51, 156,
    158, 160–61, 164, 165, 167, 179–80, 185, 186
Bonaparte, Joseph, 137–38
Bonaparte, Lucien, 88

Bonaparte, Napoleon. *See* Napoleon
Bordeaux, 91, 100, 103, 107, 212n3
Boston, 20, 21, 23–26, 33–34, 36
Boston Massacre, 26, 34
Boston Tea Party, 26, 33–34, 36
Bourbon reforms, 132–37, 156, 157, 167
Boves, José Tomás, 149, 164
Boyacá, battle of, 150, 163
Boyer, Jean Pierre, 124–25
Brabant, 86
Brandywine Creek, battle of, 37
Brazil, 94, 133, 137, 145–46
Brissot, Jacques-Pierre, 104, 107
British Caribbean, 40, 193n11; impact of
    Stamp Act, 24; population, 17; trade, 20
British North America. *See under* crowd
    action; rumors; taxation: Thirteen
    Colonies
Brittany, 83, 87
Brodhead, Daniel, 32
Brookline, 21
Brooklyn heights, battle of, 36
Brunswick, 36
Brunswick, Charles William Ferdinand,
    Duke of, 71–72
Buenos Aires, 126, 130, 138, 143–46, 149,
    153, 155, 157, 159, 160, 161, 164, 167, 173,
    228n51, 232n96
Buffon, Georges-Louis Leclerc, Count
    de, 90
Burgoyne, John, 37
Burgundy, 56, 67
Burke, Edmund, 76

Cádiz, 134, 138, 140–43, 148, 155. *See also*
    Cortes of Cádiz
cahiers de doléances, 51–53, 64, 70, 83, 106,
    181, 204n9
Campeche, 134
Canada, 9–11, 13, 25, 35, 39, 42
Cap Français, 92–94, 100, 103, 105, 107,
    109–10, 112, 113, 115, 117, 120. *See also*
    Cap-Henry

Cap-Henry, 123, 125, 222n119
Cape of Good Hope, 138
Caracas, 129, 139, 146–49, 157–58, 162–63,
    164, 173
Caribbean, 6, 10, 11, 19, 38–40, 46, 91, 97,
    98, 105, 127, 132, 139, 156, 172. *See also*
    British Caribbean
Carolina backcountry, 27
Cartagena de Indias, 149, 163–64, 166, 184,
    227n46
Casanare, 150
Castelli, Juan José, 229n64
Catherine the Great, 147
Cayenne, 91. *See also* French Guiana
Central America, 127, 131, 154, 159, 167, 168,
    180, 186
Champ de Mars massacre, 69, 77
Chandernagor, 101
Charles III, King of Spain, 10, 129, 132, 157
Charles IV, King of Spain, 135, 137, 139,
    176, 186
Charles Town, 38
Cherokees, 11, 30, 31, 174
Chesapeake, 14, 16, 38
Chestertown, 196n. 49
Chiapas, 153–54
Chile, 127, 131, 139, 154–55, 158, 159, 161,
    164, 166, 167, 175, 180, 184, 186
Chilleau, Marie-Charles, Marquis du, 101
Christophe, Henri, 114, 117–25, 186
Civil Constitution of the Clergy, 60–61,
    83, 135
Clarkson, Thomas, 186
clergy: in Europe, 5–6; in British North
    America, 28; in France, 51–52, 54. *See*
    also priests
Club du Panthéon, 87
Code Noir, 96–97, 99, 104
Coll y Prat, Archbishop Narciso, 165
Colombia, 167, 180, 184. *See also* Gran
    Colombia
Committee of General Security, 80
Committee of Public Safety, 80, 122

committees, revolutionary, 27–28, 66
Concord, 1, 33
Condorcet, Marie Jean Antoine Nicolas de Caritat, Marquis de, 109
Connecticut, 17, 47, 184
Conoghquieson, 12
Constituent Assembly, 2, 80
Constitutional Convention, 46, 180
constitutions: Argentina, 184; Cádiz, 143, 153, 155, 168, 176; Cartagena de Indias, 184; Chile, 180; Cundinamarca, 184; France, 54, 62, 68–70, 72, 78, 85, 177; Georgia, 43; Gran Colombia, 184; Great Britain, 27, 29, 184; Haiti, 121, 123; Mexico, 184–85; New Hampshire, 43; New York, 43; North Carolina, 43; Pennsylvania, 43; Saint-Domingue, 117; South Carolina, 43; United States, 178; Vermont, 46
Continental Army, 35–36, 38
Continental Congress, First, 27, 28, 32; Second, 34, 43, 48
contraband trade, 20, 131, 132, 134, 171
Convention, 72–77, 80, 82, 84, 86, 87, 111–12
Cornwallis, Charles, 38, 45, 61
Coro, 148, 173
corporations, 5–6
Cortes of Cádiz, 140–43, 166, 167, 171, 174, 176
Coshocton, 32
Costa Rica, 153
Council of the Indies, 126
creoles: in Saint-Domingue, 99, 102; in Spanish America, 127, 129, 131, 133, 135, 136, 139, 143, 144, 146, 151, 152, 154, 156, 158, 161, 163
crowd action: France, 1, 50, 55, 56, 64–66, 69; Saint-Domingue, 111; Thirteen Colonies, 21, 26, 28, 44
Cry of Dolores, 151
Cuba, 39, 109, 112, 114, 118, 127, 131, 134, 142, 156–57, 167, 176, 186

Cumaná, 149
Cundinamarca, 149, 158, 184
Curaçao, 176
Cuyo, 164
Cuzco, 136, 154

Danton, Georges, 72, 83
Dartmouth, Earl of, 33
Daufuskie Island, 41
Dauphiné, 91
Dauxion Lavaysse, Jean-Joseph, 122
David, Jacques-Louis, 77
Declaration of Independence, 29, 33, 34, 43, 184
Declaration of the Rights of Man and Citizen, 62, 64, 102, 186
Declaration of the Rights of Woman and Citizen, 64
Declaratory Act, 20
Deerfield, 41
Delaware, 17
Delaware River, 13, 36
Delawares, 9, 30, 32
democracy. See elections
Desmoulins, Camille, 83
Dessalines, Jean-Jacques, 114, 116–21, 124, 182, 186
Diderot, Denis, 3, 97
Dinwiddie, Robert, 9
Directory, 85, 87, 88, 116, 179, 211n114
Dominica, 11, 40
Draco, 178
Drayton, William Henry, 31
Duane, James, 33
Dublin, 76
Dufay, Louis, 111
Dunmore, John Murray, Earl of, 30, 45–46, 176
Dutch Republic, 7, 35, 49, 78, 89, 176

East Florida, 40, 42
East India Company, 25–26
El Salvador, 153

elections: British America, 15; France, 53, 63, 66–67, 72, 88; Saint-Domingue, 99–100; Spanish America, 143, 148, 153, 154; United States, 43

Electoral College, 47

Elío, Francisco Javier, 145

Eliot, Andrew, 20

Elisabeth, czarina of Russia, 191n28

emigration, France, 61, 69, 173; Saint-Domingue, 109; British North America, 173, 183

émigrés, 61, 68, 69, 70, 83, 87, 88, 173

Enlightenment, 2–4, 7, 34, 61, 62, 101, 132, 179, 180–82

environmental disaster, 60

equality: in Enlightenment thought, 2–4, 97; and French Revolution, 54, 59, 60, 62–64, 69–70, 71, 87; and Haitian revolution, 112; in Helvetian Republic, 185; in Spanish America, 163, 164, 166, 167, 177, 182

Esparbès, Jean-Jacques d', 109

Estates General, 51, 53–54, 83, 89, 99, 105, 169–71, 204n8

Ethiopian Corps, 46

Family Compacts, 10

Ferdinand VI, King of Spain, 132

Ferdinand VII, King of Spain, 137, 139, 143, 170

Ferrand, Louis, 121

festivals, 75, 180

feudalism, 59–60, 69, 185

Flanders, 86, 172

Florida, 11, 18, 25

Flushing, New York, 42

Fontainebleau, 76

Fort Stanwix Treaty, 30

Fraize, 52

France, 49–125

Franche-Comté, 56

Francia, José Gaspar Rodríguez de, 146

Franco de Medina, Agostino, 122

Franklin, Benjamin, 23, 34, 46, 179

Frederick the Great, King of Prussia, 10, 147

French Guiana, 88

frontier, 12, 14, 17, 18, 19, 20, 30

fur trade, 26

Gage, Thomas, 33

Galbaud, François Thomas, 110

Garrigus, John, 97

Gates, Horatio, 37

Geneva, 50, 89, 185

George II, King of Great Britain, 8

George III, King of Great Britain, 23, 28, 170, 176

Georgia, 17, 27, 31, 38, 42, 43, 45, 47, 96

German Luxemburg, 86

Germans: settlers, 12, 14; soldiers in British service, 27, 34, 35; soldiers in Continental service, 35

Germantown, battle of, 37

Germany, 12, 76

Gibbon, Edward, 147

Gibraltar, 37

Girondins, 77, 82, 84, 85

Glorious Revolution, 14

Gnadenhütten, 32

Godechot, Jacques, 2

Godoy, Manuel, 137

Goethe, Johann Wolfgang von, 81

Gold Coast, 98

Gorée, 11

Gouges, Olympe de, 63–64, 177

Gran Colombia, 123, 151, 166, 167, 168, 180

Grande Anse, 184

grands blancs, 94–95

Grasse, François Joseph Paul, Count de, 38

Great Britain: abolition of slave trade, 186; attacks on Buenos Aires, 138, 144–45; and Haitian Revolution, 113–14, 117, 122, 123, 186; involvement in Spain, 139; and Spanish empire, 133, 135, 137, 169

Great Fear, 58, 106, 181, 237n21

Grégoire, abbé Henri, 76, 102, 150
Grenada, 40, 114
Grenadines, 11
Grenoble, 92
Guadalajara, 152
Guadeloupe, 10, 91, 92, 94, 105, 106, 114, 118
Gual, Pedro, 166
Guanajuato, 135, 152
Guatemala, 127, 140, 153
Guatemala City, 154
Guayaquil, 156, 163
Guerrero, Vicente, 163
Guillotin, Joseph, 81
Guinea, 164
Guridi y Alcocer, Miguel, 166

Hainault, 56
Haiti, 119–25, 150, 165, 166, 174, 176, 178, 182, 183, 186–87
Halifax, 26
Hamilton, Alexander, 147
Hamnett, Brian, 161
Hancock, John, 26
Hanover, 8, 10
Havana, 10, 18, 62, 133
Haydn, Joseph, 147
Hédouville, Gabriel d', 116
Helvetian Republic, 185
Hesse, 34
Hessians, 35
Hewes, George Robert Twelves, 36
Hidalgo, Miguel, 151–53, 181
Honduras, 154
Hood, Samuel, 39
Howe, William, 36, 46
Hudson Valley, 37
Hugues, Victor, 219n77
Hulton, Henry, 21
Humboldt, Alexander von, 136, 141
Hutchinson, Thomas, 21

Igé, 58
Iguala, Plan of, 153, 163

India, 8, 10, 11
Indians: in the Americas, 6, 174; in North America, 9, 11, 12–13, 17–19, 26, 30–33, 48; in Spanish America, 126, 127, 129–31, 133, 135, 136, 143, 151–52, 154, 158, 161–62, 163, 167, 171, 180
indirect rule, 7
Ireland, 26, 36, 211n114
Irish settlers, 14, 35
Iroquois Confederacy, 13, 17, 30, 32. *See also* Ohio Iroquois; Six Nations
Italy, 8, 133
Iturbide, Agustín de, 153–54, 163
Ivory Coast, 98

Jacobins, 70–73, 75–76, 77–84, 88, 89, 90, 107, 109, 111, 173, 177, 179, 181, 185. *See also* Montagnards; Neo-Jacobins
Jacobite rebellion, 8
Jamaica, 40, 45, 47, 93–94, 109, 113–14, 117, 122
James River (Virginia), 14, 38
Jean-François, 107, 112–15, 219n82
Jefferson, Thomas, 18, 32, 33, 34, 45, 62
Jérémie, 113, 120
Jesuit order, 133, 135, 142
Jews, 60, 69–70
Joly, Étienne-Louis Hector de, 102
Joseph II, Emperor of Austria, 68

Kentucky, 30, 32
King's Proclamation, 18
Kingston, 122
Kongo, 98, 107, 164, 176

La Paz, 144, 154
La Rochelle, 91, 103, 107
Lacroix, Pamphile de, 121
Lafayette, Marie-Joseph Paul Yves Roch Gilbert du Motier, Marquis de, 61, 62, 147
Lake Erie, 9
Laveaux, Étienne, 113, 114

Le Hâvre, 103
Leclerc, Charles Victor Emmanuel, 117–19, 121
Lee, Wayne E., 31
Leeward Islands, 40
Lefebvre, Georges, 56, 58
Legislative Assembly, 70, 71, 83
Leonardo da Vinci, 76
Les Cayes, 100, 121, 150
Lexington, 1, 33
Lima, 126, 130, 131, 134, 140, 144, 154–56, 157, 163, 164
Liniers, Santiago de, 144, 229n64
Lisbon, 137
Llaneros, 148, 164
Loire River, 82
Loménie de Brienne, Étienne Charles de, 50
London, 76, 147
Lorraine, 52, 68, 69, 172
Louis XIV, King of France, 7, 8, 79, 96, 123
Louis XVI, King of France, 50, 54, 71, 74, 77, 80, 84, 89, 170, 172, 181
Louis XVIII, King of France, 87, 122
Louisbourg, 8, 9
Louisiana, 9, 13, 39, 134
Louverture, Toussaint, 112–18, 119, 123, 124, 125
Loyalists, 31, 37, 38, 40, 41–42, 173, 201n98. *See also* Tories
Luzerne, Anne-César, Chevalier de la, 101
Lycurgus, 178, 179
Lynch, John, 160
Lyon, 81, 82, 84, 86

Macaya, 112
Machiavelli, Niccolò, 178
Mâconnais, 56, 58
Madison, James, 178, 180
Madras, 8
Maipú, battle of, 155
Malcom, John, 21, 22
Manhattan Island, 36

Manila, British capture of, 10, 133
Mansfield, William Murray, Lord, 45
Margarita, 134, 149
Marie-Antoinette, 65, 68, 80
Mariño, Santiago, 160
marronage, 94, 99, 135
Marseille, 82, 84, 103, 181
Martinique, 10, 39, 91, 92, 94, 105–6, 114
Maryland, 17, 18, 25, 201n98
Massachusetts, 15, 17, 22, 25, 26, 28, 33, 34, 47
Massiac Club, 101
Mayhew, Jonathan, 21
McIntosh, Duncan, 120
Mediterranean, 8, 37
Mendelssohn, Moses, 147
mestizos, 6, 129, 135, 136, 143, 144, 152, 159, 174
Methodists, 46
Metternich, Matthias, 76
Mexico, 123, 127, 135, 139, 151–54, 156, 159, 160, 162, 163, 167, 171, 172, 184, 186
Mexico City, 126, 131, 143, 151, 152, 154, 157
Mill, James, 147
Mingos, 13, 30
Miranda, Francisco, 147–48, 165
Mississippi River, 11, 17, 30
Mohawks, 26
Moïse, Hyacinthe, 116
Molasses Act, 20
Môle St. Nicolas, 100, 113
Montagnards, 77, 82, 85
Montesquieu, Charles-Louis de Secondat, baron de la Brède et de, 43, 123
Monteverde, Domingo, 148
Montevideo, 138, 144–46, 161
Montmédy, 68
Moravians, 32, 198n68
Morelos, José María, 152–53, 163
Morillo, Pablo, 149–51, 163, 164, 166
Mount Pichincha, 150
mulattoes, in the Americas, 6, 174; in the Caribbean, 6; in Saint-Domingue, 94,

96, 97, 102–5, 112, 113, 114, 115, 118, 124, 175; in Haiti, 121–22, 124; in Spanish America, 129, 130, 142, 151, 161, 162–64, 166
Munsee, 32

Nago, 98
Nantes, 82, 83, 91, 93, 103
Naples, 78, 137
Napoleon, 62, 88, 117–18, 120, 122, 125, 137–39, 143, 147, 151, 169, 170, 179, 185
Nassau (Bahamas), 41
Nateiu, Anselmo, 240n59
National Assembly, 54, 59, 60, 62, 64, 65, 68, 76, 77, 81, 101–3, 105, 107, 141, 170, 174, 181
Navigation Acts, 15
Necker, Jacques, 50–51, 54–55
Neo-Jacobins, 88
neutrals, 42
Nevis, 23
New England, 33, 37, 46, 93, 172, 173, 174
New France, 9, 11, 17
New Granada, 126, 127, 135, 146, 149, 150, 151, 154, 158, 161, 162
New Hampshire, 17, 21–22, 43, 47
New Jersey, 15, 17, 36–37, 44, 47, 173, 184
New Mexico, 141
New Spain, 35, 126, 127, 134, 135, 140, 142, 153, 159, 237n21
New York, 15, 22, 27, 34, 40, 42, 43, 44, 47
New York City, 23, 24, 28, 36, 38, 39, 41, 147, 196n49, 200n89
New Zealand, 14
Newfoundland, 8, 10, 17, 40
Newport, 38
Nicaragua, 154
Nice, 78
Nîmes, 82, 84
Nine Years' War, 11
Noailles, Louis-Marie, vicomte de, 61
nobility: Europe, 5–6, 7; France, 49, 51, 54, 61, 67, 69, 70, 87, 181; Saint-Domingue,

94; Spanish America, 126, 127, 129, 130, 159
nonimportation, 24, 27
Norfolk, 41, 45, 172
Normandy, 56
North Carolina, 17, 31, 38, 42, 403, 201n. 98
Northwest Ordinance, 48
Nova Scotia, 17, 25, 27, 40, 42, 46

Oaxaca, 153, 163
Ocumare, 149
O'Donoju, Juan, 153
Ogé, Vincent, 105
O'Higgins, Bernardo, 154
Ohio Company, 9
Ohio Country, 12–13, 30
Ohio Iroquois, 30
Ohio River, 30, 32, 48
Ohio Valley, 9, 12
Oliver, Andrew, 21
Oneida, 12, 32
Osorio, Mariano, 154–55
Ottawa Indians, 17

Páez, José Antonio, 160
Paine, Thomas, 29, 30, 33, 43, 147, 170, 173, 184, 240n59
Palloy, Pierre-François, 55
Palmer, Robert Roswell, 5, 67, 173
papacy, 60
Paraguay, 127, 133, 134, 146, 159, 166, 167, 173
Paris, 1–2, 50, 55, 56, 59, 64–65, 68–69, 70, 71, 72–74, 79, 81–83, 86, 87–88, 101, 102, 103, 105, 107, 109, 111–12
Paris, Treaty of (1763), 17
Paris, Treaty of (1783), 42
Paris, Treaty of (1814), 122
parlements, 49, 53, 60, 93, 170; Bordeaux, 100; Paris, 50, 51, 109, 204n8
Pasto (New Granada), 161
Patriot revolt (Dutch Republic), 49
Pauw, Cornelius Franciscus de, 97

Paxton Boys, 18
peasants: France, 52–53, 56, 58–60, 79, 82, 83, 98, 106, 181; Spanish America, 140, 161, 163; southern Netherlands, 86; western Europe, 5–6
Peckham, Howard, 39
peninsulares, 127, 129, 133, 141–42, 143, 151, 158, 163, 237n21
Pennsylvania, 9, 13, 15, 17, 18, 29, 32, 36, 42, 43, 47, 184
Pensacola, battle of, 39, 147
Peru, 126, 127, 133, 134, 135, 136, 142, 151, 154–56, 165, 166–67, 174, 180, 183
Peter III, czar of Russia, 191n. 28
Pétion, Alexandre, 117–19, 122, 123, 124, 150, 165, 186
petits blancs, 95, 115
Pezuela, Joaquín de, 155
Philadelphia, 24, 25, 27–28, 30, 34, 37, 42, 44, 46, 172
Philip V, King of Spain, 132
Phrygian Cap, 71, 159
Piar, Manuel, 235n129
Picardie, 172
Pierrot, Jean-Louis, 112
Pitt the Elder, William, 23
Pitt the Younger, William, 76, 147
Polverel, Étienne, 109–11, 116
Pontiac's War, 18, 19
population growth, 7, 14, 16
Port-au-Prince, 93, 94, 100, 105, 109, 113, 120, 121, 150
Portugal, 3, 133, 137
Potosí, 183
priests: France, 52, 54, 56, 61, 65, 66, 70, 72, 75, 78, 82, 85, 88; Saint-Domingue, 120, southern Netherlands, 86; Spanish America, 130, 133, 135, 139, 155, 165. *See also* clergy
Princeton, battle of, 37
privilege, 1, 5–7, 29, 51–53, 59–60, 64, 67, 89, 127, 129, 132, 141, 170, 173, 177, 181, 182. *See also* equality

Protestants, 60, 69
Provence, Louis-Stanislas-Xavier, Count of, 87
Prussia, 9–11, 37, 78, 147; army in France, 71–72, 74
public opinion, 51, 71, 78, 89, 106, 170
Puebla, 153
Puerto Rico, 114, 127, 131, 134, 148, 156, 167
Pumacahua, Mateo García, 154, 156

Quakers, 14, 46
Quebec, 18, 40, 42
Quebec Act, 30
Queens County, 42, 173
Quito, 127, 150, 151, 156

Raimond, Julien, 104
Raynal, abbé Guillaume Thomas François, 97, 150, 181
redcoats, 18, 25, 48, 172, 236n6
Rhineland, 78, 185
Rhode Island, 17, 22, 38, 47, 201n98
Rigaud, André, 113, 115–17
Rio de Janeiro, 137
Río de la Plata, 126, 127, 131–34, 138, 144, 145, 154, 159, 168, 173, 180, 184, 186
Rivadavia, Bernardino, 159
Roberts, John Morris, 77
Robespierre, Maximilien, 77, 80, 84, 85, 180, 181
Rochambeau, Jean-Baptiste Donatien de Vimeur, Count de, 38
Rochambeau, Donatien-Marie-Joseph de Vimeur, vicomte de, 118–19
Rodney, George, 38–39
Roman Catholicism, 60, 85, 117, 123
Rome, 29, 78
Romero, Pedro, 163–64, 166
Rouen, 74, 103
Rousseau, Jean-Jacques, 3–4, 53, 62–63, 178, 179, 180, 181
Royal Navy, 10, 21

royalists: France, 84, 88; Saint-Domingue, 109, 114; Spanish America, 144, 145, 146, 148–50, 153, 154, 155, 156, 161–65, 174, 229n64

Ruault, Nicolas, 179

rumors: Americas, 176; France, 56, 64, 66, 84; Gran Colombia, 166; Martinique, 106; New Spain, 237n. 21; Saint-Domingue, 106, 175; Thirteen Colonies, 31, 175

Russell, William, 36

Russia, 66, 78

Ryerson, Richard, 43

Saint-Antoine, 65, 73

Saint-Domingue, 39, 91–119, 122, 125, 156, 165, 169, 171, 174, 175, 181, 182, 186, 212n3

Saint Marc, 105, 124–25

Saint-Just, Louis Antoine Léon de, 75, 79, 81, 84, 180

Salat, Jakob, 3

Salem, Massachusetts, 20

Salem, Pennsylvania, 32

San Ildefonso, Treaty of, 137

San Luís de Potosí, 135

San Martín, José de, 144, 155–56, 164–65, 175, 229n64

sans-culottes, 71, 72, 73, 78, 80, 84, 88, 89, 112, 174, 181

Santa Marta, 158, 159

Santiago de Chile, 131, 154, 229n65

Santo Domingo, 112, 117, 121, 127, 134, 156

Saratoga, battle of, 37

Saumur, 83

Savannah, 38, 96, 114

Savoy, 78

Saxony, 10, 11

Schiller, Friedrich, 77

Schoelcher, Victor, 182

Scots, 14

Scotch-Irish, 14, 18

Ségur, Philippe Henri, Marquis de, 66

Senecas, 13

Senegambia, 98

September Massacres, 74, 77

Seven Years' War, 9–11, 13, 17–20, 21, 23, 31, 36, 39, 93, 95, 96, 125, 133, 169, 170

Seville, 138, 146

Shawnees, 9, 13, 30, 32

Shelby, Evan, 31

Shy, John, 42

Sieyès, abbé Emmanuel-Joseph, 53–54, 88, 173

Silesia, 11

Simolin, Ivan, 77

Sint Eustatius, 35–36, 38–39

Sipe-Sipe, battle of, 164

Six Nations, 13, 17. See also Iroquois Confederacy

slave trade, 11, 102–03, 106, 122, 159, 166, 186

slavery: abolition of, French colonies, 63, 97, 103, 110–12, 169; Spanish America, 166, 167; United States, 46, 47

smuggling. See contraband trade

Society of the Friends of the Blacks, 102–5, 107

Solon, 178

Somerset, James, 45

Sons of Liberty, 21

Sonthonax, Légér Félicité, 109–12, 114, 115, 116

South Carolina, 17, 27, 31, 38, 41, 42, 3, 45, 174, 175, 176, 186

Spain, 3, 8, 10, 16, 91, 126–68, 170, 176; and French Revolution, 78; and Haitian Revolution, 113–14; and War of American Independence, 29, 37, 39

speculators, 9, 12, 13, 18, 30, 44

St. Kitts, 23

St. Lucia, 114

St. Vincent, 11, 40

Stamp Act, 21–24, 45, 172

Steuben, Friedrich von, 37

Sucre, Antonio José de, 156

Sugar Act, 20, 22
Sullivan, John, 31
Suriname, 47
Susquehanna River, 13, 30
Switzerland, 185

Taino, 110
taxation: France, 49–52, 54–56, 58, 63, 67, 69, 73, 81, 82, 89, 98, 177; Saint-Domingue, 104; Spanish America, 126–27, 131, 134–35, 160, 161, 167, 223n4; Thirteen Colonies, 14, 20, 23, 27, 169; United States, 43, western Europe, 5–7
Tea Act, 25–26
Tennis Court Oath, 54
Tenochtitlán, 140
Terror, 80, 83–84, 88, 173, 174, 180
Third Estate, 51–54, 61, 70, 89, 141, 170, 171
Tlaxcala, 166
Tobago, 11, 40, 41, 114
Tories, 27. See also Loyalists
Tortola, 176
Toulouse, 50, 82
Townshend, Charles, 23
Townshend acts, 23–24
Trafalgar, battle of, 137
Treaty of Amity and Commerce, 37
Trenton, battle of, 37
Trinidad, 134
Tuileries Palace, 65, 72, 74
Túpac Amaru, 136, 154

United Irish, 211n114
United States, 43–44; example for France, 85; example for Spanish America, 184–85; trade with Saint-Domingue, 100–101; treaty with Saint-Domingue, 117
Upper Peru, 127, 144, 156, 161–62, 164, 173, 229n64
Uruguay, 134, 146, 167, 184. See also Banda Oriental

Valencia, 148
Valladolid, 151–52
Van Schaick, Goose, 31
Varennes, 68–70, 78
Vendée, 83, 85, 87, 116, 119, 172, 174
Venezuela, 114, 127, 131, 134, 136, 136, 146–51, 157, 158, 160, 162, 164, 165–67, 172–76, 180, 184, 185
Venice, 78, 185
Verdun, 72
Vermont, 46
Verona, 87
Versailles, 51, 54. 64–65, 102, 123
Virginia, 9, 14–18, 25, 27, 30, 31, 32, 34, 35, 36, 38, 39, 40, 41, 45, 172, 173, 184, 186, 236n14
vodou, 99, 123, 218n68
Voltaire, 1–2, 3, 179, 181

War of American Independence, 10, 34–39, 61
War of the Austrian Succession, 8, 11
War of the Spanish Succession, 11
Washington, George, 9, 18, 31, 36, 38, 40, 45, 61, 147, 178
Wellesley, Arthur, 138–39
Welsh, 14
West Florida, 39
Whately, Thomas, 23
Wilberforce, William, 150
Williamson, Adam, 113
Williamson, David, 32
Women: in the American Revolution, 24, 41, 44, 202n. 106; in the French Revolution, 63–65, 67, 77, 79, 177, 204n9; in Saint-Domingue, 95, 99, 105, 114, 120; in Spanish America, 158, 159

Yorktown, battle of, 38, 39
Yucatán, 134

ABOUT THE AUTHOR

Wim Klooster is Professor of History at Clark University. He is the author or (co-)editor of many books, including *The Dutch Moment: War, Trade, and Settlement in the Seventeenth-Century Atlantic World*; *The Atlantic World: Essays on Slavery, Migration, and Imagination*; and *Illicit Riches: Dutch Trade in the Caribbean, 1648–1795*.